World Power Shifts and Strategic Transition in South Asia

World Power Shifts and Strategic Transition in South Asia

Capt. R. K. Sirohi

PRASHANT PUBLISHING HOUSE
DELHI-110094

Published by :
PRASHANT PUBLISHING HOUSE
C-34, 28 Foota Road, Gali-3,
West Karwal Nagar, Delhi-110094
Phone : 011-22963970, Mob. : 9810396373
e-mail.: prashantpublishinghouse@gmail.com

World Power Shifts and Strategic Transition in South Asia

First Published 2017

ISBN : 978-81-934253-5-0

PRINTED IN INDIA

Published by Mr. R.K. Jha M/s Prashant Publishing House and Published at H.S. Offset House Press, Delhi.

Contents

Preface

Global power shifts are strategically and politically significant as normally they are rare and chronologically well-spaced out. Global power shifts tend to displace or restructure existing international orders and are therefore prone to generating strategic and political turbulence.

The global strategic landscape and political and financial structures so far have been dominated by the United States and Europe. Asia remained dominated by European colonisation for nearly two centuries and was thereafter dom inated by the United States comprehensively and strategically for another century. Asia's economic resurgence and cumulative financial strengths over the last two decades have largely contributed to the global shift of power to Asia. Today, Asia overshadows the United States and Europe in economic and financial strength. This has greatly contributed to Asia's growing political leverages internationally.

Major shifts of power between states, not to mention regions, occur infrequently and are rarely peaceful. In the early twentieth century, the imperial order and the aspiring states of Germany and Japan failed to adjust to each other. The conflict that resulted devastated large parts of the globe. Today, the transformation of the international system will be even bigger and will require the assimilation of markedly different political and cultural traditions. This time, the populous states of Asia are the aspirants seeking to play a greater role. Like Japan and Germany back then, these rising powers are nationalistic, seek redress of past grievances, and want to claim their place in the sun. Asia's growing economic power is translating into greater political and military power, thus increasing the potential damage of conflicts. Within the region, the flash points for hostilities -- Taiwan, the Korean Peninsula, and divided Kashmir -- have defied peaceful resolution. Any of them could explode into large-scale warfare that would make the current Middle East confrontations seem like police operations. In short, the stakes in Asia are huge and will challenge the West's adaptability.

In tandem with Asia's economic resurgence has taken place the fast-track military modernisation and expansion of Asian military capabilities. The continued growth of Asian economic, political and military strengths have contributed to the emergence of Asia's leading countries –China, India and Japan –as global players on an ascending trajectory.

Global power no longer resides in the trans-Atlantic region. The global shift of power to Asia portends that an "Asia unbound" and consciousness of its comprehensive strengths would now increasingly demand greater say in the strategic, political and economic future of the world.

Asia's combination of geostrategic locations and energy-rich regions as well as vibrant and dynamic economies imparts to Asia an unrivalled geostrategic and geopolitical significance in global power play. Thus, when the global economic and political centres of gravity shift to Asia, global power-play is significantly affected. Geostrategically, the global shift of power to Asia marks the end of the United States' unipolar comprehensive domination of global affairs. Multi-polarity with Asian powers emerging as multiple poles will replace the existing unipolar global strategic structure.

Asia's military rise of its leading powers—China, India and Japan—fuelled by sustained economic growths is reducing the military power differentials with the United States.In terms of advanced weaponry and military hardware, Asia's military profiles are rising and budgetary constraints are limiting military profiles of United States and Europe. Asia today boasts of six nuclear weapons states with sizeable missiles arsenals.

As the book addresses this crucial issue quite deftly, it is hoped that it would prove to be a source of great information for the reader.

—*Editor*

1

Introduction

GLOBAL POWER SHIFT

During the mid-2000s, when emerging markets were growing at breakneck speed, the cavernous gap separating industrial and developing economies began to close. This convergence took place against a backdrop of economic liberalization, built on the idea that the financial systems of all nations would dovetail.

That period is now over. Emerging nations are no longer growing as rapidly as they were, particularly in comparison with developed economies; further, the fissures among different systems have become more evident. In PwC's 19th Annual Global CEO Survey, only 35 percent of the corporate leaders who responded said they believe the world is moving toward greater economic union. Instead, 59 percent of these chief executives believe that multiple models will coexist and compete. Consider, for example, how differently government and business investment is conducted in the United States, China, India, Japan, and the European Union. These nations and regions operate with fundamentally different assumptions about the way an economy should be organized. The tension among these assumptions is growing, not diminishing.

In short, a new global economic order is now emerging to replace the one that has existed since the end of World War II. For the foreseeable future, the global economy will be defined by a complex and continuously shifting set of economic relationships. They will be increasingly interconnected, to be sure, but with ever-changing rules for conducting business across borders. As a business leader, how can you manage this complexity? How can you cross the threshold to the next economic order with confidence and skill? The most effective way is to pay attention to three basic trends: the dispersion of economic power, the continuing evolution of state-directed growth models, and the accelerating disruption felt by business from technological change. These trends may seem self-evident. But none of them is quite what it seems to be at first glance. Further, they will continue to evolve along uncertain paths. None is likely to progress simply as a continuation of what we have seen in the past few years. By looking at these trends closely, you can help your organization take the substantive steps needed to thrive in the new global economic order.

ASIAN POWER GOES GLOBAL: CHINA AND INDIA

A shifting global power balance from West to East has become a much remarked upon phenomenon of recent years, but it has antecedents in earlier decades. The first country to present a modern "Asian challenge" was Japan, one of the defeated powers of World War II. In 1960, Japan was still considered to be a struggling developing country, poorer than Argentina. By the 1970s it had emerged as the leading Asian economy, welcomed as a founding member of the elite club of the Group of Seven industrialized nations (G7) and en route to global great-power status. On a lesser scale, South Korea was also being recognized as a low-income nation that was lifting itself up mightily and moving to the head of the class of the newly industrializing countries.

What is different about the current attention to rising Asia is the sheer magnitude of the transformational processes occurring simultaneously in the world's two most populous countries.

Much of the globalization with which we are familiar has been led by the G7 and OECD countries. In the future, globalization could have more of an Asian face. In the words of the U.S. National Intelligence Council study, "Asia will alter the rules of the globalizing process. By having the fastest-growing consumer markets, more firms becoming world-class multinationals, and greater S&T [science and technology] stature, Asia looks set to displace Western countries as the focus for international economic dynamism – provided Asia's rapid economic growth continues." Asian powers are also expected to dominate global politics later in this century. The ability of Western countries, notably the United States, to accommodate that fact could therefore be crucial to the future of world order.

Within Asia, the most attention is clearly focused on its pre-eminent emerging global players China and India, both of which are adding enormous numbers of new workers and consumers to the global economy while developing huge middle classes larger than the entire populations of most G7 countries. As a recent business article surveyed the prospect:

The postwar era witnessed economic miracles in Japan and South Korea. But neither was populous enough to power worldwide growth or change the game in a complete spectrum of industries. China and India, by contrast, possess the weight and dynamism to transform the 21st-century global economy. ... even America's rise falls short in comparison to what's happening now. Never has the world seen the simultaneous, sustained takeoffs of two nations that together account for one-third of the planet's population. For the past two decades, China has been growing at an astounding 9.5% a year, and India by 6%. Given their young populations, high savings, and the sheer amount of catching up they still have to do, most economists figure China and India possess the fundamentals to keep growing in the 7%-to-8% range for decades. (...) In the coming decades, China and India will disrupt workforces, industries, companies, and markets in ways that we can barely begin to imagine.

Other projections have come to similarly dramatic conclusions about the impacts of these two emerging powers on both the geo-economic and geo-political global landscape. The NIC study suggests that a combination of sustained high economic growth, active promotion of high technologies, population size, expanding military capabilities and international policy ambitions will fuel their rising power on the world stage. Among the expected manifestations are the following:

- The demographic weight of China and India will be such that they will not need to approach Western standards of living to achieve great-power standing.
- China will become the leading centre of world manufacturing and exports. ("Competition from 'the China price' already powerfully restrains manufactures prices worldwide.")
- "China's and India's perceived need to secure access to energy supplies will propel these countries to become more global rather than just regional powers ...."
- "China's desire to gain 'great power' status on the world stage will be reflected in its greater economic leverage over countries in the region and elsewhere as well as its steps to strengthen its military. East Asian states are adapting to the advent of a more powerful China by forging closer economic and political ties with Beijing, potentially accommodating themselves to its preferences, particularly on sensitive issues like Taiwan."

- "China will overtake Russia and others as the second largest defence spender after the United States over the next two decades and will be, by any measure, a first-rate military power."
- "The rise of India also will present strategic complications for the region. Like China, India will be an economic magnet for the region, and its rise will have an impact not only in Asia but also to the north – Central Asia, Iran, and other countries of the Middle East."
- The China-India relationship will be one to watch. Some may see India as a potential "counterweight" to China's influence. But their trade with each other will rise rapidly and they could form a potent strategic alliance.
- "The United States and China have strong incentives to avoid confrontation, but rising nationalism in China and fears in the US of China as an emerging strategic competitor could fuel an increasingly antagonistic relationship."
- Since "China's ability to sustain its current pace is probably more at risk than is India's ... India could emerge as the world's fastest-growing economy as we head towards 2020."

So far there is little sign that China's torrid economic pace is slowing, with the latest figures showing an expansion of 9.9% in 2005, recently overtaking the United Kingdom and France in economic size, and likely Germany in 2008. However, there are a number of downside risks and disruptions that accompany this extraordinary rise: massive internal migration from the countryside to the cities, fragile financial systems and state-owned enterprises, pervasive corruption, rising socio-economic inequalities, inadequate social safety nets and health-care systems in the face of an ageing population and epidemic diseases, growing levels of unemployment and civil unrest, demands for political as well as economic liberalization, for democracy and rights as well as market freedoms, and the spectre of conflicts involving Taiwan or North Korea.

Indeed, some argue that China's combination of a neo-Leninist state and rampant crony capitalism is not sustainable and is more likely to lead to decay than democratic transition. As one sceptic puts it: "For the moment, China's strong economic fundamentals and the boundless energy of its people have concealed and offset its poor governance, but they will carry China only so far. Someday soon, we will know whether such a flawed system can pass a stress test: a severe economic shock, political upheaval, a public health crisis, or an ecological catastrophe. China may be rising, but no one really knows whether it can fly." About 800 million people, 70% of the population, still live in the countryside, and the gap between the rural poor and urban elites is larger than at any time since the 1949 revolution. As a recent *Economist* article put it: "A spectre is haunting China – the spectre of rural unrest." How well, or badly, China is able to manage multiple transitions and surmount potential internal challenges will be critical to its role in shaping world politics in the coming years.

At the same time, it is undeniable that China's growing weight in political and military as well as economic terms is already reshaping the strategic balance in Asia and globally. Much of the attention has focused on China's aggressive diplomacy, an uneasy United States-China relationship and closer United States-India relations. A report prepared for members of the U.S. Congress prior to the first East Asia Summit in mid-December 2005 – a new formation that excludes the United States, unlike broader forums such as APEC (Asia Pacific Economic Cooperation) – suggests that: "Fundamental shifts underway in Asia could constrain the U.S. role in the multilateral affairs of Asia. The centrality of the United States is now being challenged by renewed regionalism in Asia and by China's rising influence."

According to James Hoge: "Suspicious Americans have interpreted larger Chinese military budgets as signs of Beijing's intention to roll back America's presence in East Asia. Washington is thus eager to use India, which appears set to grow in economic and military strength, as a counterbalance to China as well as a strong proponent of democracy in its own right." That in turn feeds Chinese suspicions of current United States-India military cooperation (which also raises sensitive nuclear nonproliferation issues) as part of a policy of "soft containment of China." An article on the eve of President Bush's March 2006 visit to India refers to "China's fear that America's grand strategic design is to encircle it and block its rise as a great power." Military historian and journalist Gwynne Dyer goes so far as to suggest that "Washington and New Delhi are laying the foundations for a new Cold War in Asia." But other analysts point out that "India is far too canny, and cares too much about its own China relationship, to be drawn into such a game." (Interestingly, India has also been improving relations with Taiwan, with the launching of a Taiwan-India Cooperation Council in February 2006.)

Implications for Canada

Canada is not a major player in any of the above strategic manoeuvres and calculations, but it will be affected by their result. And like all countries, including the United States, Canada will have to adjust its policies to accommodate the "Asian face" of globalization and the growing global power and influence of China. That includes coming to terms with China's inroads into Canada's principal market, the United States. In July 2005, for the first time, China overtook Canada to become the largest exporter of goods to the United States. While China does not yet tend to compete in the same products as Canada, its continued rapid rise does raise concerns about whether Canada will remain up to the competition in future. Even Canada's established markets cannot be taken for granted. Moreover, China has now replaced Japan as Canada's second-largest trading partner. According to a March 2006 Statistics Canada study, China's growing role in global trade is a main factor in the U.S. share of Canada's imports dropping to its lowest level since the 1930s.

An awareness of the rising role of Asia goes back some decades. For example, a 1975 study sponsored by the Ottawa Defence Research Board and the Canadian Institute of International Affairs described both Japan and China as having "entered officially a new age of global influence and responsibility." As well, it was foreseen that "the Chinese seem certain to widen their lead over the Japanese in terms of regional power and global political-diplomatic influence." Recognition of the importance of Asia was advanced by the creation of the Vancouver-based Asia Pacific Foundation of Canada (APFC) by Act of Parliament in 1984 and by Canada's multilateral participation in APEC.

However, as several recent APFC publications warn, Canada could be sidelined politically by the advent of new Asia-only forums; and given that Canada's share of the Chinese market is actually declining, a broader, more strategic approach is needed to the region than just occasional "Team Canada" trade missions. Canadian experts on the region have argued that, notwithstanding official recognition of the importance of emerging powers in the 2005 *International Policy Statement*, Canada still lacks a significant presence. As a recent roundtable report put it: A point that came out more than once during the discussion of our relations with China and India is that people in those countries, and elsewhere in Asia, have no very clear impressions of Canada. In economic terms we are still seen as a vast repository of natural resources. We have to do a much better job of 'branding' ourselves, or portraying ourselves as more than that, as a country with many strengths and much to offer. Promotion of new technologies, including for environmentally sustainable development, of globally competitive education and skills development, and of a western Canadian "Gateway" to the Asia Pacific are some of the initiatives being advanced to respond to this challenge.

China is clearly the most important Asian country in terms of building a beneficial long-term relationship, and it represents a challenge that engages every facet of international policy: not only diplomacy, development, and trade and commerce (including controversial investments in Canada by Chinese state-owned firms), but also security, human rights, democratization and governance issues, the environment and climate change, public health concerns, and so on.

In terms of the bilateral economic relationship, as previously noted, China is by far Canada's dominant partner among the BRICSAM countries. But even so, China still accounts for only about 4% (2004 figures) of Canada's total two-way global trade flows (in a substantial deficit position, given a trade imbalance of just 1.6% of Canadian exports compared to 6.8% of imports). And looked at from China's perspective, Canada has only a 1.5% share of Chinese trade with the world. The investment relationship is even less, with Canada receiving under 0.1 % of China's overseas foreign direct investment (FDI) and Canadian FDI in China still small at US$500 million in 2004. During 2005, which marked 35 years of official diplomatic relations with the People's Republic under the "One China" policy, the Canadian government made a commitment to double economic ties by 2010 and to upgrade relations to the level of a "strategic partnership." Strategic working groups were launched in January 2005 in the areas of trade and investment, energy and resources, science and technology, and multilateral cooperation. According to Paul Evans of the Asia Pacific Foundation, China's rise as a world economic power and global diplomatic player carries a number of implications for Canada:

- Increasing prices for commodities, natural resources and energy based in large part on growing Chinese demand.
- Increasing trade and investment volumes with China accompanied by a growing trade and, at least in the short term, investment deficit. In addition to formulating rules to protect Canadian investment in China, a major new development is the prospect of increasing substantially larger Chinese investment and acquisitions in Canada. The increased volume of trade poses major issues for air and port infrastructure and has the potential to affect the course of deeper North American integration.
- Increased pressure for Chinese professional and business people to emigrate to Canada and to press for more flexible visa, taxation and citizenship rules.
- Increased opportunities in areas of non-tradable service including education, health care and tourism. The level of human interactions is destined to grow, perhaps dramatically, with significant implications for new opportunities in connecting immigration, education and

tourism. There will be new pressures for alterations in visa, citizenship and taxation rules.

- Increased opportunity, and need, for working with Chinese officials on virtually the full spectrum of Canadian diplomatic and developmental priorities.

Canada's engagement with India is at a considerably lower level despite the fact that India is the world's largest democratic emerging power. The relationship has never been very deep and was vexed for decades following 1974 when India exploded a nuclear device using Canadian technology. Canada has had to come to terms with India as a nuclear power. While bilateral sanctions were lifted several years ago, diplomatic strains remain in a number of areas notwithstanding recent prime ministerial and ministerial visits and trade missions. Moreover, India, unlike China, is no longer a direct recipient of Canadian official development assistance.

Canada's trade and investment relationship with India is growing but remains very small. India is only Canada's 18th-largest export market, and India accounted for just 0.3% of Canada's two-way trade flows in 2004 (0.2% of exports and 0.4% of imports). Canada in turn represents about 1.0% of India's global trade. The investment relationship is even smaller, with about $250 million of Canadian FDI in India in 2004, versus only $62 million of Indian investment in Canada, mostly in the information technology sector. At the same time, a significant trade developing in commercial services is probably under-reported in the official statistics. In contrast to China's reliance on low-cost manufacturing, much of India's dynamism is due to the burgeoning services and high technology sectors.

Another potentially important factor in reinvigorating the bilateral relationship is a rapidly growing Indo-Canadian community that is approaching one million strong. In recent years India has been the second-largest source country for immigrants to Canada, accounting for approximately 10% of the annual total.

In addition to those ties, India, as the leading democratic economic power in Asia after Japan, would seem to be a particularly attractive country with which to pursue partnership arrangements in trade and other areas. Yet Canada-India relations have a lot of ground to make up. As pictured by several analysts, "Canada's India policy, ranging in the past from indifference to neglect, presents an image that is best described as a 'bazaar relationship': shopping around for one-off trading opportunities but lacking a sustained and diversified relationship." The increasing prominence of India in the world economy and in multilateral forums may finally provide the spur for Canada to move its diplomacy with India to a higher level.

CHINA AND THE WORLD: THE VIEW FROM SALZBURG, THEN AND NOW

When the National People's Congress met this month and named Xi Jinping China's President (and thereby completed conferral of the triple crown worn by top Chinese leaders: state President, Communist Party General Secretary and Central Military Commission Chairman), Xi and his near-colleagues formally fully took the helm of a nation with capacities, options and challenges strikingly different from those that had characterized China under Jiang Zemin—Xi's predecessor's predecessor and the man whose acolytes and kindred spirits hold most of the seats on the Politburo Standing Committee installed last November. There are many ways to try to capture the evolution of China and its place in the world over the intervening period: statistics about economic growth, trade or military spending, journalistic accounts of progress and problems at home and abroad, big-picture policy and scholarly debates about whether a rising China will sustain, accept or challenge the current international system and the postwar and post-Cold War order.

One evocative glimpse of these patterns and trends (and assessments of their significance) comes from comparing the snapshots offered by two sessions of the Salzburg Seminar, one held in mid-1995 and another at the end of 2012. The ageless Baroque castle and the implausibly picturesque alpine setting that are home to the Seminar throw into sharp relief the dramatic transformation of China and its international roles. The timeless venue also underscores the persistence—or the intractability—of many of the issues affecting China and its relations with the U.S. and with the wider world.

More than fifty faculty and fellows—from across East Asia, North America, Europe and elsewhere, and from academia, government, international organizations, think tanks, civil society, journalism and beyond—gathered for each of the two iterations of nearly-week-long intensive discussions.

They grappled with questions that remained—in broad outlines—remarkably similar despite the passage of nearly twenty years and the almost completely non-overlapping sets of participants: Do deep and growing economic interdependence within Asia and between Asia (including China) and the West (including the U.S) and shared interests in a stable and peaceful regional environment mean that it will be possible to contain pressures for protectionism and other illiberal trade policies in economically troubled rich countries and rapidly rising developing states?

Do these and other factors mean that the major powers will be able to avoid conflict despite rising nationalism (especially in China, but also in Japan), crisis-prone territorial disputes (primarily along China's maritime periphery, including the South China Sea) and other long-running regional security challenges (particularly North Korea)?

How will the U.S., in relative decline from its postwar and post-Cold War dominance, cope with an economically dynamic Asia, including a steeply ascendant China? How are the foreign policy calculi of China and U.S. allies and near-allies in the region affected by the U.S.'s waning dominance and regional states' growing doubts about Washington's commitment to remaining fully engaged in underwriting stability and security in Asia? Can a more powerful China be integrated effectively into the existing order, or does China's ascent mean pressure or demands for relatively radical change? Do China's recently stalled economic reforms, long-highly-constrained political reforms and seemingly deeply flawed institutions pose serious threats to the sustainability of China's economic growth, social stability, and willingness and capacity to take on greater and status quo-supporting roles in regional and international regimes?

How can the U.S. (and like-minded states) best promote human rights, democracy and the rule of law in China (and elsewhere in the region)? Which are the more promising policies for pursuing those ends: those that sharply criticize China's practices and strongly press human rights ideals on a recalcitrant China, or those that take lower-key and more collaborative approaches, offering support for civil society, the rule of law and institutional capacity-building and stressing smart deployment of the U.S.'s (and other liberal-democratic states') "moral capital" (or, as it would come to be called during the period between the two Salzburg sessions, "soft power")? What are the implications for relations with China, and East Asia more broadly, of the perennial tension in U.S. foreign policy between traditional concerns of strategic and economic interests and more ameliorative, values-based agendas? What are the consequences of the prevalent view in China that the U.S. is leading a "containment" strategy against China, and what can or should be done about that perception?

Will Japan be able to overcome economic stagnation or decline, political sclerosis and dysfunction, and persisting impediments—including "history questions" in relations with nations it once conquered and the pacifist provision in its constitution—to Japan's becoming a "normal country" with a larger regional security role? Is European foreign policy sufficiently focused and coherent in engaging Asia, and China in particular? Do domestic interest groups and ideological politics produce policies toward China that are unstable and ill-serve national interests in the U.S. and elsewhere in the West? Do deepening economic ties among Asian states and efforts to promote a sense of Asian identity or values threaten U.S. economic interests, political influence and, in turn, security objectives in Asia? Is a stronger regional institutional order achievable and, if so, what benefits could it bring to states in East Asia and interested states outside the region?

While many such questions from 1995 would remain strikingly pertinent nearly two decades later, the context in which they were asked would shift fundamentally, changing their meaning and also bringing new issues to the fore. In the first half of the 1990s, it was still possible to think of questions of fostering mutual understanding and managing difficult relations between East and West partly—even primarily—in the shadow of the Cold War concerns that had motivated the creation of the Salzburg Seminar during the early postwar years. The fall of the Berlin Wall and the dissolution of the Soviet Union were still relatively fresh memories. The new order for Europe—a continent devastated by violence in the decades preceding the tense and troubling stability that came with its division into Western and Soviet-dominated blocs—was still taking shape. To be sure, China already had marched relatively far down a path of reform, opening and development in the first nearly twenty years of the Post-Mao Era. But China was still in the early phases of its reemergence from the setbacks to domestic reform and international engagement that followed the violent suppression of the Tiananmen protests in 1989. A few years after Deng Xiaoping's last great intervention in Chinese politics to restart reform with his 1992 "southern tour," China could still seem to be something less than the central question in international or "East-West" relations, at least to those viewing such issues from a global or non-East Asian regional perspective.

This perspective—and appreciation of the growing need to move beyond it—were reflected in the 1995 Salzburg Seminar session. The first of the Seminar's sessions devoted entirely to East Asia policy issues, it was tellingly dubbed "U.S. Foreign Policy toward Asia: Adapting to Change." As the title reflected, much of the analysis and discussion concerned the U.S as the key player and the actor with the most room for choice. Much of the focus was on what Washington should do and the potential impact on China's rise and trajectory of U.S. policies that might engage—or seek to contain—China. Whether the U.S. should delink China's most-favored-nation trading status from Washington's reviews of Beijing's human rights record, and support China's accession to the newly established WTO, was seen as a decision largely within the U.S.'s discretion and one with weighty implications for China's prospects for economic development and full-fledged (re-)entry into the international system after Mao-Era isolation and post-Tiananmen Incident opprobrium. The notion that U.S. policy would be facing much less passive partners in its relations with China and other Asian states was new enough to warrant discussion as a significant development. To be sure, the issue—chronic since the early 1970s—of the U.S.'s relative decline in power in East Asia was a major and predictable theme, but it was relatively muted amid the lingering afterglow of the collapse of the Soviet Bloc, the emergence of a one-superpower world and a positive turn in the U.S. economy.

As the second half of the 1995 session's title also suggested with its general language, there was no single "change" in Asia that defined the challenges—and opportunities—that U.S. policy faced. Accounts offered at the Seminar depicted a messy landscape of seemingly unconnected or uncertainly interconnected trends. Some of the broadest developments would persist, or return, nearly twenty years on: China's remarkable ascension, economically and militarily; Japan's deepening economic difficulties and what they foretold for Japan's role as a regional power and U.S. ally; the threat to China's economic success and political stability posed by increasingly troubling weaknesses in its political system, rising social unrest, and growing doubts about the sustainability of its model for growth; the problems for regional and international economic integration posed by signs of newly illiberal economic policies; and the perils for regional security fed by escalating nationalist friction between China and Japan and provocative antics from North Korea.

Other aspects of "change" in Asia that seemed noteworthy nearly two decades ago—but are much less so now—point to how much "change" has changed, and how much more central an issue a much more formidable China had become, almost two decades later. In the mid-1990s, the demise of the Cold War logic behind bilateral security ties and recrudescent trade frictions raised concerns about the health of the U.S.-Japan relationship. More than two years before the Asian Financial Crisis, the East Asian Model for economic development seemed robust and perhaps to promise continued dynamism even for relatively developed East Asian states and for China as well (although perhaps only to the extent China continued reforms that followed the model's prescriptions). With the third wave of democratization recently having crested in the region, the view that East Asian states would converge politically with U.S. or Western or universal norms—at least in a general way—gained substantial traction and invigorated a debate about whether modernization meant Westernization or left open the possibility of a meaningfully different path based in part on "Asian values." To some, it seemed plausible to imagine ASEAN as the focal point of a more institutionalized regional international order. To others, it seemed necessary to debunk the idea of a U.S.-centered post-Cold War "New World Order." To a few, Japan seemed possibly poised to reclaim some of its former prominence in the realms of regional economics and security.

For many, China's prospects appeared to be the biggest uncertainty in 1995. A mere six years after the setbacks that followed the violent suppression of the student-led movement at Tiananmen and the ouster of top leaders who had supported energetic reforms, rising economic and political nationalism appeared to have the potential to derail China's nearly twenty year-long and impressively successful pursuit of openness and engagement. There was much concern about the possibly dire consequences of China's seemingly weakly institutionalized politics: Would an orderly process or potentially severely disruptive elite infighting characterize the eventual succession from Jiang Zemin (whose elevation to the top posts had come in the wake of the purge of two prior heirs-apparent to the great architect of the Post-Mao Reform Era, Deng Xiaoping)? Would the leaching of political power from the center to localities continue and imperil the state's capacity to pursue further reforms and check local authorities' abuses (which seemed to undermine growth and erode public tolerance for the regime)? With the passing of Deng and the revolutionary generation of leaders and their unique credibility with the military, and with the use of the army at Tiananmen still a relatively recent event, were civil-military relations stable in China and was Mao's dictum that the Party must command the gun fully in force? With political institutionalization suspect and communist ideology a spent force, could the regime sustain its legitimacy based on economic performance alone? Was such performance-based legitimacy itself imperiled—even at China's still relatively low level of wealth and development—by barriers to continued growth inherent in China's semi-reformed economy?

Eighteen years later, a session of the renamed Salzburg Global Seminar addressed some broadly familiar—and other more novel—questions in a very different context. In the intervening period, aspects of China in particular and China in a wider context—industrialization, environmental challenges, legal development, differences and commonalities in "values" between Asia and the West and so on—had become topics for the week-long symposia at the postcard-perfect castle by the lake.

At Salzburg, as elsewhere, relations between East and West had come to mean relations between a broadened "West" that incorporated the much-expanded group of European Union states, Western hemisphere countries and—in interest and orientation if not geography—countries in other regions, including many of China's neighbors. The triangular China-U.S.-Japan focus of the 1995 Seminar had given way to something far more multifaceted. China's relations with the non-West, including South, Central and West Asia, the Middle East and Latin America had grown thick and complicated enough to be addressed as distinct topics at the Seminar. Much of the discussion focused on how states in the West, East Asia and beyond were cooperating, or might coordinate, in their responses to a much more powerful and in some respects much more disconcerting China.

As with geography, so too with subject matter: the traditional, fundamental concerns of regional and global security, international trade and investment, and human rights and other values-related issues were hardy perennials. But the salient issues in assessments of China and its external relations had come to include much more.

Deepened linkages among national economies had brought attention to Chinese outbound investment and its impact on sectors ranging from raw materials extraction to high technology, the likely effects of Chinese domestic demand on exporting countries' economic health and global energy markets, and the implications for China's growth path of the lasting decline in markets for Chinese exports.

China's environmental challenges had emerged as an evident threat to China's and, in turn, the world's growth (and, especially, sustainable growth) and as a major contributor to climate change and associated dangers of economic crisis, political instability, and worse. China's voracious demand for energy, prospects for greatly increased fossil fuel production in North America and the likely substantial hydrocarbon reserves beneath the sharply contested waters of the South and East China Seas were reshaping great power interests and international relations in a world where secure access to foreign oil resources had long been a major focus of national security and economic security.

Such issues, which formed major foci of discussion at the Seminar, are among the consequences of China's rise to become the world's second largest economy, largest trading state and soon-to-be largest economy and its growth as a key economic partner for countries far from its borders. Such concerns are also the fall-out of China's emergence as a formidable regional military power with proven ability to sow insecurity among neighbors (especially those embroiled in territorial disputes) and with growing capacity to impede the U.S.'s ability to conduct military operations near China.

The 2012 session's title reflected the recognition of how the world and China's place in it had changed: "China in the 21st Century: What Kind of World Power?" Attempts to answer this question necessarily come with caveats about China's stature. China still lags far behind the U.S. in military capacity and possesses very limited ability to project force beyond its immediate region. The clout seemingly implied by China's impressively large and growing GDP and its massive foreign exchange reserves have to be discounted by China's still relatively low per capita income and the paucity of options for converting piles of largely U.S.-dollar-based holdings into useable power in international affairs. The prospect of a global power that is a developing country—and formally socialist (and at least residually Leninist) as well—has no precedent. Nonetheless, the indicia of China's major power status and global reach are manifest and pervaded discussion at the Seminar: the China-centered structure of the East Asian economic order; speculation that China aimed to revive the Sinocentric regional order that predated the nineteenth-century impact of the West; China's prominent place in formal and informal regional and global entities that had not existed in the middle 1990s, including the BRICs, the Shanghai Cooperation Organization, ASEAN-plus groupings, the G20, the East Asia Summit and so on.

To be sure, much of the discourse and debate at the Seminar addressed the threats to continued ascension that an incompletely risen China still faces. Some—but not all—of the apparent risks are descendants of those that had been principal concerns at the 1995 session. In 2012, what had seemed to have become an orderly and stable process for succession at the top had suddenly become badly unstuck when the Bo Xilai affair prompted old-style factional infighting, revealed a surprisingly robust challenge to a seemingly closed and largely top-down process, and triggered an awkward, several-week postponement of the Party Congress that would anoint the post-Hu Jintao leadership. It also spotlighted intra-elite divisions over agendas for economic reform and governance (ranging from Bo's neo-Maoist, quasi-populist hard-edged authoritarian "Chongqing Model" to Wang Yang's more popular-preference-accommodating and rights-regarding approach that had emerged through the provincial Party chief's response to widely publicized discontent over land-takings and the scuttled local elections in Wukan, Guangdong). Even though the expected accession of Xi Jinping, Li Keqiang and other members of the top echelon of the Fifth Generation leadership ultimately held, critical accounts depicted problems of declining capacity and pointed to an ongoing oligarchy of the mediocre (compared to the exceptional, if sometimes badly flawed, leaders of the revolutionary generation), the long term erosion of the central authorities' ability to control local powerholders and the retreat of the state from its former capacity—and will—to control Chinese society.

Skeptical questions about China's ability to extend its remarkable record of rapid growth and economic transformation were serious, numerous and strikingly varied in discussions at the Seminar. Was China finally reaching the limits to growth inherent in the authoritarian developmental state model or, less fundamentally, the limits of what could be achieved without undertaking major and perhaps politically infeasible further reforms?

Would China become ensnared in the "middle income trap"—the tenacious plateauing of economic growth that has bedeviled many countries when they have reached, roughly, China's current level of per capita income? With China's Gini coefficient—the ubiquitous measure of inequality—among the world's highest, would stark and severe maldistribution of wealth and opportunity, or the social unrest it was fueling, or the possibly growth-compromising costs of ameliorating inequality flatten or reverse China's already-falling growth rate?

Would long-deferred environmental costs, tightening energy constraints, the resurgence of state-linked enterprises and concomitant retreat of a vibrant private sector, or a rapidly aging population (partly the product of thirty years of restrictive population policies) mean the end of China's remarkable run of rapid growth? Could potential crises in local government finance or the bursting of a real estate bubble or non-recovery (or re-collapse) of rich country demand for Chinese products bring more sudden and severe hits to the economic performance that has brought China internal stability and international power and influence? Amid revived territorial disputes and soured relations with China's neighbors, were China's leaders becoming more inclined—or more constrained—to sacrifice national economic interests in international cooperation on the altar of assertive and prickly nationalism?

Would the long-resilient authoritarian regime deploy adequate methods of "social management" (the slightly Orwellian phrase favored by official Chinese sources) or—more promisingly and more hopefully—find means to accommodate a much-changed and rapidly changing society?

From the diverse perspectives of the Seminar's participants, threats to stability, risks of repressive reaction and hope for liberalization lay in the emergence of social media and other spaces for the expression of independent and critical views, vastly expanded access to ideas and information from abroad, rising rights-consciousness and demands for government accountability among ordinary citizens (spurred by official rhetoric that has endorsed the rule of law), the growth of a vast and economically insecure population of internal migrants, and the increasingly clear failures of repressive policies toward restive ethnic-religious minorities in Tibet and Xinjiang.

Although these are indeed daunting challenges and possibly serious perils with deep roots in China's Reform Era and the longer PRC Era, such difficulties face a country that has achieved a level of wealth, power and influence far greater than that which seemed certain—or perhaps even possible—a mere eighteen years earlier. Despite all the troubles actually or potentially besetting China in 2012, the relevant question is no longer whether China will become a global power but rather, as the 2012 Seminar asked, what kind of world power China will be.

As the 2012 Seminar title's also implied, China—not the United States—is now at the center. Where the 1995 session had focused significantly on the U.S.'s options and actions in responding to changes in Asia, many of the questions now are about China's choices. What path will Chinese foreign policy take now that China's power and prominence were consigning to the dustbin of history Deng Xiaoping's dictum of taoguang yanghui (often rendered—unfairly sinisterly—as "hiding brightness and biding time")?

What balance will China's policymakers strike between the Reform Era's traditional pragmatic developmentalism and the more recently ascendant and sometimes provocatively assertive nationalism? Are the ever-more-benign sounding doctrines of "peaceful development," "peaceful rise" and "harmonious world" sincere and sustainable? Are there still reliable foundations for a pro-status-quo foreign policy in the leadership's apparent preoccupation with domestic challenges and China's continued interest in a peaceful and stable external environment to support economic development at home?

Or, instead, will leaders in Beijing overestimate China's new clout, underestimate the U.S.'s resilience, and overreach in pressuring China's weaker neighbors? Are there indications of a broad inclination to use economic leverage to political ends in such moves as a threatened rare earth export embargo against Japan and moves to punish Norway over the Nobel Peace Prize for dissident Liu Xiaobo or the Philippines over the South China Sea island disputes?

Are prospects for cooperation with the U.S., the West and East Asian states severely undercut by perceptions of a U.S.-led plot to encircle China or keep China down, by exaggerated fears in Beijing of foreign-fomented secessionism in China's far West, or lingering and recrudescent senses of "victimhood" rooted in China's bitter nineteenth to mid-twentieth century experiences of colonial and quasi-colonial encroachment?

Are there meaningful signs that China will become a "responsible stakeholder" in the international system in its assertion and assumption of a major role in the G20-centered process for addressing the Global Financial Crisis, its ever-expanding participation in international regimes (particularly economic ones) and the relaxation of its once-uncompromising commitment to state sovereignty as a shield against human rights critiques and sanctions targeting problematic regimes? Or do the more significant harbingers lie in China's chafing at what it sees as politically motivated resistance—ostensibly on national security grounds—to Chinese outbound investment and high-technology imports, in chronic frictions with WTO partners over intellectual property, market access and unfair trade practices, and continuing preferences for bilateral over multilateral arrangements and recommendatory over binding processes for resolving disputes?

Is China's ability to craft and implement a stable, coherent and national interest-serving foreign policy increasingly at risk? The question has seemed increasingly relevant as the Chinese actors with stakes in China's external relations have grown in number, variety and clout: state-owned enterprises, sub-national governments, private firms, multinational corporations, new and traditional media, hordes of Netizens and public intellectuals from across China's broadened spectrum from radical reformist to New Left, from cosmopolitan globalist to ardent nationalist.

Questions of how the U.S. will deal with the most dramatic change in Asia had shifted in the opposite direction (if not quite to the same extent) during the eighteen years between the two Salzburg Seminar sessions. The long-term trends of relative U.S. decline and absolute Chinese rise meant much-reduced room for U.S. choice, much less U.S. diktats. A recurrent theme at the Seminar was the waning of the leverage that U.S.—and other, weaker states—held over China. Some argued that phrases such as "engaging China" or "integrating China" were outdated, misleading and insulting in their implications that the U.S. or others had the discretion and ability to grant or deny China stature in—much less access to—the international system. Many cautioned that simply hectoring or condemning China on human rights or greenhouse gases or intellectual property rights or other issues offered little hope for impact and risked being counterproductive. Human rights especially pointed to the complexity of the options facing the U.S. and other foreign states in dealing with a more powerful, confident and recalcitrant China. While few saw promise in the old approach of naming, shaming and threatening (but rarely imposing) sanctions, views were more varied or syncretic about what should replace it: cooperative approaches that stressed capacity-building, civil society development, progress toward the rule of law and other aims that were not obviously threatening to the regime's hold on power and that resonated with articulated regime interests and goals; and, perhaps at the same time, continuing to stress universal human rights (especially civil and political liberties), partly to remain true to our own values and partly to support those inside China who form a receptive audience and include brave advocates for positive change in China.

Dealing effectively with a large range of international issues, including volatile territorial disputes along China's maritime periphery, post-Global Financial Crisis international economic affairs, nuclear proliferation in North Korea, Iran and elsewhere, and climate change and other non-traditional security issues, requires finding ways to work with China. Policies toward China have come to be important to other states' national interests—so much so that there were multiple warnings at the Seminar that domestic politics in the U.S. and Europe (and other countries) too often produced ill-considered policies and political rhetoric toward China that poorly served national interests.

A broad and stark variation of the 2012 Seminar's titular question—"What Kind of World Power?"—loomed over the discussion of specific issues: Should the U.S., China's neighbours and pretty much everyone else proceed from the assumption that an increasingly powerful China will—or can be steered to—remain broadly accepting of the international status quo and, beyond that, become a bearer of a greater share of responsibilities to provide regional and global public goods? Or should other countries' policies be based on the premise that China will be—or at least very well might be—a revisionist power, potentially as disruptive to the largely U.S.-led current order as the rise of Germany and Japan were to the international relations and international systems of an earlier era? For advocates of both views, China's contemporary rhetoric and action—and contending theories of international relations as well—provide ample support.

With such basic questions not amenable to consensus answers (and with any answers being of limited relevance to near-term and specific policymaking), more disaggregated assessments and more nuanced prescriptions become the pressing issues. As the balance of "hard power" has shifted toward China, balancing and hedging have become evident and seem (as they did to many at the 2012 Seminar) to be wise and inevitable approaches. Examples include: the U.S.'s "pivot" or "rebalancing," other U.S. efforts to reassure China's nervous neighbours of Washington's commitments to the region, and Asian states' pursuit of closer alignment with the U.S. in a more partnership-like approach to regional security and stability. Facing a much more China-focused East Asian and, increasingly, global economy, the U.S. has understandably and sensibly (in the view of many Seminar participants and many other observers) sought—openly if not clearly successfully—to parry the trend through such initiatives as a Trans-Pacific Partnership among the U.S. and market economies in Asia and other endeavors to foster trade liberalization in the wake of the belatedly approved U.S.-Korea Free Trade Agreement. While China's rise has brought shifts in its favor in military and economic power, soft power appears to be a persisting and relatively growing strength for the United States. Across the wide spectrum of perspectives and backgrounds represented among the Seminar's participants, there was striking agreement that China's soft power has remained weak and has recently declined. China's implicit social-political model holds little appeal abroad. Values from China are stubbornly cast in parochial rather than universal terms. And Beijing's once seemingly formidable charm offense became a casualty of China's increasingly aggressive stance on territorial disputes and other foreign policy issues and the worries in Asia and beyond inescapably generated by China's great and growing clout.

With China's relations with the U.S., China's neighbours and the rest of the world having grown so much denser, complicated and ambivalent, a Salzburg Seminar-style approach may be more necessary than ever. Gathering participants from every relevant line of work, area of study, stage of career and region of the world can be a powerful solvent to the institutional and intellectual stove-piping and siloing that surely ill-serve the ends of crafting official policies and private sector approaches to the now-pervasive questions of China and its interactions with the world. Removing such people from their ordinary professional lives with their focus on immediate problems and specialized fields, and cloistering them in an intellectually open (and embarrassingly idyllic) space, creates an all-too-rare opportunity to slough off conventional wisdom, consider alternative perspectives and think outside the box. To be sure, the seeds sown on such occasions may not yield a harvestable crop until much later. But, given the magnitude and complexity of the challenges posed by a changing China and its changing place in the world, we cannot afford to eschew any promising method, not least the Seminar's eclectic version of crowd-sourcing among leaders and future leaders in a world where we all must be China hands now.

THE PATHWAY TO POWER: RUSSIA

In just a few months Putin was catapulted from relative obscurity to the pinnacle of political power. The story of his rise contains the usual mixture of serendipity and predictability to be found in any political biography. But unlike most politicians, Putin showed little political ambition throughout his career. The first election he ever contested was that for President of Russia. Political power fell into Putin's lap almost by chance. But, when the opportunity arose, he showed consumate political skills. His lack of background in politics turned out to be an asset: both in the eyes of Russian voters, and in his ability to examine Russia's problems with a dispassionate eye.

Putin was born in 1952. His father worked in a factory and his grandfather had been a cook for Stalin. They lived in a communal flat in Petersburg, sharing the kitchen with two other families. He studied law and German at Leningrad State University from 1970-75, and became an expert in judo, winning the city championship. He joined the KGB, which was his goal even before entering college. He worked in foreign intelligence in Leningrad, and was sent to East Germany in 1985, rising to the relatively modest rank of lieutenant-colonel. He witnessed the trauma of the GDR's collapse at first hand, graphically describing how he held off an angry mob outside the KGB offices in Dresden in November 1989. A call for help to the nearest Soviet army barracks went unanswered for several hours: in his words, "Moscow was silent."

Returning to Russia he worked for the KGB at Leningrad University, but then was recruited as an aide by the liberal mayor Anatolii Sobchak, his former law professor. On the first day of the August 1991 coup, Putin resigned from the KGB. Under Sobchak Putin was responsible for handling contacts with foreign companies and helping joint ventures overcome bureaucratic hurdles, and apparently he did a good job.

Sobchak lost office in 1996, falling to an electoral challenge from his former deputy Vladimir Yakovlev. Out of a job once again, Putin was tapped to join the presidential administration in Moscow, as deputy head of the powerful Kremlin property agency run by Pavel Borodin. His sponsors were the liberal Petersburg economists Anatolii Chubais, at the time deputy prime minister, and Aleksei Kudrin.

In March 1997 Putin was promoted to deputy presidential chief of staff overseeing relations with the regions, and a year later to first deputy chief of staff. In July 1998 Yeltsin appointed him head of the Federal Security Service (FSB). The influential oligarch Boris Berezovsky claims to have had a hand in Putin's rise, although the precise extent of his role is a matter of controversy. Berezovsky says he first met Putin in 1991, and as evidence of their close ties he claims that in early 2000 was still talking with him by phone once a month. Berezovsky also says that in February 1999, when he was under investigation form corruption, Putin unexpectedly came to his wife's birthday party in a show of support.

Putin's biography suggests a man of humble origins and modest ambition: intelligent, competent and loyal; an organization man and a team player. He is a populist in the sense that he understands ordinary people and speaks their language; but he is also a functionary, a bureaucrat. Service of the state and concern about the common people are the twin poles of his philosophy. He was a product of the Soviet state and its loyal servant. He was also a product of the Yeltsin state and *its* loyal servant.

Judging both by his personality and his public statements, Putin feels more comfortable in the post-1991 Russia than in the pre-1991 USSR. He is the first post-Soviet leader, a man who understands how life works in the "New Russia," with all its pluses and minuses. His life story contains evidence for both the "closet liberal" and "closet authoritarian" interpretations. He spent 16 years in the KGB – but helped bring capitalism to Petersburg. He was the first Russian leader since Lenin to speak a foreign language and live abroad – but he did so as a KGB man, in East Germany.

What is clear is that he was able to win the confidence of leading officials, and to rapidly climb the very greasy pole of Kremlin politics. What is also indisputable is that his biography provided the raw material to fashion a political persona which Russian voters found powerfully attractive.

Note that Putin rose through patronage, and not by competing in elections or working inside a political party. He was selected as a trustworthy aide by officials at ever-higher levels of responsibility. Patron-client relations were central to cadre policy in the Soviet era, and paradoxically became even more dominant as a vehicle for elite recruitment during the Yeltsin years, when Russia was becoming a democracy. This was true even for the teams of liberal reformers led by Anatolii Chubais and Boris Nemtsov, which were recruited through patronage networks.

The Chosen Successor

Putin's rise to the presidency was rapid and unexpected. In March 1999 a distinguished group of scholars assembled in Washington DC to discuss the likely candidates for the June 2000 presidential election. Papers were delivered on the leading contenders: then-Prime Minister

Yevgenii Primakov, Communist party leader Gennadii Zyuganov, Moscow mayor Yurii Luzhkov, liberal economist Grigorii Yavlinsky, and ex-general Aleksandr Lebed. The name Vladimir Putin was not mentioned – not even among the dozen or so possible outsider candidates. Nor for that matter did anyone mention the name of Sergei Stepashin, the interior minister who just one month later was appointed prime minister, only to be dismissed after four months in office.

The lesson is clear: Russian politics is highly unpredictable. Moreover, one can argue that this uncertainty is not merely a contingent factor, a product of the idiosyncracies of Boris Yeltsin's personality. Rather it is a systemic feature, due to the failure to develop robust political and economic institutions, such as stable parliamentary parties from which familiar leaders could emerge, in the decade since the collapse of communism.

Although Putin himself seemed to come from nowhere, there was one aspect of his rise that was predictable: the institutional mechanics of his elevation. Yeltsin created a political system that was held together through patronage, and in which political succession hinged was the prerogative of the incumbent leader. There were two other striking regularities of political succession under Yeltsin: the use of the post of prime minister as a sounding-board for potential successors, and increasing reliance on the security organs as a source of candidates. (Three of the four prime ministers appointed in the last 18 months of Yeltsin's rule came from the security apparatus).

Yeltsin had created a super-presidential system, where presidential power exceeded that of the legislature and was unconstrained by the emaciated judicial branch. Klyamkin and Shevtsova have described this system as an "elective monarchy," where the president rules like a monarch, but is subject to periodic election. It is natural in such a system to expect that the president will select his successor. In Mexico, for example, another super-presidential system, the practice was for the president to stay only one term in office but have the privilege of picking his successor (a process known as finger-pointing, or *dedazo*). Yeltsin failed to develop an institutional procedure for handling the transition of power and had to rely on the Russian equivalent of *dedazo*.

Yeltsin spent much of his time in office fending off challenges to his rule, primarily emanating from the Communists who with their allies had a majority in the State Duma after the December 1995 election. Although Yeltsin managed to secure re-election in June 1996, his ill- health made him a vulnerable target, and the Communists persisted unsuccessfully in their efforts to impeach the president. More attention was devoted to Yeltsin's ability to cling to power than the question of his likely successor.

However, speculation about who would succeed Yeltsin intensified after as the severity of his medical problems became clear. (Yeltsin's heart condition kept him physically out of the Kremlin for eight of the 12 months following his re-election.) In spring of 1997 Yeltsin signaling that the youthful governor of Nizhnii Novgorod, Boris Nemtsov, who he appointed first deputy prime minister might be a worthy successor. Nemtsov's liberal reforms ran into opposition from regional and industrial elites, and he fell from grace. In March 1998 Yeltsin abruptly fired the dour Viktor Chernomyrdin, prime minister since December 1992, viewing his efforts to raise his public profile as a sign of presidential ambitions.

Chernomydrin's replacement was the bland and inexperienced Sergei Kirienko, a 35-year old banker from Nizhnii Novgorod. But the August 1998 financial crash, with a dramatic foreign debt default and 75% devaluation of the ruble, forced the resignation of Kirienko. After the Duma twice rejected Yeltsin's proposal to reappoint Chernomyrdin as premier, Yeltsin agreed to accept a compromise candidate – Foreign Minister Yevgenii Primakov. Primakov appointed several communist ministers and started to cautiously chart a new course: tightening controls on export earnings, trying to rein in Russia's autonomous regions. In January 1999 Primakov proposed a compromise with the Duma that would have significantly curtailed the president's powers: in return for an end to impeachment hearings, Yeltsin would promise not to dismiss the Duma (his constitutional prerogative). In February Primakov ordered prosecutors to investigate corruption in the Central Bank and in two organizations with close ties to the Yeltsin family and their key financial backer Berezovsky, Sibneft oil company and Aeroflot. In March Procurator General Yurii Skuratov, who was in charge of these investigations, was blackmailed into resigning with a tape of him in bed with two prostitutes. Skuratov went public, the Federation Council refused to accept his resignation, and the tape was leaked to national television. In April the procuracy issued a warrant against Berezovsky – but Interior Minister Sergei Stepashin, the head of the police, refused to serve it, and Berezovsky retreated to France. Presumably in response to these anti- corruption efforts, Yeltsin fired Primakov on 12 May. Three days later the Communists put impeachment to the vote in the Duma, but failed to win the necessary two-thirds majority. Yeltsin nominated Stepashin as premier and the Duma meekly concurred. By August, however, Stepashin himself had been fired, for his failure to prevent two developments: renewed fighting in Chechnya and a new political alliance between Primakov and Moscow Mayor Yurii Luzhkov. He was replaced by Putin.

Thus Yeltsin went though three premiers (Kirienko, Primakov, and Stepashin) in 12 months before hitting upon the relatively unknown Putin. Yeltsin was using the post of prime minister to vet a presidential successor, rather than to provide a well-led government. He seemed indifferent to the resulting chaos in Russia's political system, not to mention its domestic and foreign policy.

Yeltsin had very practical reasons for being concerned about the identity of his successor. In the winner-take-all world of Russian politics, there were no guarantees that a future Russian president (under pressure from the Duma, for example) would not seek to strip Yeltsin of his government-provided villas, medical services, and other privileges, and even sanction his criminal prosecution. The same held true for the members of Yeltsin's circle: his daughter and "image consultant" Tatyana Dyachenko, his other daughter's husband Valerii Okulov, an Aeroflot executive, and the rest of his entourage known as "the Family." Again, however, it is important to remember that Russia is not unique in facing this problem of indemnifying corrupt or repressive leaders as an unpleasant precondition for removing them from office. It is a feature of democratic transitions from Indonesia to Chile. (Yeltsin's case differs slightly, in that he is a transitional figure, intermediate between the old regime and a democratic future.)

Putin, the ever-loyal apparatchik, was trusted to meet this criterion for office. The day after Yeltsin's surprising resignation on 31 December, Putin as "acting president" signed a decree granting Yeltsin and his immediate family immunity from prosecution. (The same day he also made a well-publicized trip to Chechnya.) Putin the pragmatist did what was necessary to become president. More charitably, one can suggest that Putin was less interested in an abstract search for justice than in forestalling a tide of retribution which could have had disruptive and violent consequences. His action was in keeping with the amnesty the Duma granted in1994 to the leaders of the August 1991 coup and October 1993 parliamentary rebellion – a step which Yeltsin had opposed at the time.

Putin enjoyed a vertiginous rise in popularity following his appointment as prime minister in August 1999. Polls indicated those willing to vote for him as president climbed from 2% in August to 4% in September, 21% in October, 42% in November, 50% in December and 59% in January.

By then his approval rating as prime minister was 79%. In contrast, for the past several years Yeltsin's approval rating had been in the single digits. Putin's rise was fueled by two factors, analyzed in the following sections: the war in Chechnya, and the strong showing of the pro-Putin Unity party in the December 1999 Duma elections.

As Putin's rating rose the Yeltsin camp became increasingly confident that they had found the ideal successor. Yeltsin's decision to step down and appoint Putin "acting president' nevertheless came as a great surprise – not least because of the drama of its announcement on 31 December, at the dawn of a new millenium. Yeltsin had clung to power with such determination over the preceding decade that it was hard to imagine that he would leave before the end of his term, in June 2000. But in retrospect it is easy to explain why Yeltsin resigned in December. By selecting his own successor, Yeltsin underlined his historic legacy as Russia's "first president" (which is his official designation, as opposed to "former president").

More importantly, it boosted Putin's chances of winning the election. Putin would have the crucial advantage of incumbency: the ability to use the presidential office to mobilize support and cultivate an image of leadership. It seemed that Putin's popularity had already reached its peak and would erode over time – especially if Russian forces were to suffer setbacks in Chechnya. Yeltsin's resignation minimized this risk by bringing forward the election from June to the end of March, since the constitution decrees that elections must be held within three months of a presidential resignation.

2

India's Leading and Super Power Shift in Asia

Singapore's defence minister Ng Eng Hen stated last month that his country wanted India to play a bigger role in the South China Sea. The leaders of Vietnam and the Philippines have also made similar statements in recent years. This "invitation" extended to India by the leaders of Southeast Asia to participate in that region's security affairs is tantamount to India's emergence as a great power in Southeast Asia, and by extension, in Asia itself. Southeast Asia connects the Indian and the Pacific Oceans, and includes some of the most important maritime chokepoints, is likely to be the site of order-making in Asia in the context of the rise of China.

Thomas Donilon, who was the American National Security Advisor when the US said its "pivot/rebalancing" has explained that the pivot is not just about "rebalancing towards Asia" but also includes rebalancing "within Asia" as America has begun to focus "in a renewed way on Southeast Asia and Asean." Furthermore, the Asian-institutional architecture is Asean-centric and Asean-led. Therefore, India's emerging profile in Southeast Asia is significant and marks its arrival as a great power.

Solid grounds

There are two main reasons that explain the benign perception of India's rise in Southeast Asia. First, there are no territorial disputes between India and its immediate neighbours in Southeast Asia. India has a land border with only one Southeast Asian state, Myanmar, which was fixed by their British colonial rulers in 1937. India has maritime borders with three Southeast Asian states: Myanmar, Thailand, and Indonesia. India's maritime boundaries with

Thailand and Indonesia were fixed through a trilateral agreement in 1978, while India's maritime boundary with Myanmar was finalized in 1987.

Second, India is not pursuing any unilateral or hegemonic policies towards Southeast Asia. In 2012, former Prime Minister, Manmohan Singh, explicitly noted that New Delhi believes that "Asean centrality is essential in the evolving regional architecture," endorsing Asean's leading role in regional diplomacy. Similarly, at the military/maritime level, India not only prefers to be invited into the region , but former defence minister, Pranab Mukherjee, noted in 2006 that India was willing to assist the regional states in "any capacity" for security in the Strait of Malacca subject "to the desire of the littoral states."

In other words, despite India's more advanced military capabilities, New Delhi is not claiming the mantle of leadership there but prefers to work in accordance with the local norms and mores. Therefore, it is not surprising that Lee Kuan Yew, Singapore's recently deceased statesman, welcomed India's presence in Southeast Asia in 2007 by noting that there was "no fear" that India had "aggressive intentions." India has now transcended its home region of South Asia due to its growing power in Southeast Asia, thus becoming a key component of the Asian security architecture along with the region's other great powers: the United States, Japan, and China. Notably, all three Asian great powers also seem to be willing to work with India in Southeast Asia.

Strategic edge

US President Obama has urged India to "act East" on a number of occasions. Furthermore, the US and India released a joint vision statement earlier this year in which they specifically called for "safeguarding maritime security and ensuring freedom of navigation and over flight throughout the region, especially in the South China Sea." On his part, Japanese Prime Minister Shinzo Abe sees the India-Japan relationship as a "confluence" of the Indian and Pacific Oceans.

Notably, Southeast Asia is geographically — and geopolitically — located at this confluence. The Japan-India statement on their strategic and global partnership that was released last year especially noted the launch of their "bilateral dialogue on Asean affairs." Finally, China also seems to be willing to work with India, even if begrudgingly, in the region's economic and institutional affairs.

Through their 2008 shared vision document, China and India agreed to "explore ... a new architecture for closer regional cooperation in Asia, and to make joint efforts for regional integration of Asia." This statement, which explicitly identified the Asean-led East Asia Summit as an avenue where

China and India can work together is significant simply because China was hitherto unwilling to recognize India as a major power in Asia beyond South Asia.

In other words, the regional states of Southeast Asia, as well as the great powers active in Southeast Asia, now seem willing to grant India the status of a great power in that region.

This has two noteworthy implications. First, these acts 'legitimise' India's status as a great power in Asia as well as its role in the security affairs of a region outside of India's home region in South Asia. As such, India is not seen as an interloper. Second, this empirically demonstrates that the rise of a new great power need not disrupt the extant order as is normally assumed. In fact, the rise of a new great power — in this case, India — can be seen as contributing to the maintenance of the regional order.

Security angles

India has three main security-related interests in Southeast Asia. First, as noted by Mukherjee in 2005, India's "Look East" strategy is based on the principle of "the maintenance of an equitable strategic balance."

India does not want Southeast Asia to be dominated by any single great power. Consequently, India is upgrading its naval and air assets in the Andaman and Nicobar Islands. Located at the mouth of the Strait of Malacca, India's maritime and air capabilities in the Andamans help India meet its second security interest in the region: the security of the Strait itself. Finally, India's growing maritime and air capabilities — cantered on diverse platforms such as the P-8I aircraft, the C-130Js, the C-17 Globemasters, Sukhoi-30 MKIs, aircraft carrier(s), nuclear submarine(s), and landing dock(s) — allow India to project military power into the South China Sea from the Andamans.

After all, India's third security interest in Southeast Asia is to ensure the freedom of navigation in the South China Sea. In fact, India's regional partnerships — including docking rights at Vietnam's Nha Trang port — may further augment India's capabilities. At the same time, India has been providing a range of security-related public goods in Southeast Asia such as the provision of humanitarian and disaster relief assistance as well as military capacity-building in regional states.

Despite these modest but significant efforts, Southeast Asian states want India to "do more" pro-actively. The crucial question now is whether India's political leaders will grasp the geopolitical opportunity to ensconce India in the emerging Asian order or if a lack of vision and the exigencies of domestic politics will effectively force New Delhi to squander the chance to shape Asia.

At the very least, India needs to expedite its economic engagement with Southeast Asia while enhancing physical connectivity – land and maritime – in order to demonstrate its seriousness.

INDIA AS A LEADING POWER

Prime Minister Narendra Modi's call for India to become a leading power represents a change in how the country's top political leadership conceives of its role in international politics. In Modi's vision, a leading power is essentially a great power. However, India will only acquire this status when its economic foundations, its state institutions, and its military capabilities are truly robust. It will take concerted effort to reach this pinnacle.

Realizing Unfulfilled Potential:

- When fulfilled, Modi's ambition to make India a great power will mark the beginning of a third epoch in Indian foreign policy, when its weight and preferences will determine outcomes in the global system.
- New Delhi's current ability to expand its national power is handicapped by an overly regulated economy, inadequate state capacity, burdensome state-society relations, and limited rationalization across state and society writ large, all of which have persisted throughout India's history as an independent nation.
- Whether India becomes a great power depends on its ability to achieve multidimensional success in terms of improving its economic performance and wider regional integration, acquiring effective military capabilities for power projection coupled with wise policies for their use, and sustaining its democracy successfully by accommodating the diverse ambitions of its peoples.
- Even if India manages to undertake the myriad reforms necessary to achieve these aims, many analyses suggest that it will be the weakest of the major poles for decades to come, geographically located uncomfortably close to a powerful China.

WHAT INDIA MUST DO TO BECOME A LEADING POWER

Complete the structural reforms necessary to create efficient product and factor markets. India has lost too many opportunities to build efficient markets that foster innovation and accelerate long-term trend growth. The government needs to redirect its activities toward producing better public goods, while establishing an institutional framework that stimulates private creativity and increases rationalization across Indian society.

Create an effective state to leverage India's capacity to build its national power. Without a vastly improved presence in society as well as better extractive and regulatory capacities—all of which require a more autonomous state—India cannot accumulate material capabilities to rapidly become a great power.

Foster a strong relationship with the United States. The United States is an important host for India's skilled labor; remains a critical source of capital, technology, and expertise; and constitutes the fulcrum of strategic support for India's global ambitions.

If India maintains robust ties with the United States, even as it strengthens relations with key U.S. allies in Asia and beyond, it will continue to gain indispensable benefits.

Less than a year after he took office in May 2014, India's Prime Minister Narendra Modi challenged his senior diplomats "to help India position itself in a leading role, rather than [as] just a balancing force, globally." Elaborating on this idea, the foreign secretary, Subrahmanyam Jaishankar, later noted that Modi's dramatic international initiatives reflected India's growing self-confidence, declaring that the country now "aspire[s] to be a leading power, rather than just a balancing power."

When this ambition is realized, it will mark the third and most decisive shift in independent India's foreign policy, one that could have significant consequences for the future international order. It will take concerted effort, however, to reach this pinnacle in the years ahead: New Delhi will have to reform its economy, strengthen its state capacity, and elevate the levels of rationalization across state and society writ large so that India may be able to effectively produce those military instruments that increase its security and influence in international politics.

FROM BALANCING TO LEADING POWER?

For the longest time, India's foreign policy was essentially defensive. Its early rhetoric was bold—championing, in former prime minister Jawaharlal Nehru's words, a "real internationalism" that promoted global peace and shared prosperity. Yet its material weaknesses ensured that its strategic aims in practice were focused principally on protecting the country's democracy and development from the intense bipolar competition of the Cold War. Although the character of India's international engagement varied during these years, its broad orientation did not: remaining fundamentally conservative, India's nonalignment aimed mainly at preventing U.S.-Soviet hostility from undermining its security, autonomy, and well-being at a time when the country was still relatively infirm.

In retrospect, this effort turned out to be more successful than was imagined initially. India survived the Cold War with its territorial integrity broadly intact, its state- and nation-building activities largely successful, and its political autonomy and international standing durably ensconced. In the process, it created some impressive industrial and technological capabilities, but its obsession with "self-reliance" unfortunately also ensured the relative decline of India's economic weight in Asia and beyond.

After 1991, when it was freed from the compulsions of having to avoid competing alliances at all costs, India entered into the second phase of its foreign policy evolution. Pursuing a variety of strategic partnerships with more than 30 different countries, India sought to expand specific forms of collaboration that would increase its power and accelerate its rise. The domestic economic reforms unleashed in the very year of the Soviet Union's collapse paved the way for consolidating India's path toward higher growth. From the abysmal 3.5 percent annual growth witnessed until the 1980s, the 1991 reforms accelerated the improving 5.5 percent growth rate to the 7 percent demonstrated since the new millennium, leading the U.S. Central Intelligence Agency to conclude that India was likely to become the most important "swing state" in the international system. This assessment suggested that India's significance in global politics lay mainly in its being a balancing power. That is, even if it were not strong enough to be an independent pole, its presence in any particular international coalition would strengthen that grouping significantly.

Since the presidency of George W. Bush, this realization has driven the United States to consciously assist the growth of Indian power. On the assumption that New Delhi and Washington share a common interest in preventing Chinese hegemony in Asia, the United States has sought to bolster India as a counterweight to China, fully appreciating that India would pursue an independent foreign policy but expecting nonetheless that it would concord with larger U.S. interests in the Indo-Pacific. Even if India were to eventually become a true pole in international politics, U.S. calculations would not in any way be undermined: shared democratic values would then position India as a valuable partner for the United States, while its growing national capacities would help to create those objective constraints that check the misuse of Chinese power in Asia in the interim.

Modi's clarion call for India to assume a leading, rather than merely a balancing, role signifies larger ambitions. Jaishankar summarized these aims succinctly when he stated, insofar "as larger international politics is concerned, India welcomes the growing reality of a multi-polar world, as it does, of a multi-polar Asia." In other words, India, by its choices at home and its actions abroad, would seek to create the distribution of capabilities at both the global and the continental levels that would accommodate its presence as an authentic great power. Although these aspirations are conveyed by the more modest locution "leading power," Modi's vision, strictly speaking, envisages India becoming a traditional great power—an inescapable conclusion if the desire for multipolarity at the global level has any consequential meaning.

Contrasting the concepts clarifies the point abundantly. From a structural perspective, great powers in international politics are genuine poles: their number defines the configuration of the global system, and their preferences regulate its institutions and determine the ways in which its constituent entities relate to one another. Great powers, accordingly, are system makers. Leading powers, in contrast, are not genuine poles. They exist within the dispositions defined by the great powers, and while they do influence various issues, they cannot determine outcomes pertaining to the fundamental questions of order against the core inclinations of the great powers. Leading powers, therefore, can at best be system shapers. Minor powers, in even greater contrast, are unambiguously system takers. They cannot impose their desires on others, and they can secure their national aims only through aid from other states and institutions or at the sufferance of stronger powers.

Clearly, Modi seeks to transform India from being merely an influential entity into one whose weight and preferences are defining for international politics. While this desire is laudable, it appears that India's climb to great power status will take time. Although contemporary projections of global growth out to 2050 suggest that India will become a true pole by then, they also conclude that it will remain the weakest of the principal entities—China, the United States, the European Union, and India—dominating the international system at that time. A detailed analysis from 2012 suggested that India, representing only 7 percent of the global product in 2050, will remain well behind China at 20 percent and the United States and the European Union at 17 percent each, though it will be somewhat ahead of Japan at 5 percent and comfortably lead Russia and Brazil at 3 and 2 percent, respectively. Assuming that current U.S. alliances survive until then, the Western democracies and Japan will still reign supreme with 39 percent of the global product, almost double that of China's and similarly close to double China's and Russia's gross domestic products (GDPs) combined.

It is in the greater Asia-Pacific region, however, that India can make a dramatic difference to the continental balance. If India allies with the United States and Japan, the resulting 29 percent of the global product will easily exceed China's 20 percent in contrast to only the marginal advantage that the two democracies will enjoy if India sits out. Against China and Russia together (a total of 23 percent), India's contribution will become even more valuable because it will erase the slight inferiority that will otherwise mark the collective U.S.-Japanese product.

Such projections help to characterize India's value in the larger geopolitical context, and their underlying insight is sobering. Although India will likely be transformed into a genuine pole by 2050, it will remain fundamentally a balancing power—a swing state—rather than a colossus capable of either holding its own against a major rival such as China or defining the international system to its advantage in the face of possible opposition.

To be sure, all long-term economic projections are fragile for various reasons. But insofar as such forecasts represent disciplined analysis, any differences between their predictions and the actual outcomes are likely be of degree rather than of fundamental mischaracterization.

This does not imply that Modi's vision of India as a leading power ought to be jettisoned. Far from it. It should in fact be pursued even more vigorously to protect the possibility of India becoming a true pole by 2050 with material power exceeding what the current prognoses suggest—an outcome that will require New Delhi to purposefully expand its own national capabilities in ways that other great powers have done before.

INDIA: THE FIGHT TO BECOME A SCIENCE SUPERPOWER

With her jeans, T-shirt and spirited attitude, Tapasya Srivastava could pass for a student as she works in her brightly lit cancer-biology lab on the University of Delhi South Campus. Srivastava, who oversees a team of eight researchers, is thrilled that she earned "a small research space of my own" in 2010, while still in her thirties. "With a decent list of publications under my belt, I am one of the few who have studied and undergone training entirely in India," she says.

Eight kilometres away, in the chemical-engineering department of the Indian Institute of Technology Delhi, Shalini Gupta's team is developing sensors to detect early-stage sepsis and typhoid. Gupta did her doctorate in the United States but returned to India to focus on its needs: "I am more connected to society and its challenges," she says.

Srivastava and Gupta are part of a wave of young Indian scientists convinced that they can do high-quality research at home rather than having to move abroad. Such optimism reaches all the way to the top: in January, Indian Prime Minister Narendra Modi told an assembly of scientists to "dream, imagine and explore. You will have no better supporter than me." India has much to be proud of. Last year, it became the first to reach Mars on its initial attempt. It boasts a thriving pharmaceutical industry that produces low-cost medications that are desperately needed by the developing world. And in his first year in office, Modi launched an ambitious plan to make India a leader in solar power.

Such successes cannot hide the huge challenges facing this country of 1.3 billion people, which leads the world in tuberculosis incidence and maternal deaths, and lacks electricity for one-quarter of its citizens. India is expected to become the world's most populous nation within a generation, and it will require a robust science and technology sector to supply the needed energy, food, health care, jobs and growth. Yet researchers in India and abroad say that the country has a relatively weak foundation in science and engineering.

Indian research is hampered by stifling bureaucracy, poor-quality education at most universities and insufficient funding. Successive governments have pledged to increase support for research and development to 2% of India's gross domestic product (GDP), but it has remained static at less than 0.9% of GDP since 2005. Despite its huge size, India has a relatively tiny number of researchers, and many of its budding scientists leave for other countries, never to return. Only by tackling its systemic problems can India compete with other emerging powerhouses such as Brazil and China.

"The density of scientists and engineers in India is one of the lowest in the world," says Sunil Mani, an economist at the Centre for Development Studies in Trivandrum, who is assessing Indian science and engineering for an upcoming report by the United Nations Educational, Scientific and Cultural Organization. "There are very many important areas where we are not able to do research."

Space to grow

In one of the cleanest rooms in India, Mylswamy Annadurai is busy conducting fitness tests on a 750-kilogram patient — a gleaming satellite called ASTROSAT. The probe is strapped to a table, where it is being shaken at six times the strength of gravity to simulate the intense forces of lift-off. ASTROSAT must also pass tests in extreme high and low temperatures and vacuum conditions, followed by checks on its solar arrays and antennas.

If all goes well, the satellite will blast into orbit by September, armed with two telescopes and four other instruments to study both nearby and distant stars.

Annadurai, who is head of the satellite centre of the Indian Space Research Organisation (ISRO) in Bangalore, says that ASTROSAT will be India's "first full-fledged science mission" in space. It will carry instruments ten times heavier than those on India's first mission to the Moon, 2008's Chandrayaan-1, and its 2014 Mars Orbiter Mission, nicknamed Mangalyaan.

With its run of recent accomplishments, India has earned international acclaim for its ambitious space programme, which includes launch vehicles, communication satellites and one of the world's largest constellation of remote sensing satellites, as well as its science missions. Since ISRO was founded in 1969, the government has invested heavily in it, and even established a dedicated university in 2007 to train personnel. "The ISRO technical test, assembly and launch facilities are first class," says Paul Spudis, senior staff scientist at the Lunar and Planetary Institute in Houston, Texas, who was the principal investigator for one of Chandrayaan-1's experiments.

Chandrayaan-1 carried an orbiter and a 35-kilogram probe that took images as it smashed into the Moon at high speed. ISRO plans to follow it in 2017 with Chandrayaan-2, which will gently set down a lander and a six-wheeled rover; together with an orbiter, they will study the composition of the Moon's surface. Up next after that is the Aditya mission to study the Sun's corona, in 2018.

Spudis is critical of last year's Mars mission, calling it "largely irrelevant" and saying that it would have been better to return quickly to the moon. ISRO, he says, "seems to lack a strategic vision of what it wants to accomplish in space". But the agency counters that it is pursuing several missions in parallel; the Mars mission just proceeded faster than Chandrayaan-2. And the success in reaching Mars has convinced others at ISRO that they can carry out world-class space-science missions, says Annadurai. "The Mars mission experience has once again strengthened our belief that we can."

Biotech bonanza

In Genome Valley, a biotechnology park in Hyderabad, entrepreneur Krishna Ella is confounding expectations. Ella returned home from the United States in 1996 with a 12-metre shipping container filled with vaccine-making equipment to support his grand plan of producing a US$1 vaccine for hepatitis B. That goal, which would make his vaccine at least an order of magnitude cheaper than the available one, struck investors as crazy, he says. But within three years, Ella's company Bharat Biotech International Limited (BBIL) succeeded in producing the Revac-B+ hepatitis vaccine at $3 a dose, which has since dropped to 30 cents per dose. It went on to develop vaccines against

Japanese encephalitis, rabies, haemophilus influenza virus B and, most recently, rotavirus. Each costs barely a dollar per dose.

Affordable medicines are the cornerstone of India's health-care sector, where publicly funded hospitals struggle to provide treatment. The country has long battled infectious diseases such as tuberculosis, malaria and dengue, but is now facing rising numbers of non-communicable illnesses, including diabetes and coronary heart disease. A 2014 report from the World Economic Forum and Harvard School of Public Health estimates that non-communicable diseases and mental illness could cost India $4.58 trillion by 2030.

Low-price vaccines and generic drugs have helped India to carve out a niche in the international pharmaceutical industry. The global medical charity Médecins Sans Frontières (also known as Doctors Without Borders), which relies on Indian generics for 80% of its anti-HIV drugs, hails the country as the "pharmacy of the developing world". Other international organizations, including the UN children's charity UNICEF and the Global Fund to Fight AIDs, Tuberculosis and Malaria, routinely use Indian vaccines and generic drugs to treat infectious diseases (see *Nature* 468, 143; 2010).

But India is battling criticism over the quality of some of its pharmaceuticals. In 2012, for example, the World Health Organization took BBIL's hepatitis B vaccine and oral polio vaccine off the list of drugs preapproved for use by the UN. Ella says that the issues related to documentation submission and that they have since been sorted out. The vaccines are now back on the list.

In 2014, the US Food and Drug Administration (FDA) sent warning letters to seven Indian firms over various concerns relating to pharmaceutical production there. An FDA spokesperson told *Nature*: "While some Indian companies meet US product quality standards, others have been found to lack sufficient controls and systems to assure drug quality, both of finished product and active ingredients." The FDA has an India office to work closely with Indian drug regulators to solve those problems.

And some in the biotech sector warn that India has a long way to go to create a thriving enterprise in developing new drugs. The country's success in the generics industry relies on a different set of skills: reverse-engineering pharmaceuticals created elsewhere by breaking them into their components and remaking them through cheaper routes.

"The challenge for the sector will be to graduate from reverse engineering to new-drug discovery," says Pallu Reddanna, a biotechnologist at the University of Hyderabad. "There is need for incentives and promotion of academy–industry interactions."

The government and private sector are trying to jump-start such efforts by setting up incubators that help transfer university and lab know-how to industry, and provide infrastructure and financial support to start-ups. Such incubators are the "greatest changer in the drug-discovery sector in India", says P. Yogeeswari, a chemist at the Hyderabad campus of Birla Institute of Technology and Science.

Krishnaswamy VijayRaghavan, secretary of the government's Department of Biotechnology, commends "incredible growth" in India's biotech entrepreneurship — despite the lack of big drug companies and the relatively low domestic investment in drug discovery. International and industry collaborations with academia are helping to advance the sector, he says. In 2013, the department started two major projects seeking drugs for drug-resistant tuberculosis and chronic disorders such as heart disease. In early leads, scientists have zeroed in on some human proteins that are crucial for the survival of multidrug-resistant tuberculosis strains. Proof-of-concept studies in mice have demonstrated that targeting such host proteins could help to kill the drug-resistant strains, says VijayRaghavan (S. Jayaswal *et al. PLoS Pathog.* 6, e1000839; 2010). "We are at an exciting early applied stage," he says.

Power hungry

Nearly 2,000 kilometres north of Genome Valley, 9.7 hectares of solar panels cover a building in Punjab state, generating 7.5 megawatts of electricity. This project is India's largest roof-top solar installation that is connected to an electrical power grid, and it signals India's outsize ambitions in renewable energy.

Coal supplies two-thirds of the electricity in India and will remain king for some time. But the government has set aggressive goals for installing solar-energy capacity. In 2014, Modi's government announced that it would develop 100 gigawatts of solar-energy capacity by 2022. This is a huge leap from the existing 3.7 gigawatts of solar capacity — just 1.4% of India's total electricity generation today.

"India is one of the most attractive markets in the world," says Pashupathy Gopalan, Asia Pacific head of SunEdison, a global solar-energy company based in Maryland Heights, Missouri, which is joining Adani Enterprises of Ahmedabad to build India's largest solar-panel-manufacturing facility. "We are entering a new era where solar electricity is competitive and has achieved 'socket parity' with other sources of energy in India."

There are other big international collaborations. The Solar Energy Research Institute for India and the United States was established in 2012 to target emerging research areas. In one project, researchers are trying to generate solar thermal power by using sunlight to heat up a highly compressed fluid form of carbon dioxide so that it turns electricity-generating turbines. This could be used in much smaller plants than conventional steam-driven turbines.

But some analysts say that India suffers from "gigawatt obsession". The focus on giant solar plants comes at the expense of smaller facilities that do not require large parcels of land, but could provide electricity to isolated towns, even without being connected to the grid.

"The gigawatt rush must pay attention to the pace with which the capacity is to be built in India," says Satish Agnihotri, former secretary of India's Ministry of New and Renewable Energy. Plans to build large plants could run into opposition in densely populated or heavily farmed areas, and in remote areas it can be difficult to hook gigawatt projects up to the electrical system.

News and debates about the government's current focus on solar power have overshadowed past successes in wind energy. India has more than 23 gigawatts of installed wind-power capacity, which puts it roughly even with Spain as the world's fourth biggest producer. And Mumbai-based Suzlon is the world's seventh-largest turbine manufacturer.

India has been able to develop its wind power in part because of long-term government policies and financial incentives, as well as a growing interest from independent power producers and financiers, says Shantanu Jaiswal, lead analyst at Bloomberg New Energy Finance in New Delhi. But some of the concerns about solar power also hamper wind projects, which face difficulty acquiring land, encounter lengthy permitting processes and often have trouble connecting to the electrical power grid.

Education outlook

Back on her leafy campus in Delhi, Srivastava and her fellow young faculty members are less concerned about big national projects than about producing their own high-quality research. They are lucky, they acknowledge, to work in one of India's top federally funded universities, which has superior faculty members and equipment.

Others are not so fortunate. India has some 700 universities of varying quality, from the elite institutions funded by the central government to more than 300 state universities and about 200 private ones. "The landscape of science education is uneven," says Sri Krishna Joshi, former director-general of India's Council of Scientific and Industrial Research (CSIR) and former chair of the advisory committee of the University Grants Commission, which funds and oversees university education in India.

"We are caught in a vicious circle of mediocrity." In the top institutions, he says, "science students are doing world-class research, publishing in leading journals and boosting the global reputation of our country". National scientific research institutes and leading universities have all contributed to India's growing strengths in research: the country's output of scientific publications quadrupled between 2000 and 2013.

Even so, India is not keeping pace with some other emerging nations, which have increased their scientific output more quickly (see page 142). And the advances in India's global science metrics mask some signs of declining quality in university science education, especially at the cash-starved universities funded by state governments that account for the majority of India's science undergraduates, says Joshi. Publicly supported universities depend on the Ministry of Human Resource Development for funds, and the higher-education budget was hit by a 3% cut in the 2014–15 budget cycle.

"Lack of even bare, minimal and sustainable funds for teaching, let alone research, has seriously plagued the quality and standards of science education," says Krishna Ganesh, a chemist and director of the Indian Institute of Science Education and Research in Pune, one of five top universities set up in India since 2006. Many students at state universities are receiving a substandard education, says Joshi. "Here, there are no good science teachers, no good Indian textbooks, and most of the science laboratories are poorly equipped," he says.

"We are caught in a vicious circle of mediocrity," says geneticist Deepak Pental, former vice-chancellor of the University of Delhi. Most analysts are concerned over the plight of science departments in state universities. At the University of Calcutta, for example, even procuring a laptop involves endless red tape, says physicist Amitava Raychaudhuri. At some other institutions, support from funding agencies helps to purchase equipment, but there is a shortage of qualified faculty members to train the students.

Beyond questions of quality, the quantity of available university spots is a persistent problem. India has gone through a university building boom, but there still is a huge shortage of slots for students (see *Nature* 472, 24–26; 2011).

"There is a rise in the number of students going for higher education in India, which reflects the rising aspirations of its society. But this rise should be matched by better infrastructure and financial support," says Joshi.

Research investments

Investments in science have also dragged. India's research intensity — the share of its gross domestic product devoted to research and development

(GERD) — remains lower than those of many other nations, including Brazil and Russia. Twenty years ago, India's GERD exceeded China's. Now, it is less than half.

But those numbers do not tell the whole story, says Ashutosh Sharma, secretary of the government's Department of Science and Technology — one of India's largest research-funding agencies. "The total funding is, perhaps, not as poor as it seems in terms of absolute numbers, because the number of full-time scientists doing research is also low."

India averages about 4 full-time researchers per 10,000 people in the labour force, whereas China boasts 18 and nations with advanced science and technology sectors have around 80. "India spends about $150,000 per scientist per year, which is probably not too far from the optimal levels," says Sharma.

India's notorious bureaucracy deserves part of the blame for the problems afflicting science education and research. The administrators of several state universities are political appointees rather than leading academics. "Often the appointed person has never been exposed to a good university in India or abroad," says Kizhakeyil Sebastian, chair of the science-education panel of the Indian Academy of Sciences in Bangalore. "There is over-bureaucratization within the universities and their controlling bodies," says Pental. It often takes two years to recruit an academic after announcing an open post, which means that the best applicants can slip away, says Raychaudhuri.

The governmental quagmire has begun to affect some elite national research institutes, too. Of the 38 national laboratories that are part of the CSIR, only 25 have full-time directors. The rest are making do with acting directors, or temporary arrangements. Even the CSIR headquarters in New Delhi has been without a full-time leader since January 2014. Interim director-general Madhukar Garg says that "the current situation is indeed challenging. CSIR is the backbone of scientific and technological research in the country. In case the prevailing scenario continues, it will affect the national innovation system as a whole."

Sharma acknowledges that red tape is "all-pervasive", but he says that the challenges are not bogging down Indian science. "In terms of output indicators such as the number of papers per dollar spent, Indian science is among the very top performers in the world," he says.

And there are some signs that India might be slowing its debilitating brain drain. Although the vast majority of Indians who obtain science doctorates in the United States remain there for at least 5 years after graduation, the proportion has declined: from 89% in 2001 to 82% in 2011, the most recent year for which data are available.

Kaustuv Datta, a geneticist at Delhi University South Campus, is one of those who returned. Datta may "hate the red-tapism" at universities in India, but he still prefers doing research back home. "My parents are here, in India. And academics have a strong, positive influence on the next generation of students," says Datta. "I wanted to make that contribution in India".

INDIA: A CENTURY OF STRUGGLE AND THE RISE OF A SUPERPOWER

The monograph "A History of India: The Twentieth Century" is an outstanding work embracing the eventful period of Indian history, from political processes in colonial India to India's path of development today. In this major work, the authors present a thorough, in-depth analysis of the crucial socio-political and economic processes taking place in contemporary India.

The monograph offers readers a definitive, multifaceted study. The first part of the work reviews key political processes in colonial India and the history of the country's struggle for independence, in which Mahatma Gandhi played a major role. The second part analyses the formation and implementation of socio-political and economic policy in India since independence. The third part explores the fundamental priorities of the foreign policy in independent India, as well as its military doctrine and the build-up of its armed forces.

The work investigates the activities of India's key political parties, above all the Indian National Congress and the Bharatiya Janata Party, as well as achievements and failures of left-wing and regional parties. A study of the role of religions and religious castes constitutes an integral part of the study of India's domestic political processes.

Some chapters address specific aspects of the formation and implementation of economic strategy in modern India that can be traced to the time when the governments of both Jawaharlal Nehru and Indira Gandhi, and parties opposing the Congress Party were in power. The review of India's economic reforms of the 1990s emphasises that, despite its focus on economic liberalisation, India did not renounce its previous achievements, specifically national economic planning. The market economy can and must be used as a measure of the exigencies and requirements of the people.

The work stresses the positive role of the Indian diaspora, numbering over 25 million people. Remittances from emigres make a significant contribution to the country's balance of payments. By the same token, Indians living abroad are proactively and successfully lobbying for India's interests in relation to the commerce, economies and political lines of their countries of residence. Furthermore, they even helped India secure the right to use the know-how they had accumulated to develop and upgrade its own economy.

India's social development experience since independence has demonstrated that its progress resulted from a national focus in the social, economic, and political development model. India's search for development options has been based largely on its own historical traditions. In its political practices, as well as in building its political and social systems, India has been relying on methods rooted in the specifics of Indian society. This, however, has not implied creation or pursuit of any autarchic model. Indians have localised the best achievements of other nations (for instance, the democratic system of governance) and cautiously, without ever forcing them on society, built them into their system of values, lending them a national hue.

Meanwhile, India's spiritual and political elite has never given up the further search for solutions to outstanding problems and new challenges. The key criterion in this search has been the capacity of a particular model to solve problems rather than a commitment to a certain ideology.

The section of the book that provides an overview of the foreign policy of independent India, including its contribution to the Non-Aligned Movement and the nature of its relations with its major international partners: the Soviet Union (succeeded by Russia), the United States of America and China, deserves separate mention. It deals largely with a study of India's policies in South Asia and the Asia-Pacific region, armed conflicts and wars with China and Pakistan.

The monograph emphasises that at all stages of India's independent development and its foreign policy have served as a major tool for securing its national interests based on equality, justice, and democratisation of both economic and political international relations. Simultaneously, India has always sought to respond flexibly to global changes by making tactical adjustments, yet remaining adamantly committed to consistently observing the fundamentals of its foreign policy that go back to the first years of its independence.

India's evolution into a nuclear superpower is discussed in this work separately. The monograph highlights the role of India's confrontation with Pakistan, specifically the Indo-Pakistani war of 1965, and the armed conflict with China in 1962, in India's emergence on the nuclear arena.

Still, India's way of securing an independent nuclear position cannot be called easy or, still less, rash. The book discusses why India, which had repeatedly promoted moves to create a nuclear-free world, nevertheless refused to sign the Nuclear Non-Proliferation Treaty (1970). In 1974, the country tested a nuclear device as a warning to its rivals on the international arena and demonstrating India's scientific and technological potential. And finally, 24 years later, in May 1998, it test-fired a nuclear weapon. After the breakup of the USSR and the end of the bipolar world, India was faced with reinforcing its national security in the new environment, including through use of nuclear weapons.

The monograph is a fundamental work, building its conclusions on a broad reference base. This book's clear advantage is that, alongside official documents, works by Russian and foreign India-scholars and researchers engaged in broader studies, as well as press publications from all over the world, it features personal observations and assessments by its authors formed resulting from many years spent working in India.

The wealth of information and the unconventional assessments and conclusions this book features make it an interesting reading not only for specialists in Oriental studies, but also a wider readership.

INDIA AS A RISING MILITARY POWER

China has taken serious note of India's growing military power over the last decade. India, which has traditionally talked of the power of argument began to talk of the argument of power. In fact, the 1998 nuclear tests themselves were indicative of the fact that India had begun to realize the role of hard power in securing its national interests and also in making her voice heard in international politics. India's growing military profile is especially evident in the maritime domain. The Indian navy has emerged as the net security provider in the Indian Ocean over the last decade. In 2004, it unveiled its first-ever naval doctrine that defined India's legitimate areas of interest stretching from the Persian Gulf to the Malacca Straits. It released its updated version in 2009, incorporating the rapid changes in the geo-strategic environment involving India. India's defense ties with the US have developed at a frenetic pace, which has played the central role in India's military modernization. For example, recent defense contracts signed with the US include US$ 1.1 billion for C-130J Super Hercules transport planes and US$2.4 billion for 10 Globemasters airlifters. In January 2009, the Indian Navy signed an agreement with the U. S. to buy eight P-8I planes worth nearly US$2.1 billion, so as to replace the aging long range aerial reconnaissance fleet of eight Russian-made Tu-142s and five IL-38 planes.

The tests of its China-centric Agni series missile systems and the development of a Ballistic Missile Defense system. India's future military plans are even more ambitious, which further complicates China's strategic calculations. For example, the Indian Ministry of Defense in late 2011 announced its biggest expansion package to date, a US$13 billion military modernization plan. Under this plan within next five years, the Indian army is set to deploy 90,000 more soldiers and raise four new divisions along India's border with China, the largest such mobilization since the Sino-Indian border clashes of 1962.

India's Poly/Multi-aligned Diplomacy

The India that China defeated in 1962 was guided by a foreign policy doctrine called *non-alignment* vis-à-vis the superpower rivalry, and it remained the cornerstone of India's international diplomacy for more than four decades. However, this foreign policy paradigm underwent a U-turn when it metamorphosed into *poly/multi-alignment* under the new leadership in New Delhi in 1998. The new foreign policy outlook broadly had two components, namely, *improving relations with the US* and its *Look East Policy-II.*

The turnaround in India-US relations from being "estranged democracies" during the Cold War to "engaged democracies" in the 2000s has played a central role in bringing out a shift in China's India posture over the last decade. The anti-China element in the dramatically improving Indo-US relations was not very difficult to discern. Chinese scholar Jing-Dong Yuan notes that the warming of US-Indian relations took place at a time when China-US relations were undergoing serious setbacks in the late 1990s. In 1999, NATO bombed the Chinese embassy in the former Yugoslavia (the only embassy that it targeted); in May of that year, the Cox Report charged Chinese nationals with nuclear espionage and accused China of proliferation activities. hostile attitude toward the PRC further exacerbated tensions in early 2001. Also, the revised Nuclear Posture Review (NPR) included China as a nuclear target.

Meanwhile, in a diametrically opposite turn of events, India-US relations suddenly displayed signs of dramatic improvement. US President Bill Clinton visited India in March 2000 (the first presidential visit since Carter's visit in 1978). The US' National Security Strategy Report of 2002 released by the White House redefined India-US relations, stating that because of "India's potential to become one of the great democratic powers of the twenty-first century," the United States would "invest time and resources [for] building strong bilateral relations with India," and "work hard to transform our relationship accordingly." Consequently, the years 2002-03 witnessed a series of high-level meetings and substantial cooperation between the two democracies. Yet another contrast was the U.S.'s approval of Israel's sale of the Phalcon airborne warning and control systems to India in 2003 after the blockage of a similar sale to China in 2000.

Another Chinese security analyst Du Youkang argues that the US strategy of maintaining the balance of power in South Asia during the Cold War has gone beyond the balance of power and has tilted toward India. He cites the Clinton administration's pro-India attitude during the Kargil conflict, and his subsequent official tour to South Asia, where he spent six days in India compared to five hours in Pakistan. The growing strategic ties between the two countries provides a dangerous historical precedent for Beijing. During the Cold War, China perceived India-USSR relations in terms of an anti-China alliance in South Asia. So the strategic partnership between India and the US in the 2000s is, from China's perspective, the revival of the same anti-China alliance – the only difference being that the US has replaced the Soviet Union. Zhang Guihong compared the US-India Western Pacific.

The other pedestal of India's multi-aligned diplomacy included its *Look East Policy-II*. India's Look East Policy-I was officially initiated in 1992. Like most of the previous Indian policies it was reactionary and an outcome of ad hoc-ism. The main driver behind this policy was the economic doldrums of early 1990s, and India saw Southeast Asia as a springboard to join unfolding globalization. However, India displayed an uncharacteristic proactiveness in projecting the Look East policy in its second incarnation in the first-ever India ASEAN summit in Phnom Penh, Cambodia in 2002. India added a politico-security dimension to this policy. It developed security ties with the ASEAN group. From ASEAN's perspective, developing such ties with India (apart from the US presence in the region) provided them a sense of strategic reassurance given their territorial disputes in the South China Sea with a rapidly growing, authoritarian China.

An important highlight of India's Look East Policy-II, from China's viewpoint, has been a transformational improvement in India-Japan relations. Although the ice between their relations was broken with the visit of Prime Minister Mori Yoshiro to India in August 2000, their relations broadened and deepened in the second phase. The April 2005 joint statement issued during Koizumi Junichiro's visit to India introduced a "strategic" dimension to the partnership. The establishment of the Strategic and Global Partnership between India and Japan in December 2006 elevated relations to a new level. In 2006 Japan became only the second country with which India had a bilateral annual summit apart from Russia. When then Prime Minister Shinzo Abe visited India in August 2007, the joint statement sought to provide a roadmap for new dimensions to the strategic and global partnership. The October 2008 joint statement during Prime Minister Manmohan Singh's visit to Japan mentioned the advancement of the strategic and global partnership, making Japan the only country Partnership Agreement (CEPA) which came into force in August of the same year. In late December 2011 India's External Affairs minister visited Japan in October 2011 for the Fifth round of the India-Japan Strategic Dialogue. Japanese PM Yoshihiko Noda visited India for the sixth annual meeting of the leaders of India and Japan. It was the success of India's Look East Policy-II (and not Look East Policy I) that made China remark that India's Look East Policy is "look to encircle China."

India Emerging as an Economic Giant

India and China had similar per capita income by 1974. However, China surged well ahead of India thanks to its deep economic engagement with the US after the Policy of Reform and Open Up (*gaige kaifang*) by Deng Xiaoping in 1978. While China's Open Door policy was a well-thought-out initiative, India, following its legacy of taking radical initiatives only while in crisis, embarked upon its own version of Open Door policy in 1991. The much-needed reforms removed obstacles to economic freedom, and India began to play catch-up, steadily re-integrating into the global economy. A Goldman Sachs report from 2007 found another watermark in India's economic history since 1991 when it pointed out that since 2003 India has been one of the fastest growing major economies, leading to rapid increases in per capita income, demand, and integration with the global economy.

The story of India's economic success has captivated Chinese attention over the last decade. Among Chinese scholars a new discourse has begun over India's economic success story, especially in the IT and consensus that China is a great success in exports, inside China, focusing on China's lag in information technology, Chinese researchers ask why India has become so competitive in the international software market when India has many unattractive features."

Chinese scholars now debate an "Indian Model" as an alternative to the "Chinese model" for developing countries. The Indian model, as understood by Chinese scholars, is characterized by avoiding its weaknesses and exploiting its strengths. For example, India leapfrogged from the primary sector (agriculture) to the tertiary sector (services) by exploiting its inherent advantages in the IT sector which includes a vast, young English-speaking population, the entrepreneurial genius of its private sector, computer literacy, a sound banking sector, and a culture that respects the rule of law. Chinese analysts have especially taken notice of what they call "India New Economy" which is acting like an engine to the Indian Model. Ma Jiali argues that although India is a baby elephant in the manufacturing industry, it is a "doughty tiger" in the information sector. Another set of scholars attributed India's success in this sector to its diaspora. It opined, "India's IT success is also attributed to the large cohort of educated overseas Indians who have good connections and invested heavily in their home country in recent years as a result of favourable government policies. The dynamism brought by the overseas Indians was comparable to the boost brought by the overseas Chinese since the 1978 economic reform in China."

India's Growing Soft Power

The drivers triggering a shift in China's India posture can be placed under the rubric of India's *hard power*. However, India's (re)rising *soft power* has also contributed to this shift in China's outlook a country's ability to alter the behavior of others through attraction rather than sticks or carrots. India has been a democracy right since its birth as a modern nation-state in 1947. However, its sluggish economic growth and weak military profile that led to its defeat in 1962 seriously tarnished this aspect of India's soft power. With the rising India story, its democracy as an important component of its soft power has again come into the global limelight. India has more than 1 billion people.

It is linguistically, culturally, racially, and religiously diverse, and it is growing economically at an enviable pace under democratic governmental institutions (except for the emergency period of 1975-77 when civil liberties were undermined). Its culture values peaceful coexistence, nonviolence, and religious tolerance. All of these factors, combined with the largest pool of English speakers outside the US, has increased India's power of attraction without need for coercion or persuasion, a fact not lost on an envious, hard power-minded China. The country to which India has projected most of its soft power is the US, through the export of highly skilled manpower, consisting mainly of software developers, engineers, and doctors. China has been keeping a close watch on the rising influence of the Indian community in the United States, especially over the last decade. In order to improve its own soft power in the United States, China has sent far more students to the United States than India. As per the Institute of International Education's annual report in the academic year 2009-10, out of 690,932 international students in the United States nearly 128,000 of them, or more than 18 percent, were from China while India sent only 107,897 students in the same academic year. However, with Oct 2011, educational exchanges between India and the US would rise much faster in the future.

CONCLUSION

Prime Minister Modi's call for India to become a leading power represents a change in how the country's top political leadership conceives of its role in international politics. Attaining Modi's ambition will require India to undergo a concerted transformation. This entails strengthening what India has most successfully achieved thus far—territorial integrity, liberal democratic politics, and civic nationalism—but drastically renovating the sclerotic elements of its economy to enable the progressive rationalization that comes, inter alia, from enlarging its market system. Deep structural reforms accompanied by carefully targeted remediation would significantly mitigate the constraints on long-term accumulation, in effect serving, as one study noted, as "positive shocks to the trend that will enable growth to pick up" and persist at high levels over time.

Concerted marketization thus holds the promise of improving India's trend growth rates, enabling appropriate redistribution when desirable, and empowering the state with the resources necessary to accomplish its international goals. Achieving durable success, however, will require strengthening India's state capacity along multiple dimensions in order to mitigate the weaknesses, as one scholar put it, that affect "both [the country's] ability to grasp the big strategic picture and [its] ability to get the nuts and bolts right."

Prime Minister Modi is cognizant of the need for comprehensive transformation if India is to one day become a genuine great power. But his efforts thus far in promoting such change, though laudable in many ways, have been unduly conservative. He has certainly embarked on several high-profile projects intended to stimulate growth and development, but he has yet to articulate an overarching defense of systemic reform, and he has shied away from undertaking those consequential initiatives that would appropriately reposition the Indian state within the national economy while simultaneously strengthening it.

This hesitation is obviously shaped by the realities of Indian politics. When Modi was chief minister of Gujarat, his most audacious policies materialized only during his second term in office, and he may well be following a similar script in New Delhi. But, even if true, this approach harbors risks for his ambition to make India a great power quickly if its "persistent, encompassing, and creative incrementalism," as the Ministry of Finance described it, either falters or proves to be insufficient at a time when India's competitors, most importantly China, appear willing to make bolder reform decisions and implement them with greater alacrity.

It bears remembering that even as all these tasks are satisfactorily completed, most compelling analyses of the future global economy suggest that India will remain the weakest of the great powers for a long time to come. Given this possibility—and the likelihood that a rising China will challenge Indian security in ways that New Delhi has never had to cope with before—finishing the renovations necessary to make India a great power cannot be either put off or approached lackadaisically as has been the case thus far.

Modi's invocation that India become a leading power, consequently, offers transformative possibilities if it drives the speedy acquisition of great power capabilities and makes their procurement a formal object of Indian national policy. If this vision takes root, perhaps the most important immediate change engendered would be the imbuing of self-assurance within the Indian polity, its elites, and its leaders. For all the distinctive shifts that have occurred in Indian foreign policy in recent times, it is remarkable how large segments of the intellectual, bureaucratic, and political classes are still fundamentally insecure about their country's capacity to engage with the world on its own terms. This is partly a legacy of colonialism and partly a consequence of India's persisting material weaknesses in international politics. Yet it is nevertheless unsettling because among India's native strengths has been the capacity to assimilate diverse foreign ideas, cultures, and peoples over the millennia—enriching both the entrants and the host in the process. Given this fact, the strong fears of the "foreign" still residing in India are disconcerting. For example, in the political class, the *Rashtriya Swayamsevak Sangh*(RSS) and the Communist Party of India today converge in their fundamental suspicion of the outsider, albeit different ones. In the Indian bureaucracy, the apprehension about external penetration strongly limits its willingness to divest control over both the economy and the state. And in the Indian military, the anxiety about penetration by powers abroad serves to curb access to the institution, while constraining its ability to sustain deep engagement with its best global partners.

These insecurities, however manifested, impede India's ability to learn from the outside world and eventually improve upon it, thus raising doubts about how a country so lacking in aplomb can become a great power swiftly. This reticence is, in fact, paradoxical not only because of India's history, which demonstrates the extraordinary absorptive powers of its civilization, but also because Indian citizens often effortlessly leave their birthplace to settle abroad and acculturate easily to their adopted homelands.

If Modi's quest for India to become a leading power, then, strengthens Indian self-confidence, the foundations would be laid for making some difficult decisions about economic reform domestically; containing those elements on both the right and the left that would disfigure India's democracy and retard its development, respectively; and articulating a clear perspective of India's role in Asia and the world without either defensiveness or hubris. The stage would also be set for cementing the strategic partnerships that India has sought to build in furtherance of its own interests, taking the initiative in developing cooperative solutions that address the most pressing regional and global challenges, and building the military capabilities necessary to protect India and to provide the public goods needed to strengthen peace and security throughout the Indo-Pacific.

A focused effort along these lines would make India's journey toward achieving great power status easier. But it would require more of Modi than has been in evidence lately. There are few leaders in India today who have the capacity to articulate the importance of this vision in ways that are comprehensible to the polity at large. And India enjoys the unique advantage of having its rise unambiguously welcomed by the most important power in the international system, the United States. Building on the initiatives first undertaken by Atal Bihari Vajpayee and then elevated to new heights by his successor as prime minister, Manmohan Singh, Modi can be justifiably proud of his own contributions to strengthening New Delhi's strategic partnership with Washington. By consummating the path-breaking Joint Strategic Vision for the Asia-Pacific and Indian Ocean Region agreed to with President Barack Obama, and complementing it with deeper economic integration with the United States, Modi can solidify a geopolitical bond that will be incredibly valuable for India as it continues along the road to becoming a real great power.

FUTURE SUPERPOWERS - THE WORLD TO 2100

Most projections of future trends in national power fail to appreciate the importance of three crucial factors: (1) the declining EROEI of energy resources (including, but not limited to, "peak oil"); (2) the importance of human capital to economic growth, especially in developing countries' attempts to "catch up" to the advanced world; and (3) the impacts of climate change, which are projected to be more and more catastrophic with every passing year. Disregarding these trends produces predictions such as George Friedman's (STRATFOR) argument that Mexico – a low human capital country experiencing plummeting oil production and growing water stress – will become a superpower by 2100. Using my current estimates of Comprehensive National Power as a base (an index of power that attempts to express a nation's economic, military, and cultural power in a single number), I will *specially stress* the above factors in my analysis of future global power trends. Some results will look plausible and familiar (e.g. China overtaking the US as a superpower by the 2020's); others will appear utterly bizarre (e.g. Canada becoming a major Great Power in by the end of the century, while India and Brazil plummet back into obscurity). But they are nonetheless all plausible and even likely outcomes, derived from bringing together worlds that all too often are considered independently of each other: the economy; human capital; geopolitics; energetics; and climate change.

There may of course be unexpected discontinuities – popularized as Black Swans by Nassim Taleb – that unravel these projections (the probability of their happening increasing exponentially over time). This will be covered in greater depth below. In the meantime, bear this caveat in mind as you read the rest of the post.

The End of Pax Americana (1980-2025)

The US is the current superpower, but China is rapidly making up ground. Its real GDP is now at $10 trillion, though according to some estimates it has already overtaken the $14.5 trillion American economy.

Some critics claim that nominal GDP is a better measure of power, even using these figures to claim that even at 10% growth it will be decades before China surpasses the US. This is a product of economic illiteracy, because it doesn't take into account the convergence of Chinese price levels to those of developed countries (its nominal GDP has been expanding *at more than 20%* in the last 5 years).

There are a number of other factors that are often quoted to predict the doom of China's rise, such as: (1) Growing regional disparities; (2) Income inequality; (3) Environmental degradation; (4) Bad loans and financial collapse, aka Japan; (5) Aging population; (6) Excessive export dependency; (7) Social unrest; (8) Authoritarian nature of its Marxist-Leninist political model.

Suffice to say that they are either common to most industrializing countries (1-3, 7); will only seriously affect it by the time its already developed (4-5); are overestimated (4, 6); or it is unclear why they should derail its economic ascent for long even if they lead to a democratizing revolution (7-8). I address all these points in detail here.

In any case, most of these are factors have yet to be realized, whereas many of the same trends undermining US power are already in evidence. You can point out the accumulating weight of China's bad loans, but it is the Western financial system that had to be bailed out in 2008 at social expense; you can argue that the aging of China's population will bankrupt its (minimal) social net, but it is the US that is facing a budget deficit of >10% of GDP and a national debt soaring into the stratosphere.

China is already the world's largest manufacturing power. On current trends, it is due to overtake the US economy by the mid-2010's (followed in nominal terms sometime in the 2020's, as restrictions on the yuan are lifted and it appreciates). Since China produces its own military hardware, real GDP is what matters; consequently, it will take *less relative effort* for the PLA to match and overtake the US (especially in the crucial East Asian region and the Indian Ocean). As Paul Kennedy noted in *The Rise and Fall of the Great Powers* (of which, incidentally, the Chinese are great fans) military and political power follows naturally in the wake of economic power, whereas trying to achieve results from the opposite directions leads to the "imperial overstretch" that contributed to Soviet collapse and is now undermining American power.

Which brings us to the last point. China's population is four times bigger than America's, and human capital among the youngest generations is now as good as the US average. This makes its per capita convergence – and consequently, its ascent to economic primacy – almost inevitable.

But rather than assessing the situation dispassionately and preparing for a strategic retreat, the US is digging in all fronts: foreign wars, deficit spending, oil dependence, political gridlock, etc. This increases the probability that US decline will take the form of a sudden collapse, as of Argentina's in 1999-2002, instead of fading away like the British Empire after 1945.

The Return of the Middle Kingdom (2020-2075)

The cultural decline will be slower. It took Latin more than a millennium after the collapse of the Roman Empire to lose its status as a *lingua franca*. Needless to say, the US will still retain a great deal of power by virtue of its large population and developed economy, it will remain in second place, almost no matter what, well into the 21st century. Furthermore, it will retain its deep ties – economic, cultural, etc. – with the Anglo-Saxon world (the UK, Canada, Australia, New Zealand) and, to a lesser extent, Europe. Hollywood, Silicon Valley, and the Ivy League will remain staples of global culture and technology.

However, there's only so much power you can exercise through the English language, Google, or even Chuck Norris. For everything else there's China – after a two hundred year break (a mere blip in its millennial history), the Middle Kingdom will have returned to its rightful place at the center of the world.

China is now roughly where South Korea was in 1990. A similar growth profile will by 2030 leave its economic power *equal to 25 of today's Koreas.* Imagine that!

It's unclear what political system China will have by then. Democratization on the Taiwanese model is not inevitable. The Chinese Communist Party (CCP) has studied the Soviet collapse in rigorous detail and is determined not to repeat its liberalizing mistakes. What I consider at least equally likely is an emergence of a "consultative Leninism", in which the current NEPist model is opened up to democratic elements (e.g. competitive local elections; policy-making based on opinion polling) but under the continuing hegemony of the CCP. This could be China's own, sovereign road to democracy.

Other possibilities are also possible, e.g. a Singaporean authoritarianism, or "managed democracy" in the style of Putin's Russia. But short of a reversion to Maoism – which is exceedingly unlikely, given that China now has a commercial class that would strongly oppose it – it's unclear how the widespread mantra that political change must be accompanied by a cessation of economic growth can be justified.

China's rise will be accompanied by the flock of BRIC's trailing in its wake: Brazil, Russia, and India. The first two will enjoy a massive resource windfall from selling their plentiful energy, mineral, and water (in the form of food) reserves to a world made increasingly ravenous by depletion elsewhere and the effects of an increasingly destructive and chaotic climate. Russia will remain a first-class Great Power, and India will join its ranks; Brazil will be the most prominent of the second-class powers, which will also include France, Canada, Germany, Japan, the UK, Turkey, and Korea.

As with China, there are many reasons cited to explain for why Russia will fail to achieve its promise, such as (1) demographic decline; (2) corruption; (3) resource-based economy; (4) crumbling infrastructure; (5) authoritarianism. All these factors are either exaggerated (1-5), typical of most middle-income countries (2, 4), or it is unclear why they are necessarily negatives at all (3, 5). But it also has great strengths. Russia combines the BRIC's fiscal sturdiness and economic dynamism (both lacking in the West) with a GDP per capita that is almost twice that of the next richest BRIC, Brazil. Its human capital is on a par with the developed world's, allowing for an easy convergence. Crucially, Russia is perfectly positioned for the coming age of "scarcity industrialism", in which food, energy, and energy prices soar and global warming opens up vast regions of the country, including the Arctic, to shipping, energy production, agriculture, and habitation. Even at current growth rates of 4% per year, Russia should converge to European income levels by 2020-25 and spend the next few decades comfortably, its energy riches shielded by its nuclear umbrella.

Obviously Russia lacks the population mass, at least at this stage, to become a true superpower (even if it absorbs the other post-Soviet nations into a Eurasian union). This is not the case for India, which will overtake China to become the world's most populous nation by 2025. But within that fast-growing population illiteracy is still rife and 47% of children remain malnourished.

Though it suffers from many the usual ailments of low-income countries – creaky infrastructure, caste-based inequalities, sluggish courts and bureaucracy, etc. – it's India's low level of human capital that is the primary cause of its falling so far behind China (manufacturing output is an order of magnitude lower, and the poorest Chinese provinces are equal to the Indian average). Nonetheless, India has the coal to power itself, and temperatures will remain within acceptable bounds for producing stagnant grain harvests for at least the next few decades. And quantity counts. That is why India will become a first-rank Great Power, equaling Russia and approaching the US.

With its ample lands and resources (e.g. iron, oil), not to mention its successes with sugar cane-derived ethanol, Brazil is set to enjoy – much like Russia – a comfortable existence as a regional hegemon in a world of high prices for food, energy and minerals. Its military strength is paltry, but irrelevant given its distance from other Great Powers. It is also the least corrupt of the BRIC's. However, its prospects for true superpowerdom are constrained by relatively low human capital; as its economy wasn't distorted by a legacy of socialist mismanagement (as with China or Russia), its GDP per capita is already, more or less, "where it should be." In the background, Canada will be getting very rich off supplying fuels and water to an increasingly parched and energy-starved US. However, for the time being its profile will remain modest.

The European Union is conspicuous by its absence. Europe is no longer united by the memory of war and the Soviet threat, and each country concerned above all for its own national interests.

This is not a stable foundation for a union, and as such it will likely retreat into something like a glorified free trade area by the 2020's. Real power will be concentrated among the big European Powers, which will carve out spheres of influence and compete with each other for neo-colonial influence: e.g. France (Maghreb); Germany (East-Central Europe); Turkey (Balkans, Azerbaijan, Arab world); the Scandinavian bloc; the Visegrad bloc. Arguably there is already evidence of this in the Anglo-French effort to oust Qaddafi.

No European Power will have the mass to become a first-rank Great Power, though it may be (marginally) possible for France and definitely possible for coalitions of European Powers. By themselves, all the European nations will be lingering near the bottom of the CNP scale.

There is no point discussing any other country or alliance. NATO is becoming more irrelevant with each passing year. Japan is technologically advanced, but reliant on the US for its security and dependent on the same oceanic supply routes as China; as soon as the latter becomes the new regional hegemon, Japan's effective sovereignty is history. Indonesia is similar India, but five times smaller.

South Africa, Mexico, Australia, Nigeria, Iran, and Saudi Arabia are all some combination of (1) too underpopulated, (2) too underdeveloped, and (3) too vulnerable to climate change.

Towards a Russian Century? (2075-?)

Beyond 2050 we are getting into very foggy territory. Just think of an educated European observing the world one century ago, in 1911 – could he have predicted Germany's utter collapse and occupation, and the rise of Russia (now known as the USSR) as a superpower along with the (vastly stronger) US superpower?

And could that observer in 1951 have predicted that a China only recently consolidated under Communist control, after a century of stagnation, invasions and warlordism, would just fifty years later have overtaken a Russia that had become a basketcase?

Any number of black swans may have intervened by 2050, steering any projections wildly of course. Here are a few examples:

- *China and the US cooperate to build a massive global geoengineering project in the 2040's that succeeds at checking global warming.* This removes the conditions for Russia's rise to a dominant position.
- *Facing desiccation in the West and flooding in the South, the US annexes Canada.* As a result, it becomes the greatest Power in the world.
- *There is a total war between nuclear Powers, perhaps triggered by a Chinese land grab for the Russian Far East.* Whoever "wins" (if that's the right term), well, wins.
- *The development of nuclear fusion, space-based solar power, or some other technology, that reverses the secular trend towards declining EROEI.* This massively undercuts the power of major resource exporters, such as Russia, Canada, and Brazil.

- *A transition to sustainable development.* With global CO_2 emissions setting a new record in 2010 (just one year after the deepest global recession in the past half-century), and setting the 2C warming target practically out of reach, there is little hope of that without geoengineering (after 2C the process is expected to display a runaway dynamic due to positive feedback loops). But miracles happen, sometimes.
- *A technological singularity.* Perhaps this catapults the nation where it first appears into a dominant leadership position, much like Britain during the industrial revolution; or maybe it is so transnational and transformative in its scope that it makes the very idea of nations and national power obsolete. By definition, a technological singularity is beyond the "event horizon" of our limited imaginations, so there's little more I can say on this.

For the purposes of completing the scenario to 2100, I will assume that the above don't occur. Instead, the dominant forces in previous decades – economic convergence; declining EROEI and minerals accessibility; accelerating climate change – remain constants.

By the second half the century, climate change will start to dominate over everything else. The latest projections tend to lean towards the high end of the IPCC's 1-6C warming range for the next century (the scariest of them show that by 2300 most of the world outside the Arctic may become downright lethal during summer).

Warming of 4C is the point at which agriculture starts to not only experience difficulties but outright collapse throughout most of the equator and mid-latitudes.

[*Map of global drought under aggregated runs of IPCC's models. Most of the US, southern Europe, the Middle East, Africa, and Latin America will be in an unprecedented mega-drought. Read more here.*]

All the problems currently experienced by China and India with stagnant grain harvests will increase further, requiring very costly counter-measures. Now this is not to say that there will necessarily be mass famine and "dieoff", as doomers like to predict. It is certainly a possibility, especially under the most severe warming scenarios, but growing food production in Russia, Canada, and even East Africa may make up the difference. In particular, China should be relatively safe, because by then it should be a developed country.

On the other hand, the Chinese state will have its hands full mitigating disaster after climate disaster. The spate of rebuilding after the flooding of

New Orleans, which actually boosted US GDP, was one thing; when commercial metropolises like Shanghai are getting flooded and coastal property prices devaluing to nothing, it is economic and financial apocalypse.

What's possible, then, is the following scenario. By the 2070's, the Chinese state becomes so preoccupied with maintaining food stability, and the energy and mineral flows that enable industrial society in general, that the surplus resources and administrative capacity to do anything else diminish.

This is not a new development in its history. For much of the 19th century, Qing China was the world's biggest economy by GDP, even though Britain was becoming far more industrialized.

This was because China was at its Malthusian limits; the population level was stable, but it was always on the edge of famine, and presided over by a government made weak by lack of taxable surpluses and unable to check the corruption and independence of its own public officials. The state was unable to defend itself, to modernize the country, or to guarantee its independence. India is in a worse bind, and not just because it will likely remain less developed than China to that time. The Chinese, at least, have the reserve option of migrating some of their surplus population to Tibet (or East Africa, if they conquer it). India doesn't have that, and faces the unwelcome prospect of a further flood of excess population – this time from a collapsing Pakistan (the Indus to run dry by late century, as Himalayan glaciers melt) and inundating Bangladesh.

A consequence is that states with far smaller populations and economies, but greater surplus resources – will emerge as new Great Powers. Primarily, this means Russia, but Canada would also be in this category, as will Scandinavia, Alaska, and (in one or two more centuries) whoever settles or controls Greenland. By virtue of their control over most of the world's *remaining* critical resources – water (not only for food, but electricity); gas; coal; metals; whatever's left of oil – they will wield unprecedented strategic power over the countries to the south.

Perhaps a colonial relationship will develop, in which the Arctic nations send resources and allow southern workers to farm their lands in exchange for selling off their industrial assets and eventually ceding political sovereignty.

In the very long term, this will logically lead to the development of caste-based societies in Russia and Canada, as the sheer magnitude of climate refugees would mean that in any integration policy, it would be the indigenous inhabitants who would have to do most of the integrating (and hence politically impracticable).

3

China's Power Strategies in Asia

CHINA'S POWER STATUS AND ITS IMPLICATIONS

The author believes that in order to study China's power status objectively, we should first understand the true nature of international power and clarify our goal for measuring the differences of national powers. If we fail to do this, then as complexity in these measurements increases, their pragmatic value actually decreases. Therefore, the results of assessment will not benefit us at all in understanding national power status.

Relativity in Assessing China's Power Status

Power status connotes relativity. It refers to ranking the power status of one state with relevance to that of other states in an international sphere. The power status of a state can be understood only through a simultaneous comparative assessment of the power status of other nations.

If there is only one nation in the world, then there is no frame of reference with which we can decide if a country's power status is high or low. This means that only when there are two or more countries in the world, that the study of a state's power status and its comprehensive national power has significance.

The term 'power status' contains a connotation of both 'the rank of power status' and 'the differences in power status'. Whereas the difference in power status decides the rank of power status, the rank of power status cannot always truly reflect the real nature and degrees of difference in power status. During the Cold War period, the United States and the Soviet Union ranked first and second, respectively, in their power status. However, the difference in power between them remained at a hierarchical level of superpowers. But in the 1990s, while the United States still kept its top ranking (regardless of which major power stayed in second: Russia, Japan or China), the nature of the ranking gap between the first and the second power states changed substantially, because it became a difference in power status between a superpower and a major power.

The power status of a state is based on, but not decided by, its national power. In other words, the increase of a state's power does not necessarily elevate that state's power status. For example, in the late 19th century during the Qing Dynasty, China had enough industrial capacity to arm its military. Its overall national power was far larger than that of the early Qing Dynasty when there was no modern industry. However, internationally, China's power status during the late Qing Dynasty was far behind that of the early Qing Dynasty. Take the current cases of The Netherlands and South Korea. In 1999, GDP in The Netherlands grew from $393.5 billion to $398.1 billion, with an absolute increase of $4.6 billion. However, according to World Bank statistics, the ranking of The Netherlands fell below that of South Korea, whose GDP in the same period increased from $317.1 billion to $406.1 billion.

The rank of a state's power status is decided by the difference between its own power status and that of other states. However, this absolute difference does not indicate the nature and extent of power differences between states. The absolute value of the disparity in power status between two states indicates which state possesses a mightier power status. Therefore, it reflects the rank of the power status of the two states. However, this absolute difference hardly displays the true nature and class difference of a state's power status. For instance, according to the 2003 World Bank GDP statistics, by currency exchange rates, the GDP difference between Japan and Germany was $1.93 trillion while the GDP difference between Germany and Brazil was $1.97 trillion. The absolute values of the two differences vary little, but this by no means indicates that the difference in economic power between Germany and Japan shares any similarity with the difference between Brazil and Germany. Common sense leads us to conclude that Germany and Japan share the same class status, but that Brazil and Germany do not.

The power status of a state depends on how its national power compares with that of other nations. We can clarify this further by looking at GDP comparisons for Japan, Germany and Brazil. In 2003, Japan's GDP amounted to $4.3 trillion, Germany's to $2.4 trillion and Brazil's to $0.5 trillion. Despite the fact that the difference in GDP between Germany and Japan almost equals that between Brazil and Germany, Japan's GDP was only 1.8 times Germany's

GDP while Germany's GDP amounted to 4.8 times that of Brazil. This helps us understand that using common knowledge leads us to conclude that Germany and Japan share the same economic class, whereas Brazil and Germany are quite different.

In short, it is the proportional relationship between the power statuses of two states, not the absolute quantity of difference that decides a state's power status. It can be expressed as: $S = A/B$, (where S indicates power status of State A in proportion to that of State B; A refers to the power of State A, and B to the power of State B.) In the reality of international politics, when two states confront each other on a specific issue, the advantages and disadvantages of their powers depend largely on one state's power in proportion to the other. As an example, assume a small military skirmish along a common border between two nations, Side A has three soldiers and Side B only one. Although Side A has only two more soldiers than Side B in absolute number, its power is 200% greater than that of Side B (i.e. the possibility of winning for Side A is three times as much as that for Side B). To cite another example, Side A has 102 soldiers and Side B 100; even if Side A has two more soldiers than Side B, its power strength gains only a 2% advantage. Therefore, the possibility of winning for either side is almost equal. In this analogy, to assess China's power status and its progression, one should focus on China's power status in proportion to the power status of other states, instead of solely on the absolute differences in the power of two states.

Importance of Assessing China's Power Status

Because power status is relative, recognizing China's power status in relation to that of other states is of immediate significance in our study. In order to further understand China's power status we consider the following three aspects. First, by understanding the relativity of power status, we can better understand the major difference in defining the 'Rejuvenation' or 'Rise' of China. In 2003, the Chinese leaders first introduced the term 'Peaceful Rise'. However, in April 2004 at the Boao Asia Forum, it was replaced by 'Peaceful Development'. This was mainly because 'Rise' has a relative meaning in terms of power status. Despite the often heated debates on 'Peaceful Rise', scholars on all sides acknowledge that the word 'Rise' implies attaining superpower status. For the Chinese, 'rejuvenation' bears a similar connotation to 'rise'. Both mean to restore China's power status to the prosperity enjoyed during the prime of the Han, Tang and early Qing Dynasties. It does not simply refer to a regression of China's comprehensive national power down to the ancient level. By early 21st century standards, China's comprehensive national power in the afore-mentioned ancient periods was only equivalent to a state of low power status in the current international system. As power status changes with time and the international environment, China's national rejuvenation will be realized only if its pace of national power growth is faster than that of other countries. Growth at any slower pace will weaken China's power status gradually and thus diminish the hopes of national rejuvenation and rise.

Second, the zero-sum nature of power status helps us understand that there will be no win–win situation in conflicts among international political entities accompanying the rise of China. Power status and international politics share the same zero-sum characteristic.

The rise of a state's power status indicates an expansion of its political power. This in turn causes the fall of other states' power status and political power. Powerful states remain a minority in the world while weaker states remain a majority. Until September 2002, no more than 10 global or regional major powers had been listed among 191 member countries of the UN.

The middle and small powers are represented in greater numbers in this ranking. As the power status of one small state increases, the relative power it gains is drawn from many other middle or small states of similar power status. Thus, an evenly spread decrease in power in every small power is not obvious, and so is unlikely to cause conflict among these states. For instance, the sum of international political power for 100 small states is fixed and stable, and each small state holds 1% of this power sum. When one small state increases its power status to 1.9% of the total power, the share for each of the remaining 99 countries is decreased to 0.99%, i.e. each country loses only 1% of its original power. On the other hand, an increase in power status for a major state usually conveys serious outcomes in this aspect. Great powers are few in number. Therefore, as a major power gains an advantage in its power status, the remainder of the few major powers feel a tremendous loss of their original power. If the dominant world power belongs to a single state, then this hegemony holds 100% of the power. When the power status of another state increases to the same level, there are two states sharing this world dominant power. That means, among those with dominant power, the former hegemony will be diminished to half, or only 50%. Since a change in a major power's power status may result in the restructuring of international relations and a rearrangement of world resources, studies on comprehensive national strength and power status are of the utmost importance only for those few major powers. The zero-sum nature in power status gives us the insight that a majority of political conflicts along China's path to her rise will bear this zero-sum nature as well. In other words, there will be few win–win situations in China's ascent to a superpower.

Third, by recognizing China's current power status, we can better perceive the strategic relationship between China and the other major powers in the post-Cold War era. In a world configured with one superpower against several major powers, the United States is destined to defend its status against any possible challenging states in the future. As one of the major powers after the Cold War, China automatically becomes an opponent of the United States.

None the less, the United States will decide whether to interpret China as its number one rival on the basis of how China's power status changes. Although China and the Western European major powers have been categorized as regional powers, the geographical distances between them cause fewer conflicts of interest.

Thus they may even forge a strategic alliance against the United States' hegemonic pressures. However, in East Asia, China and Japan have fundamental conflicts that will cause inevitable confrontations between the two.

In the early post-Cold War period, Japan was the world's second economic power after the United States, and the number one economic power in East Asia. If its economic power status decreases due to an increase in power status of other states, both globally and regionally, Japan may take several measures to protect its existing international status by strengthening its political and military power. Thus, if China's economic power status replaces that of Japan, Japan may confront China politically. A better understanding of China's power status enables us to know why structural conflicts exist in China's strategic relationships with the United States and Japan but not with the major European powers.

NATIONAL POWER AND CHINA'S POWER STATUS

After clarification that national power status is relative, we also need to clarify the nature of comprehensiveness of national power status. Even though the term 'comprehensive national power' was coined after the Cold War, the idea that national power is a combination of many different elements has been around for centuries. Nevertheless, people's understanding of comprehensive national power varies widely, i.e. people cannot reach an agreement on how to weigh the different components. In order to form an objective judgement of China's power, we need to clearly define the relationships between the different components that form national power.

Relationships Among Elements of National Power

Although scholars hold major differences of opinion regarding the fundamental components of comprehensive national power, they have reached consensus in dividing those components into 'soft' and 'hard' power. Alfred Thanyer Mahan believes that state power consists of six components; Hans. J. Morgenthau has classified nine components for his study; and Ray. S. Cline separates it into five types. However, all of them divide components of state power into 'soft' and 'hard' categories. After the Cold War, Chinese scholars applied the concepts of 'soft' and 'hard' power into their studies.

In the post-Cold War era, many scholars use Cline's Power Equation, introduced in the 1970s, in their measure of comprehensive national power. The author believes that Cline's significant contribution to the field was not his new conclusion on components of state power, but rather his inclusion of both 'soft' and 'hard' powers as factors rather than addends in his equation. Even today, many people outside of international studies have the erroneous notion that comprehensive national power is simply the sum of various power elements. The concept that comprehensive national power is a product rather than a sum of 'soft' and 'hard' powers introduced by Cline makes us realize that 'soft' power is as equally important as 'hard' power in political reality. As both 'soft' and 'hard' powers stand as factors, if one of them is zero, no matter how large the value of the other is, the total value of the comprehensive power will be zero. For instance, if the efficacy of a deterrence strategy equals its military might times its political will, the deterrence strategy will have no efficacy when either factor (military might or political will) is zero.

The power for national unification is also a produce of a state's military strength and political determination. In 1991, as the Soviet government lacked a strong will to retain military forces to protect its unification, the Soviet Union collapsed in spite of its military superpower. In reality, a state must be composed of its population, territory and economic infrastructure, or it will disappear. Therefore, it is unlikely that a state has zero 'hard' power. Rather, it is the 'soft' power that sometimes turns out to be zero. In a given conflict, if one side can no longer confidently protect its interests, the state's comprehensive power as well as its 'soft' power would vapourize. In 1931, when Japan invaded China's northeast areas, the Chinese government adopted a policy of non-resistance for the sake of avoiding escalation. With regard to protecting China's northeastern territory, both China's 'soft' and comprehensive national powers were zero. As a result, the Japanese armies occupied China's three northeastern provinces with little resistance.

The structure of power components influences the character of comprehensive national power. This structure varies from state to state. Using examples of major powers in the 21st century, Japan and Germany's economic powers are significantly greater than their political and military powers, while Russia's military is very strong in proportion to its economic power. The United States, China, France and Britain possess relatively balanced comprehensive national power structures, and their economic, political and military powers are all weighed relatively equal. Some claim that economic power is the dominant factor in comprehensive national power. In fact, this notion contradicts the connotation of comprehensive national power.

A state does not rely on abstract comprehensive national power in dealing with international issues, but rather on its specific power components.

That is to say, a state relies on military power to deal with a security threat, and relies on economic power to deal with economic conflicts, and depends on its political power to deal with political pressures. These component powers cannot be converted unconditionally. It requires a long time and many conditions to convert one power component to another. The difficulty of converting power components directly affects the efficiency of comprehensive national power. That is to say, balanced power structure has superiority over unbalanced power structure. If we agree that states have a need to maintain their economic, security and political interests, we should also agree that states with a balanced power structure will gain an advantage over those with unbalanced powers in dealing with most of their external issues.

In other words, a state with a balanced power structure has an advantageous position in comprehensive national power while a state with an unbalanced power structure can only have advantage on certain interests over the others, but it will not have any overall advantage. A comparative case study of the Soviet Union and Japan in the 1980s further supports our argument. In 1985, the Soviet Union's GDP was $741.9 billion and Japan's $1220 billion, which accounted for 18.6 and 30.6% of the US GDP of $3988.5 billion, respectively. In spite of the fact that the Soviet Union's economic capacity was less than that of Japan's, the Soviet Union possessed a military and political power comparable with that of the United States. Thus the comprehensive power of the Soviet Union was of the superpower-level, while Japan was merely a major power.

Character of China's Comprehensive Power

We will adopt a class approach to assess China's power status, in accordance with the political meaning of international status. The author's goal is to understand the differences between the status of China and that of other greater powers, rather than to accurately measure the degree of difference between them. Therefore, applying this power class analysis enables us to make sound judgements on the character of China's comprehensive power in comparison with that of other great powers, without using a complicated index system. Assigning values to each of the national power components is a very subjective process; therefore, quantitative measurements can hardly improve accuracy and reliability in research results. The goal of measuring comprehensive national power is to identify the characteristics of the differences in power, thus the essence of comprehensive national power measuring remains in establishing standards for power measurement, rather than in dissected analyses of power components.

As a further analogy, the function of a thermometer is to identify the degree of change in temperature but not to study the reasons for the change. Therefore, if a measurement can efficiently assess the different characteristics of a major powers' national strength, that measure will be sufficient for assessing China's comprehensive power. When the power difference of two states is very obvious, there will be no need to use measurement and a common sense judgement should be sufficient in order to define the stronger state. For instance, we can conclude that the comprehensive national power of the United States is stronger than that of China, China is stronger than Australia, Australia is stronger than New Zealand and New Zealand is stronger than Brunei.

China's power class using common knowledge in international relations, and then to further compare China's power structure with that of other states at the same class for the sake of judging their difference. It is common knowledge that the United States is the only superpower in the post-Cold War era. This common knowledge has significant impact on the value-vest of complicated national power measurements. All the complicated measurements vested much higher value to the US comprehensive national power than that of any other major powers'. Based on common knowledge, we can judge that China's power status has not yet reached the superpower level. Our common judgement of an international system of one superpower versus many smaller great powers after the Cold War helps us understand that China belongs to one of the major powers and her power status remains at the same echelon as Japan, Russia, Britain, France, Germany and India. Once we have clarified China's power status and its hierarchical rank, we are ready to identify the difference in China's comprehensive power with that of other major powers. For this purpose, we need to classify the afore-mentioned major states into 'strong' or 'weak' categories in terms of political, economic and military power, respectively.

With regard to military power, the data from Stockholm International Peace Research Institute shows that in 2002, based on the average of currency exchange rates and PPP statistical data, the national defence expenditures for the afore-mentioned major states ranked as follows: China, Japan, India, Britain, France, Russia and Germany.

Even if China's military expenditure stays highest among the six countries, the average value of currency exchange rates and PPP data indicated that the national defence expenditures for all the seven powers have been kept at the same level, none get into the rank of hundreds of billions (the United States' national defence expenditure was US$ 335.7 billion).

A state's military capacity over a certain period of time is an accumulated result of its military investments in the previous years instead of the defence expenditures of the current year. Therefore, to estimate and categorize the military power of the seven states mentioned earlier, we should incorporate both strategic nuclear capacity and national defence expenditures of those states. According to the same source, in 2003 the number of the nuclear warheads of the seven states listed as follows: Russia has 8332 nuclear warheads; China, 402; France, 348; Britain, 185; India, 30–40; and both of Japan and Germany, zero. Although Russia's 2003 national defence expenditure is less than that of the other nuclear states, its nuclear arsenal is superior both in quantity and level of sophistication.

The third indicator for military power is army scale which shows the quantity of conventional military armaments and number of professional trained military personnel. China, Russia and India all have forces of over 1 million personnel, while France claims a military force of 440 000 and Britain, Germany and Japan have between 200 000–300 000 personnel.

To fully consider defence expenditure, nuclear capacity and army scale as three major indicators, we can further divide the military power of the seven states into strong and weak classes as follows. Strong: Russia, China, France, India and Britain; weak: Japan and Germany. In terms of political power, China, Russia, France and Britain as permanent members of the UN Security Council, are politically strong; and Japan, Germany and India are weak as none is a permanent member of the UN Security Council. In terms of economic power, according to World Bank 2003 statistics, using the weighted average of both PPP and exchange rates, the major powers like Japan, China and Germany with a GDP of over $2 trillion can be categorized as economically strong; while those with a GDP below $2 trillion are weak, such as, India, Britain, France and Russia.

Based on the principle that 'soft' power is equally significant as 'hard' power, we can distinguish the character of China's power and the difference in power status between the United States and China. China's comprehensive power is not only inferior to that of the United States as a whole but also in every single aspect of military, political, and economic power. However, when comparing China's power component one by one with that of the United States, the difference in each comparing component varies greatly. In terms of military power, China's 2002 nuclear warheads amounted to only 5.3% of the United States' 7600 arsenal. At the average value of exchange rates and PPP calculations, China's 2003 national defence expenditure accounted for 26% of US expenditure. In terms of economic power, China's 2003 GDP accounted for 13% of the US$ 10.9 trillion GDP by exchange rate calculation, 59% by PPP rate and 36% by the average of the both. As political power can be interpreted as a state's capability of mobilization, it can be further divided into domestic and international capabilities of mobilization. With regard to domestic mobilization capability, the different political systems of China and the United States provide China with a stronger political mobilization capability than the United States as China possesses more administrative measures to mobilize its people.

Internationally speaking, China's political mobilization capability is weaker than that of the United States. However, the gap is much smaller with regard to military and economic power. For instance, between 1990 and 2001, the United States made 10 anti-China proposals to the UN Human Rights Committee over China's human rights conditions and each time they failed because of China's counter efforts. China's capability in mobilizing the international community to safeguard her own political interests concerning human rights issues is much more powerful than her capabilities in safeguarding her economic and security interests internationally. Since the end of the Cold War, China has never showed such a strong resistant capability in Sino–American economic or security conflicts. By way of the afore-discussed comparisons, we have discovered that the greatest disparity in power status between China and the United States remains in military power, with a smaller disparity in economic power, and least in political power.

CHINA'S EMERGENCE AS A GREAT POWER

The preeminent geopolitical factor in Asia for the next several decades would appear to be the emergence of China as a great power. In most discussions of the region's future, this assertion is all but taken for granted, although some observers have dissented. Those who accept this assertion can point to the following realities and trends.

Economic Growth

First and most fundamentally, China has enjoyed rapid and sustained economic growth since 1978, when Deng Xiaoping initiated the current era of economic reform. Indeed, before the Asian economic crisis erupted in 1997, this growth was so rapid that some analysts, using optimistic but not unrealistic assumptions, predicted that China's GNP—evaluated in terms of purchasing-power parity— would surpass that of the United States by 2006.2 Yet while China has escaped the immediate brunt of the region's financial crisis, the Asian economic slump has exposed and highlighted some weaknesses in the Chinese economy as well as in the "Asian model" of economic development in general.

Despite large "pump-priming" efforts by the government over the past several years, the Chinese growth rate has been slowing down.

According to some measures, prices have been falling as well, which suggests the existence of excess productive capacity. China also faces serious economic challenges not only with respect to its stateowned enterprises (SOEs), many of which have been losing money as they encounter increased competition from the private sector and from imports, but also with regard to its banking sector, which is burdened with the large nonperforming loans that are required to keep many of the SOEs afloat.

Thus, the key question for the immediate future is whether the private sector can grow fast enough to absorb those workers who would inevitably be laid off in the course of restructuring China's SOEs and reforming its banks. This reform process is likely to be accelerated when China is admitted to the WTO, thereby bringing matters to a head more quickly.

China's economic prospects for the next decades thus depend largely on whether its leadership has the political will to back economic reforms that are in the short run likely to lead to the bankruptcy of some SOEs or, alternatively, whether China will opt instead for a Japanese-style policy of putting off hard decisions. In the first two decades of economic reform, the Chinese leadership exhibited a talent for "muddling through"—i.e., for implementing enough reform to keep the economy moving forward while for the most part avoiding major shocks to the political system. However, the urban inflation of the late 1980s, which was closely linked to the public dissatisfaction underlying the 1989 Tiananmen protests, offered one instance in which the leadership's ability to strike this balance was sorely tested and ultimately found lacking. Whether China's leadership will prove capable of juggling these competing economic and social/political requirements remains an open question. This analysis proceeds on the assumption that it will, but it must be recognized that China's economic prognosis may be less optimistic than it now appears.

Technological Modernization

China's economic reform program of the past 20 years has included rapid if selective technological modernization. Nevertheless, China's level of technological sophistication is likely to prove a more significant obstacle to its achievement of great-power status than its overall economic development. Starting as it has from a very low level, China's technological progress—while relatively rapid in some areas— has a long way to go. In eight of nine technologies deemed critical for military purposes, Chinese production capabilities have been found to be significant yet limited.

The exception is biotechnology, with respect to which China has good basic research but poor production capability. Although China has access to "all but the most advanced dual-use technologies" and is able to assemble many high-tech products, it remains largely dependent on imported high-tech equipment. Nevertheless, urrent capabilities... reflect a significant improvement over the past two decades. When China's economic reform program began in the late 1970s, Chinese industrial technology was universally obsolescent. Now, while China is hardly a high-tech powerhouse, some sectors are relatively modern.

The key question for the future is the extent to which China will be able to develop a technological base sufficient to support advanced weapon production. Although China purchases some advanced weapon systems on the international market, primarily from Russia, Chinese leaders are unlikely to remain content to base their military power entirely on imported equipment. Indeed, on two occasions— in 1960 and 1989—China suffered an abrupt cutoff of foreign arms transfers from the Soviet Union and the West. Thus, putting aside questions of national prestige, China will not want to remain dependent on foreign suppliers in the future. A RAND assessment of China's future technological capability insofar as it affects the country's military potential asserted that, China's prospects for technological progress are moderate.... By many measures China's potential for technological progress looks comparable to that of South Korea or Taiwan in the 1970s. In terms such as absolute numbers of scientists and engineers or total spending on R&D, however, China already vastly surpasses smaller countries like South Korea or Taiwan.

Thus, average technological levels in China in 2020 are likely to be comparable to those of South Korea or Taiwan today, but China's greater size suggests that the number of areas in which China possesses state-of-the-art capabilities will be larger than is currently true in those countries.

It was thus concluded that, while China can expect to make significant technological progress in coming years, it is impossible that China will catch up to, much less "leapfrog," the United States... for the foreseeable future. By many measures, China's prospects ... appear comparable to those of Taiwan or South Korea in the 1970s.... Thus, it seems likely that, by 2020, *average* technological levels in China will be roughly comparable to those in Taiwan and South Korea. There may be a difference, however, due to China's scale.... [South Korea and Taiwan] have become very competitive in particular technological niches.

If China follows a similar development path, its huge size... means that the number of these niches will be far greater. Thus, while China will on average still be significantly behind the United States... technologically, its technological capabilities could be very competitive in a significant number of areas by 2020. Depending on the strategic insight with which China chooses these niches and the competence with which the relevant R&D is conducted, China could build a technological base sufficient for the development of a military force that could pose some severe challenges to the United States. To be sure, such a military force would not be the equal of that of the United States and might not be designed to defeat U.S. forces in an all-out battle—but by exploiting various asymmetric strategies, it could be used to further Chinese political interests in Asia, even against some U.S. opposition.

Military Modernization

Previous RAND research has dealt with Chinese military modernization in detail and has concluded that by 2015 China could emerge as a *multidimensional, regional competitor* to the United States—i.e., as a military power that, while not a peer of the United States, could nonetheless assert itself in its immediate region so as to thwart U.S. political-military objectives. In particular, it has been asserted that China could credibly:

- exercise sea denial with respect to the seas contiguous to China;
- contest aerospace superiority in a sustained way in areas contiguous to China's borders;
- threaten U.S. operation locations in East Asia with a variety of long-range strike assets;

- challenge U.S. information dominance; and
- pose a strategic nuclear threat to the United States.

Of course it is by no means a foregone conclusion that the Chinese military will reach this level of capability within the second decade of the 21st century. Aside from the caveats expressed in the preceding sections concerning China's economic and technological development, China would probably have to significantly increase its defence spending, continue to trade quantity for quality, and ensure that the PLA opens itself to doctrinal, operational, and tactical innovation in order to do so. Assuming that its economy continues to grow, however, China would not find it difficult to increase defence spending to a sufficient extent to meet this objective; indeed, merely keeping defence spending constant as a percentage of GNP would in all likelihood suffice. In recent years, real defence spending in China has been growing faster than GDP, although it is unclear whether this trend represents a policy shift or a confluence of other factors (e.g., the unexpectedly rapid drop in inflation and "compensation" to the PLA for relinquishing its control of many business enterprises to other governmental entities).

A NEW CULTURAL CENTER OR CULTURAL IMPERIALISM

For China, in particular, the core of soft power is the promotion of Chinese culture and language. Since 2004, China has built more than 295 "Confucius Institutes" in 78 countries. A total of 500 are projected before 2010. In Southeast Asia, there are 21 Confucius Institutes providing language courses, including 13 in Thailand and others in Indonesia, Malaysia, Burma (Myanmar), the Philippines, and Singapore. These Institutes are sites for cultural transmission, intercultural exchange, and Chinese learning, conveying China's soft power resources to its ASEAN neighbors.

To be specific, overseas Confucius Institutes have at least two purposes. One is educational. The Institutes function as Alliance Française, Goethe-Institute, British Council, Insituto Cervante, which mainly deal with language and culture learning. Although Beijing heralds that the Institute is a non-profit and non-governmental organization, its principle and its budget are guided and sponsored by "the Office of Chinese Language Council International" (Hanban) affiliated with the PRC's Ministry of Education. Such an orientation naturally associates the institutes with the underlying strategic goals of the Chinese state.

Great powers both employ cultural commodities to exploit economic markets and to pursue ideological hegemony. Undoubtedly, the statement reminds us of U.S. foreign policy since the 1950s. The United States Information Agency (USIA). The USIA exerted influence on information sharing and made efforts to broaden dialogues between the States and the rest of the world. Moreover, it sponsored exchange programs such as the Fulbright Scholarship to inculcate overseas grantees with American culture and values.

Likewise the Confucius Institute also employs at least three kinds of soft power resources. First, the very notion of Confucius Institute is to nurture a worldwide cordial atmosphere conducive to Chinese learning. Language learning is associated with Chinese art, cinema, cuisine, fashion, and lifestyle. The pop culture itself may forge a pro-China ambiance (i.e. the fervor extending from Chinese language learning to supporting the 2008 Beijing Olympic Games), and reinforce the influence of Chinese soft power. Second, the Institute also provides a "Chinese Bridge Fund," sponsoring college student exchange program and supporting the research and development of overseas Chinese education. These funding programs and activities will intensify Beijing's international cultural attractiveness and magnify the influence of its soft power at the grassroots level. Third, since 2004, China has dispatched more than 2000 volunteers and teachers to 35 countries to work on Chinese education abroad in such ASEAN states as Indonesia, Lao, Philippines, Singapore, Thailand and Vietnam. These "civil diplomats" become vital human resources to wield cultural and social influence in the region.

Beijing has reiterated the politically neutral stance of the Confucius Institutes. However, political and ideological strings are evident in organizational governance, and relevant activities and publications.

For example, the grantees of the "Chinese Bridge Fund" determined by the Hanban may reflect Beijing's strategic considerations based on national interests. In addition, the disposition of 21 Confucius Institutes and hundreds of volunteers in Southeast Asia is also decided in accordance with cultural intimacy and political amity. China has made great efforts toward its neighbors in Southeast Asia to increase its cultural centrality in the region. It is plausible that the "China Fervor" intensified by Confucius Institutes and relevant projects will lay a foundation for the perception of a "benign China" and foster an even closer relationship between China and ASEAN states.

CHINA'S RISE TO WORLD POWER: WILL HISTORY REPEAT ITSELF?

China has been growing at about 9% per annum and its goods and services are rapidly rising in quality and value. In contrast, the US and Europe have wallowed around 0% growth from 2007-2012. China's innovative techno-scientific establishment routinely assimilates the latest inventions from the West (and Japan) and improves them, thereby decreasing the cost of production. China has replaced the US and European controlled "international financial institutions" (the IMF, World Bank, the Inter-American Development Bank) as the principle lender in Latin America. China continues to lead as the prime investor in African energy and mineral resources. China has replaced the US as the principle market for Saudi Arabian, Sudanese and Iranian petroleum and it will soon replace the US as the principle market for Venezuela petroleum products. Today China is the world's biggest manufacturer and exporter, dominating even the US market, while playing the role of financial life line as it holds over $1.3 trillion in US Treasury notes.

Under growing pressure from its workers, farmers and peasants, China's rulers have been developing the domestic market by increasing wages and social spending to rebalance the economy and avoid the specter of social instability. In contrast, US wages, salaries and vital public services have sharply declined in absolute and relative terms.

Given the current historical trends it is clear that China will replace the US as the leading world economic power, over the next decade, if the US empire does not strike back and if China's profound class inequalities do not lead to a major social upheaval.

Modern China's rise to global power faces serious challenges. In contrast to China's historical ascent on the world stage, modern Chinese global economic power is not accompanied by any imperialist undertakings. China has seriously lagged behind the US and Europe in aggressive war-making capacity. This may have allowed China to direct public resources to maximize economic growth, but it has left China vulnerable to US military superiority in terms of its massive arsenal, its string of forward bases and strategic geo-military positions right off the Chinese coast and in adjoining territories.

In the nineteenth century British imperialism demolished China's global position with its military superiority, seizing China's ports – because of China's reliance on 'mercantile superiority'.

The conquest of India, Burma and most of Asia allowed Britain to establish colonial bases and recruit local mercenary armies. The British and its mercenary allies encircled and isolated China, setting the stage for the disruption of China's markets and the imposition of the brutal terms of trade. The British Empire's armed presence dictated what China imported (with opium accounting for over 50% of British exports in the 1850s) while undermining China's competitive advantages via tariff policies.

Today the US is pursuing similar policies: US naval fleet patrols and controls China's commercial shipping lanes and off-shore oil resources via its overseas bases. The Obama-Clinton White House is in the process of developing a rapid military response involving bases in Australia, Philippines and elsewhere in Asia. The US is intensifying its efforts to undermine Chinese overseas access to strategic resources while backing 'grass roots' separatists and 'insurgents' in West China, Tibet, Sudan, Burma, Iran, Libya, Syria and elsewhere. The US military agreements with India and the installation of a pliable puppet regime in Pakistan have advanced its strategy of isolating China. While China upholds its policy of "harmonious development" and "non-interference in the internal affairs of other countries", it has stepped aside as US and European military imperialism have attacked a host of China's trading partners to essentially reverse China's peaceful commercial expansion.

China's lack of a political and ideological strategy capable of protecting its overseas economic interests has been an invitation for the US and NATO to set-up regimes hostile to China. The most striking example is Libya where US and NATO intervened to overthrow an independent government led by President Gadhafi, with whom China had signed multi-billion dollar trade and investments agreements. The NATO bombardment of Libyan cities, ports and oil installation forced the Chinese to withdraw 35,000 Chinese oil engineers and construction workers in a matter of days. The same thing happened in Sudan where China had invested billions to develop its oil industry. The US, Israel and Europe armed the South Sudanese rebels to disrupt the flow of oil and attack Chinese oil workers. In both cases China passively allowed the US and European military imperialists to attack its trade partners and undermine its investments.

Under Mao Tse Tung, China had an active policy countering imperial aggression: It supported revolutionary movements and independent Third World governments. Today's capitalist China does not have an active policy of supporting governments or movements capable of protecting China's bilateral trade and investment agreements. China's inability to confront the rising tide of US military aggression against its economic interests, is due to deep structural problems. China's foreign policy is shaped by big commercial, financial and manufacturing interests who rely on their 'economic competitive edge' to gain market shares and have no understanding of the military and security underpinnings of global economic power. China's political class is deeply influenced by a new class of billionaires with strong ties to Western equity funds and who have uncritically absorbed Western cultural values. This is illustrated by their preference for sending their own children to elite universities in the US and Europe. They seek "accommodation with the West" at any price.

This lack of any strategic understanding of military empire-building has led them to respond ineffectively and ad hoc to each imperialist action undermining their access to resources and markets. While China's "business first" outlook may have worked when it was a minor player in the world economy and US empire builders saw the "capitalist opening" as a chance to easily takeover China's public enterprises and pillage the economy. However, when China (in contrast to the former USSR) decided to retain capital controls and develop a carefully calibrated, state directed "industrial policy" directing western capital and the transfer of technology to state enterprises, which effectively penetrated the US domestic and overseas markets, Washington began to complain and talked of retaliation.

China's huge trade surpluses with the US provoked a dual response in Washington : It sold massive quantities of US Treasury bonds to the Chinese and began to develop a global strategy to block China's advance. Since the US lacked economic leverage to reverse its decline, it relied on its only "comparative advantage" – its military superiority based on a world wide system of attack bases, a network of overseas client regimes, military proxies, NGO'ers, intellectuals and armed mercenaries. Washington turned to its vast overt and clandestine security apparatus to undermine China's trading partners. Washington depends on its long-standing ties with corrupt rulers, dissidents, journalists and media moguls to provide the powerful propaganda cover while advancing its military offensive against China's overseas interests.

China has nothing to compare with the US overseas 'security apparatus' because it practices a policy of "non-interference". Given the advanced state of the Western imperial offensive, China has taken only a few diplomatic initiatives, such as financing English language media outlets to present its perspective, using its veto power on the UN Security Council to oppose US efforts to overthrow the independent Assad regime in Syria and opposing the imposition of drastic sanctions against Iran. It sternly repudiated US Secretary of State Hilary Clinton's vitriolic questioning of the 'legitimacy' of the Chinese state when it voted against the US-UN resolution preparing an attack on Syria.

Chinese military strategists are more aware and alarmed at the growing military threat to China. They have successfully demanded a 19% annual increase in military spending over the next five years (2011-2015). Even with this increase, China's military expenditures will still be less than one-fifth of the US military budget and China has not one overseas military base in stark contrast to the over 750 US installations abroad. Overseas Chinese intelligence operations are minimal and ineffective. Its embassies are run by and for narrow commercial interests who utterly failed to understand NATO's brutal policy of regime change in Libya and inform Beijing of its significance to the Chinese state.

There are two other structural weaknesses undermining China's rise as a world power. This includes the highly 'Westernized' intelligentsia which has uncritically swallowed US economic doctrine about free markets while ignoring its militarized economy.

These Chinese intellectuals parrot the US propaganda about the 'democratic virtues' of billion-dollar Presidential campaigns, while supporting financial deregulation which would have led to a Wall Street takeover of Chinese banks and savings. Many Chinese business consultants and academics have been educated in the US and influenced by their ties to US academics and international financial institutions directly linked to Wall Street and the City of London. They have prospered as highly-paid consultants receiving prestigious positions in Chinese institutions. They identify the 'liberalization of financial markets' with "advanced economies" capable of deepening ties to global markets instead of as a major source of the current global financial crisis. These "Westernized intellectuals" are like their 19th century comprador counterparts who underestimated and dismissed the long-term consequences of Western imperial penetration. They fail to understand how financial deregulation in the US precipitated the current crisis and how deregulation would lead to a Western takeover of China's financial system- the consequences of which would reallocate China's domestic savings to non-productive activities (real estate speculation), precipitate financial crisis and ultimately undermine China's leading global position.

These Chinese yuppies imitate the worst of Western consumerist life styles and their political outlooks are driven by these life styles and Westernized identities which preclude any sense of solidarity with their own working class.

There is an economic basis for the pro-Western sentiments of China's neo-compradors. They have transferred billions of dollars to foreign bank accounts, purchased luxury homes and apartments in London, Toronto, Los Angeles, Manhattan, Paris, Hong Kong and Singapore. They have one foot in China (the source of their wealth) and the other in the West (where they consume and hide their wealth).

Westernized compradores are deeply embedded in China's economic system having family ties with the political leadership in the party apparatus and the state. Their connections are weakest in the military and in the growing social movements, although some "dissident" students and academic activists in the "democracy movements" are backed by Western imperial NGO's. To the extent that the compradors gain influence, they weaken the strong economic state institutions which have directed China's ascent to global power, just as they did in the 19th century by acting as intermediaries for the British Empire. Proclaiming 19th Century "liberalism" British opium addicted over 50 million Chinese in less than a decade. Proclaiming "democracy and human rights" US gunboats now patrol off China's coast. China's elite-directed rise to global economic power has spawned monumental inequalities between the thousands of new billionaires and multi-millionaires at the top and hundreds of millions of impoverished workers, peasants and migrant workers at the bottom.

China's rapid accumulation of wealth and capital was made possible through the intense exploitation of its workers who were stripped of their previous social safety net and regulated work conditions guaranteed under Communism. Millions of Chinese households are being dispossessed in order to promote real estate developer/speculators who then build high rise offices and the luxury apartments for the domestic and foreign elite. These brutal features of ascendant Chinese capitalism have created a fusion of workplace and living space mass struggle which is growing every year. The developer/ speculators' slogan "to get rich is wonderful" has lost its power to deceive the people. In 2011 there were over 200,000 popular encompassing urban coastal factories and rural villages. The next step, which is sure to come, will be the unification of these struggles into new national social movements with a class-based agenda demanding the restoration of health and educational services enjoyed under the Communists as well as a greater share of China's wealth. Current demands for greater wages can turn to demands for greater work place democracy. To answer these popular demands China's new compradore-Westernized liberals cannot point to their 'model' in the US empire where American workers are in the process of being stripped of the very benefits Chinese workers are struggling to regain.

China, torn by deepening class and political conflict, cannot sustain its drive toward global economic leadership. China's elite cannot confront the rising global imperial military threat from the US with its comprador allies among the internal liberal elite while the country is a deeply divided society with an increasingly hostile working class. The time of unbridled exploitation of China's labor has to end in order to face the US military encirclement of China and economic disruption of its overseas markets. China possesses enormous resources. With over $1.5 trillion dollars in reserves China can finance a comprehensive national health and educational program throughout the country. China can afford to pursue an intensive 'public housing program' for the 250 million migrant workers currently living in urban squalor. China can impose a system of progressive income taxes on its new billionaires and millionaires and finance small family farmer co-operatives and rural industries to rebalance the economy. Their program of developing alternative energy sources, such as solar panels and wind farms – are a promising start to addressing their serious environmental pollution.

Degradation of the environment and related health issues already engage the concern of tens of millions. Ultimately China's best defence against imperial encroachments is a stable regime based on social justice for the hundreds of millions and a foreign policy of supporting overseas anti-imperialist movements and regimes – whose independence are in China's vital interest. What is needed is a pro-active policy based on mutually beneficial joint ventures including military and diplomatic solidarity. Already a small, but influential, group of Chinese intellectuals have raised the issue of the growing US military threat and are "saying no to gunboat diplomacy".

Modern China has plenty of resources and opportunities, unavailable to China in the 19th century when it was subjugated by the British Empire. If the US continues to escalate its aggressive militaristic policy against China, Beijing can set off a serious fiscal crisis by dumping a few of its hundreds of billions of dollars in US Treasury notes. China, a nuclear power should reach out to its similarly armed and threatened neighbor, Russia, to confront and confound the bellicose rantings of US Secretary of State, Hilary Clinton. Russian President-to-be Putin vows to increase military spending from 3% to 6% of the GDP over the next decade to counter Washington's offensive missile bases on Russia's borders and thwart Obama's 'regime change' programs against its allies, like Syria.

China has powerful trading, financial and investment networks covering the globe as well as powerful economic partners.These links have become essential for the continued growth of many of countries throughout the developing world. In taking on China, the US will have to face the opposition of many powerful market-based elites throughout the world. Few countries or elites see any future in tying their fortunes to an economically unstable empire-based on militarism and destructive colonial occupations.

In other words, modern China, as a world power, is incomparably stronger than it was in early 18th century. The US does not have the colonial leverage that the ascendant British Empire possessed in the run-up to the Opium Wars. Moreover, many Chinese intellectuals and the vast majority of its citizens have no intention of letting its current "Westernized compradors" sell out the country. Nothing would accelerate political polarization in Chinese society and hasten the coming of a second Chinese social revolution more than a timid leadership submitting to a new era of Western imperial pillage.

CHANGE OF POWER STATUS AND THE SPEED OF CHINA'S RISE

Entering the 21st century, there are more and more predictions about when China will become a superpower. Some guess that China will be as strong as the United States in the coming decade, some bet that in 20 years and some predict its rise in year 2040. In spite of those disagreements among scholars, the forecasts were all based on the speed at which China's total power has been growing in recent years, without any consideration of the influences of the other powers' growth. As we are aware that China's power status is related to that of the other states, when forecasting China's future power status, we should not only take account of the speed of China's power growth but also the growth of the other states' power. To foresee the future change of China's power status, we should clarify the conditions for ascent and descent of international power status.

Conditions for Ascent and Descent of Power Status

As a state's power status is determined by quantitative comparisons of powers among states, the change in power status of a state depends on the difference in power growth rates between two states in a given period of time. Based on the afore-mentioned formula of a state's power status, the expression for the change of a state's power status should be $Sc = A(1 + Ra)/B(1 + Rb)$ " A/B, (here *Sc* refers to the result of a change in power status of two states *A* and *B*; where *A* and *B* indicate the original power for State A and State B respectively; while *Ra* and *Rb* indicate the actual growth rates of the two states, respectively). The expression shows that the change of a state's power status depends entirely upon the power growth rates (*Ra* and *Rb*) of the two states over a certain period of time.

That is, the state with a faster power growth rate will rise, and the other will fall, and the statuses remain unchanged if the growth rates of the two state powers are the same. Over a fixed time period, the difference in power growth rates for the two states may result in three possibilities for change of a side's power status: rising, falling or unchanged. The three scenarios may result from 13 different situations, in which there are five for ascent, five for descent and three for no change.

It will be a political issue if a state is able to rise to a superpower in a few decades, but only an historical issue if a state rises to a hegemon over hundreds of years. As the atrophy of a state's power is a significant factor for the rapid rise of other states' power statuses, it creates an important scenario for a shift of power between two states. Therefore, power atrophy is an important political issue deserving more attention than power growth. A state's power increases in most years, decreases occasionally and very rarely has zero growth. Thus, the probability of the 10 scenarios of power-status change varies. Often both states enjoy positive power growth simultaneously; it is less common for one state to have a positive power growth while the other has a negative one; it is rare for both states to have negative power growth and is even less common that one state incurs zero power growth. When two states simultaneously have positive or negative power growth, it takes a longer time for their power gap to change and their power statuses to shift, and the probability of power-status shift is small. If one of the two states incurs zero power growth, their power gap will change relatively rapidly and there will be a higher probability for their power status to shift. However, the fastest change in the two states' power gap or their power statuses will occur when the two states have opposite power growths, i.e. one state's power increases and the other's decreases ($Ra > 0 > Rb$ or $Ra < 0 < Rb$). Because national power grows in most years and opposite power growths of two states tend to shift power statuses easily, the factors leading to power atrophy are more significant than the factors enhancing national power in terms of changing the power gap and power status between states.

Political turbulence can cause a state's comprehensive power to diminish severely and rapidly, and it alters a state's power status at a faster rate than does economic development. Being defeated in a war, state disintegration, civil war, social turmoil and political movements all work effectively in shifting power status. The shift of power status between China and the Soviet Union after the Cold War serves as a typical example. In 1991, prior to collapse, the Soviet Union was the only competing superpower in the world rivalling the United States, and its power status drastically differed from that of China. However, as the succeeding state of the former Soviet Union after its collapse, Russia's comprehensive power endured a drastic fall and as a result its geographical area was reduced by about 24%, its population reduced by 48%, its economy decreased by 11%, and the size of its military was cut by 33.7%. At that time Russian comprehensive power was still greater than China's, however, its power status fell into the same class that China belonged to. The power gap between them was only in degree and no longer in character.

Thereafter, Russia's economy declined for years, its military capability was severely weakened, and its political power was diminished internationally. Even though it is hard for us to figure out in which specific year the power-status shift occurred, we are quite certain that China's comprehensive power surpassed that of Russia during the 1990s. Up to 1999, sustaining only military superiority over China, Russia fell far behind China in aspects of political power and economic power. In 1999, Russia's GDP accounted for only one-fourth or one-third of China's GDP of $1 trillion.

Economic crisis can cause a nation's power to decrease rapidly and it works as a faster agent than economic development in changing the power gap or power status between two states. The East Asian Financial Crisis during 1997–98 widened the power gap between China and the Southeast Asian countries and meanwhile reduced the disparity of economic power between China and Japan. The East Asian Financial Crisis decreased China's annual economic growth rate to 7% from 9% prior to the crisis while it caused negative and zero economic growth, respectively, for Indonesia and Japan. Indonesian GDP fell to $50 billion in 1998 from $190.3 billion in 1995 (in 1998 its currency exchange rate fell to US$1:IDR7500 from $1:IDR2321 in 1996) and it recovered to $208.3 billion in 2003, with only a 9.5% increase from its GDP in 1995. In that period, Japan's GDP reduced from $5083.1 billion in 1995 to $4326.4 billion in 2003, a total reduction of 15%. During the same period, China's GDP (by currency exchange rate) doubled from $704.1 billion in 1995 to $1409.9 billion in 2003. Therefore, in the eight years from 1995 to 2003, the economic gap between Indonesia and China had been widened from 3.7 times to 6.8 times, while the economic gap between China and Japan narrowed from 7.2 to 3.0 times. In terms of PPP, China's economy even surpassed Japan's, causing a shift in their economic power rankings.

Political Factors Determining the Fluctuation of China's Power Status

According to the principle that opposite power growths among states tend to change power status between states easily, we come to realize that in 10 years (by 2015) whether China can sustain the existing power status will be determined mainly by the likelihood of political crisis that may cause China's power status to descend. Since its foundation in 1949, China's power status has undergone a spell of four rising and three falling periods. During 1950–58 China's power status had been rising. During that period, the Korean War tremendously raised both China's military power status and her domestic and international capabilities of political mobilization. Between 1952 and

1958, China's GDP increased by as much as 1.9 times. During 1959–63 China's comprehensive power atrophied severely. The Anti-Rightwing Movement led the Chinese government to adopt the policies of 'Great Leap' and 'People's Commune', which resulted in an overall economic crisis. It was not until 1964 that China's economy recovered to the same level of 1960. In 1959, Sino–Soviet relations began to deteriorate and China was facing joint pressures from both the United States and the Soviet Union. During 1964 and 1965, China's national power enjoyed a brief rising period but fell again during 1966–76. In May 1966, the Cultural Revolution occurred and the country was immersed in turbulence and chaos when the government's ability to maintain order was severely hampered, economic activities stagnated, and the military weakened. However, in the same period of time, many Asian states such as Japan, South Korea and Singapore had industrialized their countries and their power status was rising rapidly in relation to China's. From 1978 to 1988 was a period when China restored its social order, increased its domestic mobilization capability and normalized relations with the United States and the Soviet Union. Consequently, China had again enhanced its international political capability, and its economy sustained an average annual growth as high as 10.2%. The political events of 1989–93 slowed China's economic growth, and dramatically reduced its domestic and international political mobilization capabilities. Thus, China's power status fell as her political power diminished in such a drastic manner. From 1993 to 2004 was the third period when China's power status ascended. During this interval, China gradually emerged from the international isolation which had started in 1989 and its capabilities of domestic and international mobilization once again increased. During 1993–2004, China's economy sustained an annual growth of 9.2% and the 1997 East Asian Financial Crisis accelerated the ascendance of China's economic power status. Ever since the founding of the People's Republic of China, each of the three major descents of China's power status was traced back to a political crisis rather than wars or economic difficulties. Therefore, we can believe that as long as there is no future political crisis, China will be able to avoid a fall in its power status.

Based on the principle that national power usually sustains growth in the majority of years, the author argues that the major external elements affecting the speed of rise of China's power status will be: (1) US military commitments and an increase or decrease of its international mobilization capabilities, and (2) the pace of political integration of the European Union (EU). According to the current growth of the comprehensive strengths of major powers, the author assumes that no other single nation, except the

United States, could have larger comprehensive power than China in the next 10 years. Although each individual European state has smaller comprehensive power than China, the EU as a unified power will have a superior status to China's. If the political integration of the EU results in an international player with national character in the next 10 years, our references for judging China's future power status should include both the United States and the EU. Some people suppose that China's future power status would fundamentally depend upon China's economic growth. They obviously have neglected the political and military powers of the United States and the EU. China possesses a huge supply of low-paid labour, therefore in the next 10 years China's economic growth will be faster than that of the United States and the EU. It is also quite possible for China to narrow its economic gap with the United States and the EU. Nevertheless, there is uncertainty with regard to the development of the military and political powers of China, the United States and the EU in next 10 years.

In 10 years from now, China may narrow its military gap with the EU but the change of its military gap with the United States will depend on its military containment against Taiwanese secessionists. A favourable security environment will constrain the EU from large military expenditure.

Therefore, in the next 10 years, China's military strength will grow faster than that of the EU and will reduce the military gap between the two. Nevertheless, the change of military disparity between China and the Unites States will be determined by the rates of military investment of the two sides. As a result of the pro-independence group introducing a timetable for Taiwan to achieve legitimate independence by 2008, the Chinese government will inevitably enhance its military capability to contain Taiwanese secessionists. If the Chinese government was to launch a military attack against Taiwan's independence, it would be possible for China to narrow its military gap with the United States.

If the United States continues to wage wars against smaller states while China has no need to attack Taiwanese secessionists militarily, the US military budget will increase faster than that of China's, thus the military power gap between China and the United States would be enlarged.

In the coming decade, China will probably reduce the disparity of its political power with that of the United States, but in the meantime her advantageous political power with relevance to the EU may diminish. In the 1990s, global democratization and marketization increased the US international mobilization capability to a historical peak. With little resistance from the UN Security Council, the United States obtained UN authorizations on waging the Gulf War in 1991, the Somali War in 1996, the war in Kosovo in 1999 as well as the war in Afghanistan in 2001.

Many countries provided military and economic support to the United States during these wars. However, the United States current unilateral policy caused its international political mobilizing capability to fall sharply from 2003. Without any UN authorization, the United States waged war in Iraq under the excuse of alleged Iraqi possession of weapons of mass destruction. The US action encountered strenuous objections from many traditional European allies, headed by France and Germany.

As no weapons of mass destruction have been discovered in Iraq, US international influence has been seriously weakened. In the next 10 years, hegemonic position will drive the United States to continue its unilateralist foreign policy. Meanwhile, China will maintain its multilateral diplomacy to harmonize relationships with her neighbours, the EU and the developing countries of other regions.

Their opposite foreign policies will reduce the political power disparity between China and the United States. Presently, China has greater political power than the EU because China is a single state while the EU is a regional organization with inconsistent foreign policies adopted by its member states. In 1999, the EU introduced the Euro which entered circulation in 2002 and finally established a single currency system on the EU market. In the year 2004, the political leaders of EU member states signed the European Constitution laying a legislative foundation for the EU to become a single state entity. If the EU constitution is approved by its member states, it will establish its own three-in-one entity of administrative institutions including a council, a committee and a foreign ministry. Future political integration of the EU will enhance its character as a large national state, which may help it to narrow its political power disparity with China.

Based on the above analysis, if we assume that both the United States and the EU act as single states, the comprehensive national power gap between either China and the United States or the EU and China will probably be narrowed by the year 2015. China's comprehensive power status may rank third in the world. In 10 years and beyond, it may be possible for China to reduce its economic power disparity with the United States and the EU even though its economic power may still be smaller than theirs. China will narrow its military power gap with the EU but its overall military strength will still be weaker than that of the United States or the EU. In terms of political power, China will narrow the gap but still cannot catch up with the United States. China may maintain her political power superiority over the EU but the disparity between the two may be reduced by further political integration of the EU if all its member states ratify the EU Constitution before 2015.

We have discussed why China enjoys the leading power status among the major powers with the exception of the United States. Based on the principle that a nation's power status ascends in accordance with a faster growth rate, we may presume that China will strengthen its power superiority over Japan, Russia and India within the next 10 years. If the EU becomes a single state entity by 2015, Britain, France and Germany will no longer be regarded as individual international players. Thus, we only assess here the power status between China and three other states: Japan, Russia and India.

With regards to economic power, low-cost labour and a rapidly expanding domestic market will ensure China a faster economic growth than Japan and Russia in the next 10 years. According to World Bank data based on PPP calculations, Japan, Russia and China have GDP per capita in 2001 of $26,940, $8230 and $4580, respectively. This indicates that China's labour wage level was less than 18% of Japan's and 56% of Russia's. Low-cost labour guarantees foreign investors long-term high profits in China. At the end of 2005, China adopted a floating exchange rate according to World Trade Organization regulations and the Renmenbi (RMB) will appreciate continuously over the next 10 years. The increase in RMB exchange rate will make China's economic growth appear even faster. Although it enjoys the same advantage of low-cost labour as China, India is far behind China in aspects of opening-up to foreign investment as well as other economic reforms. Therefore, the Indian economy will continue to grow at a slower pace than that of China.

In terms of military power, it is anticipated over the next decade none of the three states, namely Japan, Russia and India, will be involved in military conflict with the United States. Therefore, the military spending of these states will increase slower than China's. Even though India and Russia are both faced with the threat of separatism in Kashmir and Chechnya, respectively, they do not face direct military protection of these separatists by the United States. As a result, the threat to Russia and India, from the separatists in these two regions, will not be comparable to that caused by the Taiwanese secessionists. Japan is under US military protection, hence its military investment will not increase as fast as that of China. The Japanese government has decided to reduce its 2005–09 military expenditures to $233 billion, i.e. 3.7% less than its average annual military spending in the previous five years. As a result of the danger of Taiwanese independence, China is faced with potential military clashes with the United States in the Taiwan Straight. China's military spending in the next 10 years will increase much faster than that of

Japan, Russia and India. This will in turn reduce the military disparity between China and Russia and at the same time make its military superior to Japan and India.

In terms of political power, China's endeavours in East Asian regionalization will effectively enhance its ability for political mobilization over the next 10 years. China will have the opportunity to further improve its relations with the EU and that will strengthen China's influence on global affairs. India, Russia and Japan, however, will have few chances to further enhance political influence in their own regions. Although India has already been a leading nation in South Asia, the South Asian regionalization has much less momentum than the East Asian.

The Eastern expansion of the EU is constraining Russian political influence in East Europe and the former Soviet Republics. To sustain its special relationship with the United States, Japan has adopted a policy undermining the establishment of the East Asian Community. This policy is similar to that adopted by Great Britain with regard to the EU. Japan's policy against East Asian regionalization may ultimately weaken its political influence in East Asia. In terms of global affairs, both India and Japan may have the opportunity to become permanent members of the UN Security Council but they will have little chance of obtaining the power of veto. What they actually obtain may only be a position of permanent/non-permanent membership without substantially increased power. Russian political impact on global affairs will further diminish as it is still trapped in a regressive inertia following the collapse of the Soviet Union.

UNDERSTANDING CHINA'S SOFT AUTHORITY DIPLOMACY IN SOUTHEAST ASIA

ASEAN has sought to restrain Chinese power by enmeshing it in regional institutions. Whereas ASEAN is attractive China to tame the aggressive realpolitik that has characterised Chinese foreign relations, Beijing views the same institutions as a way to extend its regional influence and has sought to exclude the US. In planning for the first EAC summit, which was held in Malaysia, China tried to exclude India, Australia and New Zealand, but was overruled by Japan and ASEAN members. As China's regional influence grows, most ASEAN members are working to push against or balance Chinese power. While deepening trade and diplomatic co-operation with Beijing, many members, US allies such as Thailand and the Philippines, key 'swing states' such as Singapore, and emerging regional powers such as Indonesia, have also increased security ties with Washington.

The question is why the US has changed its policy in the region from a benign power to one almost squarely focusing on hard power balance issues including terrorism as the overall obsession. For Southeast Asia, long under the United States' political and economic influence, times are rapidly moving in a new direction. A decade ago about three-quarters of US investment in East Asia went to Southeast Asia. That figure has now fallen to 10 percent. Approximately 80 percent of US investment in East Asia now goes to China.

The United States remnants the region's single biggest destination for exports, and will be for some years to come. This is probably why the White House is on the defensive in terms of coming to grasp with the regional and multilateral setting in East and Southeast Asia. As one observer remarks: "Relations between Southeast Asia and the United States are perhaps best described as 'a policy without a strategy". Asian leaders are organizing and building new regional institutions precisely to avoid the sort of power politics that America is practicing. Progress has been tenuous but real, and most regional leaders are cautiously optimistic about Asia's future. As long as this remains true, American emphasis on balance-of-power politics will continue to meet with only limited success. Indeed, this approach is likely to be under-mined by regional players, who are more interested in participating in economic integration and building regional communities than in divisive balancing behaviour. Most troubling for the United States, it will also cede its leadership role in Asia and limit Washington's ability to influence the future shape of regional institutions in the region.

China's ultimate strategic purpose remains a subject of debate and speculation among analysts. Southeast Asia, in this respect, is the sole region adjacent to China in which Chinese influence can most easily expand. A benign interpretation would see China as simply cultivating the sort of stable, peaceful, and prosperous regional environment that is required for its own successful modernization. A more sceptical view sees China playing a long-term game designed to curtail American influence and weave a close-knit economic and security community with China at the centre.

Beijing is in fact using nationalism and the 'glories of the Chinese civilisation' to instil a sense of unity among Chinese nationals domestically and among the Chinese Diaspora in Southeast Asia. Although Beijing may acknowledge that rampant nationalism could pose a danger to its own internal stability, it has astutely harnessed it to build a new Asian pride and identity, which it hopes might help establish a new Asian system of politics, economics, security and culture within the 'ASEAN+3' framework. The PRC ardently hopes this could be transformed ultimately into an East Asian Community under its leadership (Teo 2005). To realize its peaceful rise, China is using a sophisticated blend of trade, confidence building measures, and development assistance to establish itself as an important regional-cum-global leader.

Of course the appeal of Confucianism offers Beijing a definite comparative advantage in its soft supremacy approach. Moreover, the relationship China enjoys with the Chinese Diaspora in the region, who dominate the economic and, in some countries like Thailand, increasingly the political scene, is another advantage. The immediate implications of such an approach are that it would be naive to believe that China is not interested in exerting a dominant influence over its regional hinterland; commercial and financial muscle will eventually be the levers of choice, perhaps spearheaded by a strong regional currency. As much as the Chinese may be more ethnically exclusive than Americans and some Europeans, they are every bit as eager to see Chinese culture and traditions adopted by others - as a mark of civilization.

As more and more Chinese tourists visit the region and even begin to dominate the tourist trade, the service sector response will be to tailor to Chinese taste and custom. This will inevitably result in a revival of Chinese culture and language in local communities once believed to have assimilated.

Already one of the fastest growing Chinese language media groups is based in Malaysia, where Chinese language education has an unbroken history of more than a century. Up to the present, businesses have catered to a culture that projects modernity and sophistication in a Western guise - this could change and have an impact on U.S. and European influence.

The use of culture as a tool of diplomacy highlights the sense of theatre that China skilfully deploys to exaggerate kin, ethnicity and national bonds between the Motherland and the Diaspora. It also reflects an increased appreciation by the Chinese government of the importance of norms and soft power in diplomacy.

Chinese print media, television, music, food, and popular culture are spreading around the region as never before. So, too, are Chinese tourists fanning out across the region, often filling the void left by American tourists staying home after 9/11, the Bali bombing, and tsunami; 800,000 Chinese toured both Thailand and Singapore in 2004.

In this way it is safe to say that ethnic Chinese business communities scattered in Southeast Asia have facilitated 'the rearticulation of mainland China into the global economy' not least through their reciprocal involvement in more than 100,000 joint ventures in China. It is also arguable that the Chinese Diaspora has been used not 'just as a financial resource in China to fund revolutions in the past and economic reforms in the present; they have been an important symbolic resource in the construction of Chinese nationalism'.

The combination of geo-political and geo-economic strategies and cultural expansion begs an answer to the question: 'what are the implications of China's policy of soft power for US influence in the region'? Elizabeth Economy notes the important point that, China's rise to date appears to be less about the 'inevitable conflict of rising power' theory, popular in some circles, than about creeping power transition. Chinese thinkers, themselves, have recognized that the international community is concerned by the potential implications of China's rise and have taken pains to ensure that it will be perceived as non-threatening. This is well illustrated by Li Junru, Vice-President of the Central Party School at the Chinese Communist Party (CCP), who explicitly outlined the benefits to China's neighbours, stating, 'China's rise will not damage the interests of other Asian countries. That is because as China rises, it provides a huge market for its neighbours. At the same time, the achievements of China's development will allow it to support the progress of others in the region' (2005: 3-4).

In order to understand the motives and objectives of Chinese pragmatism, it is important to put both bilateral and multilateral diplomatic initiatives and foreign policy into the overall trade and security context and understand the internal and external constraints for a Chinese expansive strategy in Southeast Asia. The region as a whole maintains a trade surplus with China of US$8 billion annually, largely from its enormous exports of raw materials and precision machinery. China also agreed to an 'Early Harvest Package' that is perceived by ASEAN as 'largely a concession' to provide benefits through tariff reductions on 573 products including agricultural and manufactured goods. Individual Chinese entrepreneurs are also now expanding China's economic reach throughout Laos and Myanmar.

In some areas, locals now use only the Yuan and speak Chinese. The forays of Chinese companies fit in with a broader strategic push by Beijing to establish closer economic cooperation with and among Asian countries. Unofficial reports by ASEAN officials claim that the foreign policy aim is part of a broader thrust by China to deploy multilateralism against what it sees as US unilateralist hegemony in the region and the world. 'This is a long-term game that China is playing,' says a senior ASEAN official. 'They want a situation in Southeast Asia that automatically takes into account China's interests. The whole objective of the policy is to avoid strategic encirclement by the U.S.' (Vatikiotis and Hiebert 2003).

Critical voices note that ASEAN's trade with Japan of $136 billion and that of the United States of more than $136 billion in 2004 exceeds trade with China. At the same time, in both Indonesia and Malaysia, people complain that jobs are being lost to China. Not least because Chinese textile exports since January 2005 have increased, thus implying down-ward competition for Cambodia and Vietnam. A growing mainland Chinese economic presence could also fuel latent resentment against the sizable ethnic Chinese economic elites in the region. In fact, almost no research has so far been done to investigate the impact of China's FDI on labour markets, environment and social issues and the question is whether China is exporting its own poor labour practices.

Factors inhibiting Chinese private investment and tourism are sensitive to the treatment of Chinese minorities in Southeast Asia and in particular in the Philippines and Indonesia. The Indonesian racial riots in the aftermath of the financial crisis in 1998 which targeted ethnic Chinese created long-term damage to the 'bamboo network'. There are also cultural impediments when it comes to expansion as noted by a senior ASEAN official: 'Unlike Americans, Chinese don't embrace foreigners - you cannot 'become Chinese''.

China's approach has been subtle, using soft power and economic diplomacy to build a benign multilateral framework in the shape of a free-trade agreement with ASEAN. 'China has shown a great deal of sensitivity,' says Singapore Prime Minister Goh Chok Tong. 'China realizes that it is a huge elephant, and even if it treads softly, it can still shake the ground.' One observer notes that 'China is seen by some to be slowly filling the vacuum left behind by the United States in the political, economic and security spheres in the region. This implies that 'U.S. Influence in Asia under Bush is Waning' (Agence France Presse, August 29, 2004.) and being replaced by China.

Beijing has also enthused the dynamics of regional cooperation in many other ways. One example is China's enthusiasm for developing the ASEAN-China dialogue into a vibrant web of multilevel and multi-sector cooperation. As noted above, the 1997 financial crisis was the main catalyst for the creation of a full-fledged diplomatic mechanism spanning summit, ministerial, and senior official levels. As Cheng-Chwee notes, the mechanism has stretched into various semi-state and civil society organizations that include research departments, media outlets, youth organizations, and the business sector. Also cooperation in agriculture, transport infraarrangement, as well as energy has been included.

Over time, these ties have interwoven into a web of interdependence between China and ASEAN. The PRC has also taken the initiative in pushing for the creation of the Network of East Asia Think-Tanks (NEAT) (2005: 115). These moves are not merely tactical but part of PRCs overall goal to utilize the ASEAN-plus-three as the main vehicle of East Asian cooperation and the creation of the hybrid East Asian Community. Although there are other factors at play, China has played a decisive role in pushing in that direction. 'China's enthusiasm for East Asian cooperation is clearly driven by its aspiration to shape the direction of the existing regional institutions' (2005: 115-116).

Diplomatically, China's goals and vision in Southeast Asia are clear as it rivals the US and Japan world-wide and regionally. Moreover it may be again considering ASEAN as its own Monroe sphere, as it was during the 400 years of the Chinese tributary system under the Ming-Qing Emperors. Southeast Asian countries appear to be accepting sub-ordination as they seek to profit from the rising China.

4

Rise of Japan and China : Global Power in Asia

THE RISE OF THE MILITARISTS IN JAPAN

While Japan was giving the appearance of being a good neighbour in the western Pacific during the 1920s by involvement in treaties designed to preserve peace, extremist elements in Japan's government, military and civilian population had privately never renounced the use of force to expand Japan's territory. Towards the end of the 1920s a combination of economic, social, and political factors played into the hands of the militarists.

Having been barely touched by World War I, Japanese industry and trade had expanded dramatically during that war to fill the gap left by Europe's devastated industries. However, most of the raw materials needed to supply Japanese manufacturing industry had to be imported because Japan possessed inadequate natural resources. This problem was compounded by substantial population increase. Between 1918 and 1930, Japan's population had expanded dramatically and outstripped the capacity of the nation's resources to support it. To sustain its population blow-out, substantial food imports were essential, but foreign tariffs imposed on its exports of manufactured goods limited the capacity of Japan to pay for its food imports. Japan had tried to deal with its population problem by encouraging emigration of Japanese to countries such as the United States, but had met resistance from Americans who feared the loss of unskilled jobs to cheap immigrant labour.

With China torn by revolution in the 1920s, Japan's militarists viewed China, and in particular, its resource-rich northern region of Manchuria, as an obvious area for Japan to expand its territory by military force and thereby solve its raw material and population problems. However, the Japanese imperial government was not responsive to proposals for military aggression against China at this time.

During the 1920s, Japanese militarists became increasingly distrustful of civilian party government. In 1922, the Washington Naval Conference had allocated to Japan a smaller naval tonnage than that allowed to Great Britain and the United States. This caused resentment in Japan, particularly in the ranks of army and civilian militarists who viewed it as a humiliation for Japan. In 1925, the Kato imperial government cut the army and navy budgets and reduced the Japanese Army by four divisions.

Between 1925 and 1928, Chinese nationalists under the banner of the Kuomintang (Nationalist Party) had begun to unite all of China's far-flung regions under a Kuomintang Nationalist government. Japan's militarists feared that a unified China under a Nationalist government would block Japanese territorial expansion into Manchuria where Japan had massive commercial interests and had achieved significant political influence. In 1927, Japanese militarists demanded action by the imperial government to block the Chinese Nationalist movement reaching Manchuria. The militarist Prime Minister Tanaka responded by sending Japanese troops to China's Shantung province in 1928 to block a union of Manchuria with the Chinese Nationalist cause.

Military Extremists take Control of Japan's Foreign Policy

When Japan acquired Port Arthur on the Kwantung Peninsular of southern Manchuria as one of the fruits of its victory in the Russo-Japanese War of 1904-1905, a Kwantung Army was established to occupy the peninsula, patrol the Japanese-owned South Manchuria Railway zone, and generally protect other Japanese commercial interests in Manchuria. The Kwantung Army included extremist officers who were well aware that senior officers of their army harboured plans to extend Japan's boundaries on the Asian mainland by military force. They were prepared to take direct action in Manchuria to force the Imperial government's hand

When Manchuria embraced Kuomintang nationalism in 1928, friction quickly developed between Chinese nationalists and Japan's pervasive and heavy-handed bureaucrats in Manchuria. The Manchurians wanted to reduce Japan's political influence in their region of China to a purely commercial presence. They also began to develop Chinese-owned railways to compete with the Japanese-owned and controlled South Manchuria Railway. Japan's militarists viewed these developments as threatening Japan's "special position" in Manchuria and their plans to seize for Japan this huge northern region of China. Extremist officers in Japan's Kwantung Army took steps intended to dampen Nationalist enthusiasm by assassinating the Chinese warlord ruler of Manchuria in 1928, but his successor was an even stronger supporter of Chinese nationalism. The murder of the Manchurian ruler was not authorised by the imperial government, but when the Tanaka government tried to punish the culprits and re-establish discipline in the army, it was blocked by the Japanese Army General Staff.

The failure to punish the murder of a foreign political leader by officers of the Kwantung Army in Manchuria clearly demonstrated that the imperial government had lost control of extremists in the Japanese Army, and the Tanaka government felt obliged to resign in July 1929. From this time onwards, the course of Japanese foreign policy became increasingly hostage to army extremists, and imperial governments and the Japanese Army General Staff were either unwilling or unable to curb them.

Intimidation and Assassination Destabilise Japanese Politics

After 1929, the extreme nationalism encouraged by the Meiji imperial government combined with traditional Japanese militarism to make life increasingly difficult, and often dangerous, for moderates in the imperial government, the Diet (parliament), and the armed services. Army and civilian extremists pointed to Japan's samurai military traditions, and accused moderate bureaucrats, politicians, and armed service leaders of disregard for Japan's national interests if they opposed increased military spending or territorial expansion by force.

Extreme nationalists branded democratic government as "un-Japanese", and called for territorial expansion and a return to traditional Japanese ways. The views of extremists would become increasingly influential in Japan during the 1930s, and they would use intimidation and assassination of politicians, businessmen and armed service leaders as means to achieve their aims.

The militarist-dominated Tanaka imperial government was followed by the more moderate Hamaguchi government which tried to curb the power of military extremists.

The extremists responded by plotting to overthrow civilian government, and Prime Minister Osachi Hamaguchi was assassinated in 1930. In March 1931, a coup involving senior military leaders was planned but abandoned. Within months, events in Manchuria would draw the focus of Japan's turbulent politics from Tokyo to that vast northern region of China.

Militarists launch Japan on the Path of Aggression by Seizing Manchuria from China, 1931

Japan's economy was seriously affected by the Great Depression which began in 1929, and with revenues from Japan's commercial interests in China's Manchurian region thought to be under threat from Chinese nationalism, military and civilian extremists found Japan's imperial government now willing to listen to their demands for a move against Manchuria.

In 1931, militarists dominated the imperial government, and all that they required was a plausible excuse for military action in Manchuria. Rather than wait for such an excuse to occur, the Kwantung Army extremists appear to have decided to create one. On the night of 18 September 1931, a bomb was exploded on the track of the Japanese-owned South Manchuria Railway. The explosion caused very little damage, and no loss of life. The Kwantung Army immediately blamed "Chinese terrorists", and without waiting for approval from the imperial government in Tokyo or producing any proof of its allegation, its troops seized the Manchurian city of Mukden.

Proclaiming a need to protect Japanese life and property, and again without approval from Tokyo, the Kwantung Army then undertook the full conquest of Chinese Manchuria. The Kwantung Army simply ignored efforts by the imperial government in Tokyo to bring its military aggression in Manchuria to a halt. When Prime Minister Inukai tried to secure Emperor Hirohito's intervention to bring the Kwantung Army back under government control, he was assassinated by naval officers in May 1932.

When the Kwantung Army had completed its conquest of Manchuria, it converted this vast former region of China into a Japanese puppet state called Manchukuo in September 1932. The last Manchu emperor of China, Henry Pu Yi, agreed to be enthroned as emperor of Japan's puppet state, and he ruled Manchukuo under the control of the Kwantung Army.

JAPAN'S QUEST FOR POWER AND WORLD WAR II IN ASIA

The World at War: 1931-1945

While the United States was still struggling to emerge from the Great Depression at the end of the 1930s, and would do so partly because of the war, Japan had emerged from its own period of depression, which had begun in 1926, by the mid-1930s. Many of the young soldiers mobilized into the Japanese army by the early 1930s came from the rural areas, where the effects of the depression were devastating and poverty was widespread.

Their commitment to the military effort to expand Japanese territory to achieve economic security can be understood partly in these terms. The depression ended in the mid-1930s in Japan partly because of government deficits used to expand greatly both heavy industry and the military.

Internationally, this was a time when "free trade" was in disrepute. The great powers not only jealously protected their special economic rights within their colonies and spheres of influence, but sought to bolster their sagging economies through high tariffs, dumping of goods, and other trade manipulation. The Japanese, with few natural resources, sought to copy this pattern. They used cutthroat trade practices to sell textiles and other light industrial goods in the East Asian and U.S. markets, severely undercutting British and European manufacturers. They also developed sources of raw materials and heavy industry in the colonies they established in Korea, Taiwan and Manchuria. Japan used high tariffs to limit imports of American and European industrial products.

The Japanese military faced a particular tactical problem in that certain critical raw materials — especially oil and rubber — were not available within the Japanese sphere of influence. Instead, Japan received most of its oil from the United States and rubber from British Malaya, the very two Western nations trying to restrict Japan's expansion. U.S. President Franklin D. Roosevelt's embargo of oil exports to Japan pressured the Japanese navy, which had stocks for only about six months of operations.

The Japanese army, for its part, was originally concerned with fighting the Soviet Union, because of the army's preoccupation with Manchuria and China. The Japanese army governed Manchuria indirectly through the "puppet" state of Manchuria and developed heavy industry there under its favorite agencies, disliking and distrusting the zaibatsu (large Japanese corporations). But the Soviet army's resistance to Japanese attacks was sufficient to discourage northern expansion.

Meanwhile in 1937, the intensification of Chinese resistance to the pressure of the Japanese military drew Japan into a draining war in the vast reaches of China proper, and in 1940 into operations in French Indochina, far to the south. Thus, when the navy pressed for a "southern" strategy of attacking Dutch Indonesia to get its oil and British Malaya to control its rubber, the army agreed.

While it seems that economic factors were important in Japanese expansion in East Asia, it would be too much to say that colonialism, trade protection, and the American embargo compelled Japan to take this course. Domestic politics, ideology and racism also played a role.

Domestic Politics

The political structure of Japan at this time was inherited from the Meiji era and was increasingly dominated by the military. During the Meiji period, the government was controlled by a small ruling group of elder statesmen who had overthrown the shogun and established the new centralized Japanese state. These men used their position to coordinate the bureaucracy, the military, the parliament, the Imperial Household, and other branches of government.

Following their deaths in the early 1920s, no single governmental institution was able to establish full control, until the 1931 Manchurian Incident, when Japan took control of Manchuria. This began a process in which the military behaved autonomously on the Asian mainland and with increasing authority in politics at home.

From 1937 on, Japan was at war with China. By the time General Hideki Tôjô became prime minister and the war against the United States began in 1941, the nation was in a state of "total war" and the military and their supporters were able to force their policies on the government and the people. The wartime regime used existing government controls on public opinion, including schools and textbooks, the media, and the police, but Japan continued to have more of an authoritarian government than a totalitarian one like Hitler's Germany. In particular, the government was never able to gain real control of the economy and the great zaibatsu, which were more interested in the economic opportunities provided by the military's policies than in submitting loyally to a patriotic mission.

The emperor has been criticized for not taking a more forceful action to restrain his government, especially in light of his own known preference for peace, but Japanese emperors after the Meiji Restoration had "reigned but not ruled." One wonders if a more forceful emperor in fact could have controlled the army and navy at this late date. The doubts are strengthened in light of the difficulty the emperor had in forcing the military to accept surrender after the atomic bombings. The emperor's decision at that point to bring agreement among his advisers was an extraordinary event in Japanese history.

Ideology

The emperor-based ideology of Japan during World War II was a relatively new creation, dating from the efforts of Meiji oligarchs to unite the nation in response to the Western challenge. Before the Meiji Restoration, the emperor wielded no political power and was viewed simply as a symbol of the Japanese culture. He was the head of the Shintô religion, Japan's native religion, which holds, among other beliefs, that the emperor is descended from gods who created Japan and is therefore semidivine. Westerners of that time knew him only as a shadowy figure somewhat like a pope. The Meiji oligarchs brought the emperor and Shintô to national prominence, replacing Buddhism as the national religion, for political and ideological reasons — since Buddhism had originated in India and come to Japan via China. The people were not allowed to look at the emperor, or even to speak his name; patriotism had been raised to the unassailable level of sacredness.

It is sometimes difficult to comprehend the extreme sacrifices the Japanese made in the name of the emperor. This can perhaps best be viewed, however, as extreme patriotism — Japanese were taught to give their lives, if necessary, for their emperor. But this was not entirely different from the Americans who gave their lives in the same war for their country and the "American" way. The kamikaze pilots, who were named for the "divine wind" (kami kaze) that destroyed the Mongol fleet in the thirteenth century and saved Japan from invasion, might be compared to the young Iranian soldiers fighting in suicide squadrons in the Iran-Iraq war of the 1980s, or even to fanatical Shiites responsible for the truck bombing of the U.S. Lebanese embassy in 1983.

Racism

The Japanese were proud of their many accomplishments and resented racial slurs they met with in some Western nations. Their attempt to establish a statement of racial equality in the Covenant of the League of Nations was vetoed by the United States (because of opposition in California) and Great Britain (Australian resistance). The Japanese greatly resented this.

The Japanese military was convinced of the willingness of its people to go to any sacrifice for their nation, and it was contemptuous of the "softness" of the U.S. and European democracies, where loyalty and patriotism were tempered by the rights and well-being of the individual.

The military's overconfidence in its own abilities and underestimation of the will of these other nations were thus rooted in its own misleading ethnic and racial stereotypes. While Asians, the Japanese saw themselves as less representatives of Asia than Asia's champion. They sought to liberate Asian colonies from the Westerners, whom they disdained.

But although the Japanese were initially welcomed in some Asian colonies by the indigenous populations whom they "liberated" from European domination, the arrogance and racial prejudice displayed by the Japanese military governments in these nations created great resentment. This resentment is still evident in some Southeast Asian nations.

JAPAN AND THE UNITED STATES AT WAR: PEARL HARBOR, AUGUST 1941

Today Japan and the United States are close allies. But between 1941 and 1945, they fought a bitter and bloody war, which many people remember well today. Why did they fight this war?

The answer on the American side is simple: the Japanese bombing of Pearl Harbor. The Americans were angry at the Japanese for their invasions of first Manchuria (1931), then China (1937), and later French Indochina (1940). After the Japanese moved into Indochina, President Roosevelt ordered a trade embargo on American scrap steel and oil, on which the Japanese military depended. But the American people felt that Asia was far away, and a large majority of voters did not want to go to war to stop Japan. The surprise attack on the Pacific fleet at Pearl Harbor on December 7, 1941 changed this, outraging the whole U.S. nation and convincing it that it must stop the Japanese army and navy.

Why did Japan attack the United States? This is a more complicated question. Japan knew the United States was economically and military powerful, but it was not afraid of any American attack on its islands. Japan did worry however, that the Americans might help the Chinese resist the Japanese invasion of their country. When President Roosevelt stopped U.S. shipments of steel and oil the Japan, he was doing exactly this: the Japanese are dependent on other countries for raw materials, for they have almost none on their own islands. Without imports of steel and oil, the Japanese military could not fight for long. Without oil, the navy would not be able to move after it had exhausted its six-month reserve. Roosevelt hoped that this economic pressure would force Japan to end its military expansion in East Asia.

The Japanese military saw another solution to the problem: if it could quickly conquer the British and Dutch colonies in Southeast Asia and gain complete control of the oil, rubber, and other raw materials it needed, then it could defend its interests in China and Indochina against those Europeans who were now busy fighting a major war in Europe against the Germans and Italians. The only force that could stop the Japanese was the American Pacific fleet — which was conveniently gathered close to Japan at Pearl Harbor, in Hawaii. Knowing that many Americans did not want to fight a war against Japan, the military thought that if it suddenly destroyed the U.S. fleet, America would simply give up and allow Japan to consolidate its grasp on East Asia.

Japan was not militarily or economically powerful enough to fight a long war against the United States, and the Japanese military knew this. Its attack on Pearl Harbor was a tremendous gamble — and though the short-run gamble was successful, the long-run gamble was lost because the Japanese were wrong about the American reaction.

But behind this mistake was another, earlier miscalculation. Ever since Commodore Perry's fleet opened Japan in 1953, in an era of great colonial expansion, the Japanese had watched the European powers dominate East Asia and establish colonies and trading privileges. China, Japan's neighbor, was carved up like a melon as Western powers established their spheres of influence on Chinese territory. After an amazingly short time, Japan was able to develop the economic and military strength to join this competition for dominance of the Asian mainland. Japan defeated China in 1895 and Russia in 1905, in battles over who should dominate Korea. Japan joined the allies against Germany in 1914-18 in a struggle to control a portion of China and then conquered Manchuria in 1931 in an effort to secure a land area rich in raw materials. The Japanese nation and its military, which controlled the government by the 1930s, felt that it then could, and should, control all of East Asia by military force.

Japan's military invasions of other Asian countries, however, brought resistance from not only the European colonial powers, but also the Asian people themselves, and finally, the United States. The Japanese military tried to convince the Japanese people that complete loyalty and obedience would make Japan invincible. Japan's early victories seemed to prove this, but the U.S. victory at Midway Island in June 1942 led to the steady encirclement of the Japanese islands, cutting them off from needed supplies of raw materials. The Japanese navy was destroyed. When this was followed by massive bombardment from the air and the final blow of the atomic bombs dropped on Hiroshima and Nagasaki, Japanese invincibility was proven to be a myth. At the end of the war, the Japanese nation was not only starving and devastated by the bombing, but bewildered and shocked by the defeat.

JAPAN'S SOFT POWER STRATEGIES TOWARD SOUTHEAST ASIA

Japan was not enthusiastic about Southeast Asian affairs during the early Cold War era. Its formal tie with ASEAN began in 1977 when Fukuda Takeo attended the 2nd ASEAN Summit in Kuala Lumpur. In the late 1980s and early 1990s, as China's economy showed remarkable growth, Japan recognized that the rise of China could weaken Japan's position in Southeast Asia. Steps toward an ASEAN-China FTA (concluded in 2004) prompted Tokyo's comprehensive strategic engagement with ASEAN. The "Tokyo Declaration" was signed by Japan and ASEAN in 2003. This declaration aimed at three things: the construction of a greater East Asia community, the realization of an ASEAN-Japan FTA before 2012, and stable official assistance of $ 3 billion which will ensure a solid Japan-ASEAN relationship in development issues. The Declaration and the affiliated plan of action consolidated Japan-ASEAN relations by deepening their economic complementarities and socio-cultural affinities.

Relations with ASEAN are important for securing Tokyo's economic leadership in East Asia. Through ASEAN, Japan seeks to maintain its position as the regional economic power and seeks to expand its international political influence in the world. In order to pursue closer relations with ASEAN states, Japan has emphasized soft power diplomacy for a decade. Like China, foreign aid, economic networking and people-to-people contact via social/cultural exchanges are the core of Japan's soft power resources. Tokyo's economic and political contributions toward ASEAN institutionalization and integration have bettered its image among Southeast Asian nations and their people.

A Trustworthy Foreign Aid Donor or Dependency Politics

Money talks. For any developing state affluence is the basis for improving local infrastructure. Most ASEAN states have long been recipients of Japan's ODA. Foreign aid, clearly, is poised to play a crucial role in regional and national development. In 1977, when Fukuda Takeo promised US$1 billion in aid to ASEAN states, Japan became the most reliable supporter of Southeast Asia nations. Tokyo's foreign aid strategy, ranging from bilateral, sub-regional, to regional assistance plans, successfully secured its political and economic interests in ASEAN states.

Japan-ASEAN aid can be traced back to the post-World War II era. Most of the ASEAN states were receiving Japan's bilateral aid as war reparations during the 1950s. Afterward the content and scope of Japan's ODA towards ASEAN states expanded. Japan extended ODA to Cambodia, Lao, Myanmar, and Vietnam (the CLMV states) by cooperating with the Initiative for ASEAN Integration (IAI) since 2001. For example, helped Cambodia in 2008 to promote poverty reduction in rural area (330 million yen grant aid), to improve health and hospital facilities (1.39 billion yen grant aid) and to give a 3.7 billion yen loan to develop a costal economic zone. Besides Cambodia, Japan contributed a 1.57 billion yen grant aid to upgrade shipping security in the Malacca straits, and a 30.77 billion yen loan to help Indonesia tackle global climate change in 2008.

At the sub-regional level, Japan has paid attention to the Mekong Basin since the Fukuda Doctrine of 1977, and has been active in the Mekong Basin development scheme since the 1990s. From 1999 to 2003, Japan invested in 55 projects (115 billion yen in all), most of which were related to the improvement of transportation infrastructure, the advancement of a special economic zone, and the upgrading of human resource and higher education in the Mekong sub-region. The East-West Corridor project (Maulamyaing-Mukdahan-Da Nang) and the 2nd East-West Corridor project (Ho Chi Minh City-Phnom Penh-Bangkok) are of particular concern to Tokyo. From 1969 to 2005, Tokyo offered over US$ 44.7 billion to all ASEAN states. In 2005, Japan provided US$ 62.5 million to the ASEAN Development Fund. In 2006, the Japan-ASEAN Integration Fund (JAIF) was set up with the financial support of US$ 70 million from Japan.

As Japan's former Prime Minister Koizumi Junichiro said unswervingly, "we want to contribute to the betterment of livelihood in areas other than military...We should come up with the most effective assistance aimed at establishing sustainability; helping countries to survive, live on their own." Koizumi's statement clearly presents one of the central philosophies of Japan's aid policy, "to support self-help efforts of developing countries." Indeed, with the inflows of Japanese ODA, ASEAN states have successfully recovered from the 1997 financial crisis, got over the threats of avian flu, and bridged difficulties during natural catastrophes. Obviously, Japan's "philanthropism" in backing ASEAN is a tactic of soft power diplomacy. Tokyo's redemption of World War II reinforced by its renunciation of pursuit of the status of "military power" seeks to gain trusts from ASEAN states. Its aid-based networking effort, in addition, is aimed at forging a "dependency politics" of ASEAN-Japan relations. The structure of dependency politics marks Japan as not only a trustworthy partner, but also an indispensable support for ASEAN development. The presence of this "decent" bilateral relationship between Japan and ASEAN counterparts under girds Japan's quest for regional leadership in East Asia.

Promoting Common Interests or Balancing China's Rising Power

Another dimension of Japan's soft power strategy towards ASEAN is to strengthen common interests with ASEAN member states, particularly in economic and trade issues. According to recent statistics, ASEAN-Japan was valued at 1.8 trillion yen in 2006. In 2007, ASEAN was Tokyo's third largest trade partner while Japan is ASEAN's fourth largest export partner and second largest import partner. Since the economic complementarity between ASEAN and Japan is distinctive, a regional FTA between Japan and ASEAN is desirable. The Joint Declaration of the Leaders of ASEAN and Japan on the Comprehensive Economic Partnership (CEP) in 2002 and the Framework for CEP between

ASEAN and Japan in 2003 opened a new page in ASEAN-Japan cooperation. This ASEAN-Japan CEP (AJCEP) could lead to the realization of a Japan-ASEAN 6 FTA in 2012 with the inclusion of CLMV in 2017. After eleven rounds of negotiation, the AJCEP Agreement was signed and entered into force in late 2008. This Agreement projects an integrated market and greater economic incentives for both ASEAN and Japan.

An ASEAN-Japan FTA would enhance Japan's competitiveness in regional integration. The strategic meaning of ASEAN-Japan trade cooperation is to balance Chinese power in the region. Japan's balancing strategies are twofold. First, ASEAN-Japan economic cooperation will project an image of a receptive and cooperative Japan. As Rahul Sen and Sanchita Basu Das argued, a more receptive Japan could offer ASEAN unique opportunities to broach sensitive issues such as agriculture and services liberalization. A free trade agreement, nevertheless, is only one part of ASEAN-Japan economic cooperation. A comprehensive scheme embodied in AJCEP Agreement, encompassing economic, scientific, technological and cultural cooperation, will provide greater incentives to ASEAN economies to embrace Japan-led regionalism.

Second, Japan's balancing strategy is to promote the idea and practice of an East Asian Community. Since 1997, the financial crisis sparked Japan's strong interests in East Asia cooperation. East Asian Community seeks to consolidate ASEAN-Japan relations and enmesh China in regional settings. The rationale for this idea is to ensure the pivotal role of ASEAN in East Asian cooperation and reconcile Japan with Southeast Asian neighbors. A viable ASEAN, for Japan, can provide stable support for Tokyo's vision of East Asian community. Tokyo has long endorsed the institutionalization and internal integration of ASEAN by making efforts to narrow the gap between ASEAN-6 and CLMV states. In addition, Japan has highlighted the importance of ASEAN as the "driving force" of East Asia economic integration in many international forums such as APEC, ARF and the East Asia Summit (EAS). In short, Tokyo's "heart-to-heart diplomacy" not only markedly "lassoes" the support of ASEAN members and their people, but also seeks to deal with China's soft power moves.

Strengthening Socio-Cultural Cooperation via Ideational Transmission

Socio-cultural cooperation is conducive to a sense of community which may forge closer ASEAN-Japan relations. Nevertheless, it reveals Tokyo's careful pursuit of regional leadership. One niche that Japan emphasizes is "ideational capacity" buttressed by economic advancement and technological innovation. As the Prime Minister Aso Taro has argued, Japan seeks to act as the "thought leader" in Asian countries. Actually, Tokyo has been actively engaging in ideational transmission to its East Asian neighbors. At the regional level, Japan has initiated the idea of the Economic Research Institute for ASEAN and East Asia (ERIA) in 2007. This think-tank, supported by the Japanese government, seeks to provide intellectual and capacity building leadership to the construction of East Asian Community in general and to the future ASEAN Economic Community in particular.

Almost every Japanese prime minister in recent decades has publicized support for ASEAN or suggested exchange programs to ASEAN states. For example, in 1977, the ASEAN Cultural Fund was designated by Fukuda Takeo to amplify intra-ASEAN cultural exchanges. Former Prime Minister Abe Shinzo announced in 2007 a program to invest US$ 315 million in a 5-year youth exchange initiative, JENESYS (Japan-East Asia Network of Exchange for Students and Youths), to students from ASEAN and EAS member states to visit Japan. In 2008, former Prime Minister Yasuo Fukuda proposed "the new Fukuda Doctrine," which promised to endorse ASEAN's single market initiative as well as the development of the Mekong Basin. Social and cultural cooperation has become a cardinal theme in ASEAN-Japan relations and a new direction for Japanese ODA in the 1990s. On the one hand, Japan believes that investing in human capital rather than physical capital will help ODA recipient countries accelerate nation-building and economic development. On the other hand, the advancement of human resources via educational, technical, and cultural programs offers a bottom-up model of nation-branding which is propitious for ASEAN-Japan relations.

With the efforts of domestic institutions such as the Japan International Cooperation Agency (JICA), Association for Overseas Technical Scholarships (AOTS), Japan Overseas Development Cooperation (JODC), financed by Japan Bank for International Cooperation (JBIC), Japan sought to work with ASEAN states in development issues such as energy, ICT industry, education, environment, infectious diseases, decreasing regional disparity, and community empowerment. Most of these projects, for example, the Japan-ASEAN Total Plan for Human Resource Development, will improve the institutional capacity of ASEAN governments to cope with socio-cultural challenges.

Additionally, the positive and progressive image of Japan in Southeast Asia provides a sound basis for sustaining ASEAN-Japan relations. In a 2008 opinion poll on Japan's image in Indonesia, Malaysia, Philippines, Singapore, Thailand, and Vietnam, the result reveal amicable ASEAN-Japan relations. 93% of respondents agreed that Japan is a trustworthy friend for ASEAN countries; 96% of respondents approved that Japan is friendly to their country; and 92% of respondents had positive images of Japan's economic and technical contribution to their country. These results demonstrate a warming attitude of ASEAN people to Japan and corroborate the efficacy of Tokyo's soft power diplomacy.

Conclusion

The application of sophisticated Chinese and Japanese soft power diplomacy toward Southeast Asia. Soft power diplomacy advocates strategies of gaining appreciation, trust and friendship, rather than muscular dominance, in the management of image change. In this regard, China wants to prove itself no longer a large and poor communist state, but a rising economic driving force and a responsible stakeholder in East Asia. Japan, for its part, devotes itself to removing the image of enemy in WWII by carefully rebuilding relations with ASEAN states.

Beijing's non-military inducement to ASEAN states, encompassing comprehensive cooperation and collaboration between different sectors and policy areas, seems efficacious. By providing foreign aid, the Chinese government has maintained leadership in cooperating with Indonesia, the Philippines, and Laos. In addition to assistance aid, China's economic foreign policy with the help of the business community has promoted large scale economic and market integration with ASEAN which strengthens its importance in the region. What's more critical, Confucius Institutes and thousands of language teachers demonstrate Beijing's flexible cultural diplomacy of promoting Chinese social and cultural attractiveness. Carefully employing these soft power resources, China intends to further engage ASEAN and its members, develop more channels of communication with Southeast Asian people, and assiduously participate in various issue-areas of regional affairs without sacrificing its economic and political interests.

Likewise, Japan has formalized its relations with the ASEAN states. The underlying rationale of Toyko's ASEAN policy has emphasized "soft power," instead of more traditional muscular approaches of engagement. The disbursement of foreign aid by Tokyo has benefited almost all members of ASEAN. In addition to financial assistance, Tokyo has further strengthened ties with ASEAN by establishing a comprehensive ASEAN-Japan partnership through economic/trade networks. Such initiatives, along with Tokyo's political support, have made Japan a trustworthy ally of ASEAN which may frustrates China's ambitions in East Asia. What is more critical is the "intellectual influence" exerted by Tokyo. This was built, and subsequently reinforced, by a series of socio-cultural exchanges and innovative regional proposals to the ASEAN states, securing Japan a leading role in the making of an East Asia community. In short, Japan's prudent cultivation of soft-power diplomacy has allowed her to link up, and act on behalf of, the ASEAN regional group to counter-balance China's rising power in the region. It has also guaranteed her strategic and economic interests in the quest for regional leadership.

"Soft power politics" is another form of struggle among big states. In this regard, patronized small states appear to be peripheral in the power structure. However, small states can still profit from soft power struggles among big states, and some may even be able to leverage their importance in the power game. The grouping of ASEAN states as a regional community, for instance, has already benefited from the Sino-Japanese competition for regional leadership. The increasing emphasis placed by China and Japan on soft power diplomacy has resulted in an abundance of economic assistance and political support from both countries, contributing significantly to the acceleration of ASEAN regionalization in general and promoting the nation-building process of CLMV states in particular. In addition, an unintended consequence of China-Japan soft power politics is a secure position for ASEAN. Soft power matters, not only for great powers, but also for small states.

JAPAN'S WILLING MILITARY ANNEXATION BY THE UNITED STATES

The Riddle: Patriotic Traitors

It is hard to believe that it happened but it did. In an 18-month working process begun in February 2005 and completed in June 2006, Japan willingly surrendered command over its military forces to the United States, committing itself unconditionally to the American empire's global strategic imperatives. It is surprising that the Japanese government made this commitment at a time when the U.S. war chariot was sinking into the bog of a "long war" it had unleashed.

If military command is the most essential element of national sovereignty, one could argue that Japan having made its military an integral part of a foreign power can no longer be considered a sovereign state. Has then Japan become a new U.S. colony? Certainly not. Nor is it ruled by the U.S. occupation as it was in the 1940s. What then is taking place?

The situation is made all the more bizarre by the fact that the political force that willingly agreed to surrender the most essential component of national sovereignty is basically the same force that glorifies Japan's imperial past and preaches patriotism and national pride to the Japanese people. Former Prime Minister Koizumi Junichiro did not hesitate to destroy neighborly relations with China and South Korea by continuing to visit the war-glorifying Yasukuni shrine. His successor, Abe Shinzo, is notorious as one of the most articulate mouthpieces in the government of the far-right's movement against the "masochist view of history." According to the views openly expressed by the rightist caucus of which Abe is a top leader, the Pacific War was a war for the liberation of Asia from Anglo-American imperialism. How can their "patriotism," ith its anti-American connotations, be compatible with the counter-patriotic act they have committed?

This riddle in fact is the key to understand the dynamics of the Japanese situation. As I have pointed out on various occasions, the postwar Japanese state is a historical construction based on three mutually contradictory principles — the U.S. imperial doctrine, the continuity (justification) of the Japanese imperial past, and the postwar constitutional pacifism. This peculiar, schizophrenic statehood came into being as the result of the postwar Japanese ruling elites "embracing defeat" so aptly stated by John Dower. Postwar Japan, created as a subsystem of the U.S. Empire, internalized the United States as a defining element of its statehood. The military alliance with the U.S. and the presence and incessant growth of the U.S.-created armed forces (Self-Defense Forces) in violation of the Constitution represented this aspect of statehood. The same state, however, has surreptitiously though obstinately retained the principle of continuity from the pre-1945 Japanese empire at its very core. This second principle, basically concealed from foreign eyes for most of the postwar years for fear of its negative political effects, has in recent years begun to be more and more openly asserted not only by the traditional ultra-right movement but also by a host of leading mainstream conservatives in power. This drive has largely succeeded in undermining the once broadly shared moderately pacifist public consensus, especially among the youth. In fact, the revisionist discourse has become close to being mainstreamed in media and political circles.

Rightists and Empire

But how can these two heterogeneous principles be reconciled at the state level? The two vectors — the thrust of the American imperial principle and that of the imperial Japan principle — if they had met horizontally, would have clashed head-on and destroyed each other.

In the actual political context, both have been deflected from the frontal collision course in the direction of fighting their common foe. The common foe is the force representing the constitutional pacifism of postwar Japan. To fight it, the two vectors fell into a V shape, producing a resultant force, turning the V into a Y. In this manner, the two political vectors, differently motivated, in effect are working together in carrying out their common project — changing the nature of the postwar Japanese state by abolishing the pacifist principle embodied in the preamble and Article 9 of the constitution.

During the past 10 years, the two horns of the Y have been extending at rapid but often uneven paces. In the past few years, it was the horn of the ultra-rightist drive that took the lead in shaping the political and ideological climate. The campaign of historical revisionists from above and "below" culminated in the rightist- and media-machinated outburst of anti-China chauvinism in May and June 2005 in the face of Chinese mass "anti-Japan" protests over Koizumi's Yasukuni shrine visit and other signs of Japan's lack of repentance of the past. The issue of abduction of Japanese citizens by the North Korean intelligence in the 1970s, admitted by Kim Jong-il in 2002, provided a rallying point for mobilization of chauvinist sentiments and victim mentality that effectively silenced voices in Japanese society calling for clear settlement of the past.

But the rightists' surge lost some of its momentum in August 2005 when their intensive drive for the adoption of their textbooks fell far short of their professed goal of getting at least 10% of the public junior highs to adopt it (in fact only 0.4% adopted it). In spite of open LDP support, they suffered this disgraceful defeat in the face of vigorous activities by local citizens and their movements to influence local boards of education. Facing this eventuality, the Society for History Textbook Reform (*Tsukuru-kai*), the rightist campaign center on the textbook issue, became split up by factional struggles. On the other hand, the worsening of Japan's relationship with China and South Korea on account of Koizumi's bigotry on Yasukuni shrine visits became a source of serious worries for big business, which badly needed better relations with China as its largest potential market. Moreover, the U.S. government, learning about the view of the last war held by the Yasukuni Shrine, felt uncomfortable with it and also began to express concern over Japan's worsening relations with China.

Not that the rightist thrust has waned or retreated. The ascension of Abe to the prime ministership shows that the far-right has now captured the helm of state. But after October 2005 the U.S. imperial thrust emerged on the stage as the looming character wielding a sledge hammer to destroy the basic assumptions of the postwar Japanese state.

REORGANIZATION INTO A GLOBAL PARTNERSHIP

On June 29 2006, Bush and Koizumi met in Washington D.C. and issued a joint statement titled, "The Japan-U.S. Alliance of the New Century." This marked the ceremonial conclusion of the intense planning process that had gone into full swing in 2005 to annex Japan militarily into the U.S. global imperial rule. The alliance of the new century, according to the statement, is not just to meet common threats but *par excellence* "for the advancement of core universal values such as freedom, human dignity and human rights, democracy, market economy and rule of law." This expression, innocent as it may appear, meant Japan's unconditional commitment to whatever military venture the United States would undertake ostensibly for the sake of these "core values." This venture is precisely what President Bush called a "long war" in his 2006 state of the union address. Japan promised to be an automatic part of it.

The press conference in June was the finishing touch to the new alliance making process that had produced three bilateral agreements: the "common strategic objectives" made as of February 19, 2005, "U.S.-Japan Alliance: Transformation and Realignment for the Future" (hereafter referred to as T&R) signed on October 29, 2005, and the ""Roadmap for Realignment Implementation" dated May 1, 2006. All these instruments worked out at the U.S.-Japan Security Consultative Committee, were signed by "two-plus-two," namely, Secretary of State Condoleezza Rice and Secretary of Defense Donald Rumsfeld for the United States and Minister of Foreign Affairs Machimura Nobutaka (Aso Taro for the Roadmap) and Minister of State for Defense Ohno Yoshinori (Nukaga Fukushiro for the Roadmap) for the Japanese government.

The legality of this process is extremely dubious as the commitment resulting from it practically repudiated the 1960 security treaty. The contents of the new arrangement therefore are of a nature that should require a formal revision of the treaty through attendant parliamentary procedures. All such legal procedures were skipped by dint of the two-plus-two expediency so that the people and their elected representatives were not to be consulted.

The major change that has been made is that under the new arrangements the alliance is to cover the "Arc of Instability" running from Korea to the Middle East, instead of just the East Asian region, as the area of U.S. military operation from Japan covered by the alliance. It should be remembered that under the 1960 treaty, the United States was "granted the use by its land, air and naval forces of facilities and areas in Japan" only "for the purpose of contributing to the security of Japan and the maintenance of international peace and security in the Far East." The Far East was defined by the Japanese government as the area north of the Philippines. The "U.S.-Japan alliance in the world" under the new arrangements has repudiated this restrictive clause and turned Japan to a major hub for American military operations all over the world and transformed the Japanese military forces into part of the globally deployed U.S. military forces.

Ten Year Process of Alliance Redefinition

While the 2005-2006 arrangement is a drastic breakthrough, it should be noted that it has resulted from a 10-year process of redefinition of the U.S. global military strategy in the U.S. search for the construction of its post-Cold War global empire. In the Pacific and East Asia, the redefining process began around the mid-1990s, and was made clearer in 1996 through the "redefinition of the U.S.-Japan alliance" in the Clinton-Hashimoto joint statement, in which the U.S.-Japan alliance was described as an "alliance in the world." Then the U.S. made it clear that, though the Cold War had ended, it would remain militarily in Asia-Pacific and would not withdraw. The Japanese commitment to this post-Cold War strategy was described as "the cornerstone" of the security setup in Asia-Pacific.

It was in 1997 that the Clinton administration adopted its national security strategy and the Pentagon its Quadrennial Defense Review, launching the "defense transformation" process to reorganize the U.S. global military posture away from the Cold War period. The key concepts of the post-Cold War U.S. strategy such as "shape, respond, and prepare" to counter "asymmetrical enemies" as well as the notion of "full-spectrum dominance" preventing the emergence of any potential hegemonic rival in the foreseeable future were already formulated in this period.

The redefinition of the U.S.-Japan alliance involving ever increasing pressure on Japan to share more of the "burden" proceeded along the line of the U.S. defense transformation. Along this line, the new Guidelines for Japan-U.S. Defense Corporation were made in 1997, replacing the 1978 Cold War version, detailed measures for the mobilization of Japanese military and civil resources in the event of contingencies arising "in areas surrounding Japan." This was already a great leap from the 1960 security treaty restriction, as the "area surrounding Japan" was defined not as a geographical concept but a situational one that can cover even the Persian Gulf if events involving Japanese security interests break out there. To implement the Guidelines, the Japanese government in 1999 railroaded through the Diet the so-called "surrounding area situation" law providing for measures to mobilize Japanese resources and systems for logistic support for U.S. military operations. But Washington felt that these Japanese domestic arrangements still fell far short of the new strategic requirements of the United States.

In October 2000, the Pentagon's special committee chaired by long-time Japan hand, Undersecretary of Defense Richard Armitage, produced a report titled, "Mature Partnership" that openly urged Japan to remove its restraints on the exercise of the right to "collective defense" as unconstitutional. According to the established government interpretation of the constitution, Japan has the right to defend itself but cannot exercise the right to fight in case its ally (the U.S.) is attacked (the right to collective self-defense). The Armitage report said this restraint was a major impediment to a "mature alliance" to be shaped after the model of the Anglo-American alliance and therefore should be removed. This was tantamount to demanding that Japan remove Article 9 by revising its constitution.

A Breakthrough to a "Mature Partnership"

After George Bush Jr. and Koizumi Junichiro came to power one after another in 2001, and especially after 9/11, Japan's military commitment to the U.S. went forward by leaps and bounds. Koizumi readily supported Bush's invasion of Afghanistan and made a special law to send a Japanese navy fleet to the Indian Ocean. When the United States invaded Iraq, he parroted the Bush rationale of the war û0WMDs û0and in a political blitzkrieg made legislation to send Japanese Ground Self-Defense Force troops to Iraq as part of the "coalition of the willing." All this would have been unimaginable a few years earlier when there was still a broad consensus that the dispatch of troops to battlefields was 100% unconstitutional. Koizumi did not even bother to plead for the constitutionality of his new military commitment, saying that the Japanese troops were sent not to war and sent only to areas where there were to be no battles. When asked how he defined such areas, he appalled the interpellator by saying, "that is (defined as) where the SDF troops are."

In the three years from 2001 through 2004, the Koizumi government forced one war-related law after another through the Diet — package of draconian laws providing for emergency measures to facilitate U.S. and Japanese military operations in and around the Japanese territory in the event of an armed attack on Japan. They include the Armed Attack Situation Law (2003), the law to facilitate the smooth operation of U.S. forces in the event of armed attack (2003), and the law allegedly for the protection of the people in emergency (2004). As a set, these wartime and emergency laws give the government the right to suspend some of the constitutional rights, and allow it to requisition public and private properties for military purposes and force residents to evacuate as military and other emergency needs dictate. These constitute a new wartime legal system that is alien to, and certainly incompatible with, the rest of the legal system that stems from the peace constitution.

With these legal and institutional receptacles having been readied on the Japanese part, the United States in January 2003 set out to remake the alliance relationship with Japan in what was called the Defense Policy Review Initiative. The full negotiation on alliance reorganization began only in October 2004 when then Secretary of State Colin Powell visited Tokyo, pressuring Japan into a reexamination of its strategy. Powell was followed by Assistant Secretary of Defense Douglas Feith who flew to Tokyo in November to tell the Japanese government that maintaining the alliance with Japan would become difficult if Japan failed to adapt to the new situation. Earlier in the year, the U.S. government adopted a "Global Posture Review" providing for "reshaping America's global military footprint" through reorganization of bases and alliances.

The new alliance making process went into full swing. It should be remembered that this process was integral to the Pentagon's new QDR making process, as a Kyodo dispatch exposed. Assistant Secretary of Defense Feith, the Kyodo report said, disclosed that the QDR would be made in consultation with Japan and other allies. "this is the first time," it said quoting Feith, "that the United States is consulting its allies in reviewing its defense systems." (Kyodo, March 18, Washington DC)

It should be noted in this context that the United States in this same process was pursuing a trilateral military arrangement. Testifying before the Senate Armed Service Committee in March 2006, Adm. William Fallon, head of the U.S. Pacific Command, said that the United States planned to "launch trilateral military cooperation with Japan and South Korea to deal not only with North Korea but also with China and terrorist threats in Asia."

In the same process as the U.S. was talking with Japan, "the United States has been working to transform its bilateral defense alliances with the two nations to deal with regional and global issues and develop them into a stronger trilateral initiative." (*The Japan Times,* March 6, 2006). The slogan for the South Korean part of the U.S. military restructuring is "trategic flexibility" under which the consolidation of U.S. bases in South Korea on a huge base complex in Pyongtaek is being carried out, involving the forced relocation of farmers, leading to fierce resistance by the victimized farmers and peace and anti-base groups.

It was in the context of this grandiose U.S. military transformation and "position review" that Japan was prescribed new, heavy military roles in the previously mentioned 2+2 documents.

Of the three documents, "U.S.-Japan Alliance: Transformation and Realignment for the Future" (T&R) should be considered the most important, as it redefines "the roles, missions, and capabilities of Japan's Self-Defense Forces (SDF) and the U.S. Armed forces" allegedly to pursue their "common strategic objectives." The "common strategic objectives" here referred to had been written in the February 19 2+2 statement, where the known diplomatic policy goals of the two countries are enumerated, including as the top global common objective the promotion of "fundamental values such as basic human rights, democracy, and the rule of law," the professed goal of Bush's war. In this document, there is also repeated mention of China, along with U.S. support for Japan's posture on the North Korea kidnapping issues and permanent membership on the U.N. Security Council.

Taking over Japanese Command

The T&R is an exacting, no-nonsense document. It lists a whole gamut of strengthened military cooperation ranging from Japan's commitment to full participation in ballistic missile defense, counter-terrorism, search and destroy operations, intelligence, surveillance and reconnaissance operations, through response to attacks by weapons of mass destruction and joint use of bases and facilities in Japan with the SDF to the U.S. use of seaport and airport facilities, roads, water spaces, airspaces, and frequency bands.

But the greatest emphasis of this document is on "close and continuous policy and operational coordination." "Recognizing the Government of Japan's intention to transform the SDF into a joint operations posture," the document states, "the Headquarters, U.S. Forces Japan will establish a bilateral and joint operations center at Yokota Base."

It goes on, "The shared use of this center will ensure constant connectivity, coordination, and interoperability among U.S. forces in Japan and the SDF." Here is the basic philosophy and practice running through the new alliance arrangements — the unification of the SDF and U.S. forces under the U.S. command. It is surprising to learn from this document signed by the two Japanese leaders that the Japanese government is willing to "transform the SDF" into this "posture." Given the power relations between the U.S. and Japanese military which are to be inter-connected, there is little doubt that these "joint operations" must end up as operations that are totally commanded by the United States.

Along with the coordination center in Yokota for the whole SDF and U.S. forces, the integration of the air force command will also be carried out. T&R reads: Japan's Air Defense Command and relevant units, currently located at Fuchu, will be collocated with the headquarters of the U.S. 5th Air Force at Yokota Air Base, strengthening the coordination between air and missile defense command and control elements, and sharing relevant sensor data through the bilateral and joint operations coordination center.

This step is considered essential to Japanese participation in the ballistic missile defense system, one of the top priority tasks assigned to Japan under this arrangement. The BMD system deployed in Japan is of course intended to protect the American mainland and for this the new U.X. X-Band radar system is to be introduced at Shariki base in Japan.

One step in this document that sheds light on the nature of the overall reorganization process is the upgrading of the Zama Camp to a global U.S. army command headquarters. "The capabilities of the U.S. Army Japan's command structure in Zama Camp will be modernized to a deployable, joint task force-capable operational headquarters element," the document states. This jargonized expression simply means that the U.S. is moving the headquarters of the First Army now located in the state of Washington to Zama to command its global operation. "The transformed command structure will provide an additional capability to respond rapidly for the defense of Japan and other contingencies." Moreover, the SDF will establish the headquarters of a Ground SDF Central Readiness Force Command in the Zama Camp for mobile operations and special tasks "thereby strengthening the coordination between the headquarters."

Another major step provided for in the document is the relocation of a carrier air wing from Atsugi Air Facility to Iwakuni Air Station. Atsugi is near Zama, both in Kanagawa Prefecture adjacent to Tokyo, where the local community has been conducting a decades-long struggle against destructively noisy night landing exercises by carrier-born planes. In successive lawsuits filed by the local citizens, the courts have repeatedly sided with the plaintiffs and the Japanese government has had to pay compensation for the noise damage. But the T&R-provided relocation of the exercise to Iwakuni Air Station is being done not in consideration of the voices of the local people. The purpose of the transfer, according to T&R, is simply "to ensure the viability of a long-term forward-deployment of the U.S. Aircraft carrier and its air wing" by using the Iwakuni base which "will have the necessary facilities and training airspace."

The single major political focus of the strategic realignment is Okinawa, where 75% of U.S. bases in Japan are concentrated causing perpetual suffering to the local people who are overwhelmingly opposed to the U.S. and Japanese military presence. As is well known, one long-contested issue is the Futenma Marine Corps Air Station located in the midst of densely populated Ginowan city. After the 1995 crisis triggered by the rape of a 12-year old girl by U.S. soldiers, Washington and Tokyo organized a special action committee (SACO), on the pretension that it would do something to meet Okinawan people's demand for alleviation of the burdens of the bases, centering on the closure of the Futenma base. SACO came out with the decision that Futenma base would be closed in exchange for a replacement base to be built off the coast of Henoko beach. This step, which would simply move the base from one location to another within Okinawa, called forth another wave of protest. Local people organized sustained non-violent action on the sea to prevent the initial sea bottom drilling and succeeded in paralyzing the construction work. In the meantime, in 2005 a U.S. helicopter from Futenma crashed at a nearby university campus, again dramatizing the danger of the base and further spurring anti-base feelings and activities. Earlier in 2003, Rumsfeld himself, visiting Okinawa to make an on-the-spot investigation, had flown over Futenma base and found it utterly impossible to continue to use it. This was the situation the U.S. and Japanese governments were facing in designing the alliance reorganization.

In the 2005 thrashing out process, the two governments found it impossible to go ahead with the original Henoko offshore base project due to the fierce opposition. Instead of abandoning the project, they improvised a new plan to build a larger base located partly inside Camp Schwab, the U.S. marines' huge training base, and protruding into sea areas on both sides of Cape Henoko. The proposed new base is to have two runways arranged in a V shape, complete with a large naval port and other facilities created through the reclamation of sea areas. The abrupt announcement of the new plan, which is far worse than the original Henoko offshore plan, set the Okinawan people aflame, spreading anti-base movement to new groups and sectors as Yui Akiko details.

The Tokyo government was certainly speculating that it could appease the Okinawans by promising to relocate 8,000 U.S. marines and their dependents to Guam Island. The government slogan justifying the whole realignment business is "alleviating burdens while keeping deterrence intact." But it could not deceive the Okinawan people. The movement of marines, having nothing to do with "burden alleviation," was solely motivated by the desire to strengthen the U.S. marine's crisis response capability by increasing flexibility. T&R introduces the transfer of part of marines to Guam as follows:

As part of its global posture realignment effort, the U.S. is making several changes to strengthen its force structure in the Pacific. Among these changes are a strengthening of Marine Corps crisis response capabilities and a redistribution of those capabilities among Hawaii, Guam and Okinawa that will provide greater flexibility to respond with appropriate capabilities according to the nature and location of particular situations.

The false rhetoric of burden alleviation for the sake of Okinawans is useful to the U.S. side, too, in the most peculiar manner. It serves to present a perverted picture of the situation — the United States is on the side of obliging Japan by agreeing to move the marines to Guam. In fact, the United States demanded that Japan meet most of the cost involved in the relocation of the marines from Okinawa to Guam, calling initially for 75% the estimated $10 billion expenditure covering the construction of the marine headquarters, other base facilities, roads, ports, and recreational facilities for use by the marines.

The Japanese government negotiated a reduction of its share and finally agreed to meet 60% but no questions were raised as to why Japan should be the host of marines stationed in Guam, a territory under U.S. administration.

This U.S. assumption that Japan should pay for the cost of moving American marines to Guam as well as the idea of locating the headquarters of the First Army for global deployment in Zama Camp in Japan betrays the prevailing American understanding behind the alliance realignment — Japan is an extension of the U.S. territory across the Pacific and the Japanese budget part of the American budget.

In this context, the T&R emphasizes general joint use of military and civilian facilities by U.S. and Japanese forces and their joint exercises.

"Recognizing the limited access that the SDF have to facilities in Okinawa," the T&R states as though Okinawa were a U.S. territory, "the U.S. underscored its willingness to implement shared use of Kadena Air Base, Camp Hansen, and other U.S. facilities and areas in Okinawa in cooperation with the Government of Japan.

While on the basis of Japan's new contingency legislation, the "use by U.S. forces and the SDF of facilities, including airports and seaports" has become possible, more "detailed surveys of civilian and SDF air and seaports" will be conducted to validate the "planning work through strengthened bilateral exercise programs." Also provided is "increasing mutual use of U.S. and SDF training facilities and areas throughout Japan" while "the training of SDF personnel and units in Guam, Alaska, Hawaii, and the U.S. mainland will also be expanded," particularly in Guam where the U.S. plans to expand its training infrastructure.

Community-Based Resistance Rises a New and Links Up

The Japanese government conducted the process of the new alliance making silently, if not totally secretly. Nor did media follow the process with sufficient attention. So, when the "Transformation and Realignment" document was disclosed in October, it came as a sheer surprise to the public, and particularly to the local communities, their people and local administration, who were going to be affected by the new arrangements. "4ÿhis is abrupt; we were not consulted" was the unanimous angry response coming from practically all the local governments in the base-bordering areas and regions.

Okinawa: Anger Mounts against the U.S. and Yamato Governments

The most vigorous opposition of course came from Okinawa. As Yui Akiko points out in her detailed report, Japan's new commitment to the global U.S. strategy has "meted out a yet more cruel fate to Okinawans" and "the treatment of Okinawa in this series of arrangements is reminiscent of the historical incident called the Ryukyu annexation (*Ryukyu Shobun*) in which the Meiji government abolished the Ryukyu Kingdom and annexed it as a prefecture of Japan." This was an affront to Okinawa, a blatant expression of discrimination against Okinawans by the Yamato (mainland Japan) government. Governor Inamine Keiichi categorically rejected the new plan. The Tokyo government responded by threatening to make a special law to deprive the governor of the powers to issue permits for the use of sea area. On the other hand, the Tokyo government promised new subsidies which would be disbursed in accordance with the progress of the base construction. Nearby communities and Nago city asked that the projected location of the base be moved a little bit further away from the populated areas. Koizumi's response was that there was no room for negotiation on the siting. "We may move it if at all by a few centimeters," he said.

As righteous anger and a growing sense of crisis take hold of the majority of Okinawans, the anti-base movement in Okinawa is gaining momentum, incorporating new groups and segments of people. Even many of those who had accepted the Henoko offshore base project changed sides in the face of the Yamato government's haughty attitude.

Simultaneously, the Okinawan anti-base movement has strengthened solidarity relationships with the Asian and Pacific sisters and brothers. For years close, day-to-day relationships have developed between Okinawa and South Korean anti-base groups and struggles through frequent mutual visits and reciprocal participation in action. Korean activists participated in the Henoko struggle and Okinawa activists joined Pyongtaek farmers' anti-base actions. It is significant that since 2005, solidarity ties have been reinforced between Okinawa and Guam (and Hawaiian) activists as well as between the Japanese and South Korean anti-base movements.

Zama-Sagamihara: Whole Cities Stand up for the Closure of Bases

Kanagawa Prefecture, adjacent to Tokyo, is next only to Okinawa in its concentration of U.S. military bases and facilities. It has been forced to be the host to strategic U.S. bases and facilities in Zama, Sagamihara, and Yamato, and the largest U.S. naval port overseas, at Yokosuka. In mainland Japan, the Zama-Sagamihara area and Iwakuni near Hiroshima are two current focuses of local communities' resistance. There, the local governments headed by the mayors have taken the initiative in expressing opposition to the imposition of the military projects, mobilizing municipal resources and powers, in collaboration with grassroots anti-base groups. These and other local movements support each other through mutual visits and exchanges of information.

Camp Zama encompasses two cities, Zama and Sagamihara, while Sagamihara also has a U.S. Sagami Depot. In the adjacent cities of Yamato and Ayase is located the Atsugi Airbase. Citizensû0movements and the municipalities involved have long been working together to get rid of the bases and their terrible effects on communities. Kaneko Tokio, a local leader of anti-base movement and a Zama municipal council representative, says that the anti-base and anti-military struggle had a long history since before the end of the war. Sagamihara people suffered seriously from Imperial Japanese Army's confiscation of land for Imperial Army facilities and military base in the 1930s and then saw the U.S. bases imposed in the postwar years. Camp Zama was formerly the Japanese Army's Military Academy and Sagamihara Depot was an Army's arms factory. "People feel that they have suffered enough. Bases are there for 70 years. They feel they have the right to demand the return of the base sites," Kaneko noted.

Moreover, Sagamihara is where in 1972 a powerful and imaginative struggle was organized by anti-Vietnam War groups against the use of the

U.S. armory for the Vietnam War. The groups attempted to block by non-violent direct action the transportation of American tanks repaired at the depot back to Vietnam from the nearby port of Yokohama. Sagamihara was turned to an arena of intense confrontation. When the tanks were being carried on lorries along Route 16, crowds of people blocked their passage before a bridge to Yokohama with the support of the Yokohama municipal government. The mayor of Yokohama invoked the traffic law that prohibited the passage of heavy weight vehicles through the bridge and on this ground banned the tanks from crossing it. The tank transportation was halted for four months.

The memory of this struggle, overwhelmingly supported and joined by local people, is still vivid in the minds of Sagamihara and Zama citizens as well as the municipal officials as a source of pride. We asked Kaneko whether the mayors and the majority of the municipal council members were not conservatives. "That's right," Kaneko said, "But they *lead* the action for the return of the bases." According to him, many citizens, who disagreed with the conservative mayors on various other issues, are now backing their mayors because they are determined to struggle to the end. In Sagamihara, there is a broad citizens' coalition demanding the return of U.S. bases. The mayor is its president and the coalition has as members the municipal office, municipal council, local PTA, and most influential local organizations. This coalition has been actively campaigning against the return of the bases for thirty years ever since the 1972 Sagamihara struggle.

This coalition has recently proposed a campaign of sending postcards to the Japanese Defense Agency director and Secretary of Defense Rumsfeld to convey citizensû0opposition to the base reinforcement. The municipal office printed and distributed to all local households 150,000 postcards and leaflets urging them to join this campaign.

The city office also printed 4,500 campaign posters that have been put up on all information billboards in the city's streets. Interestingly, the municipalities and grassroots groups in Zama and Sagamihara are competing with each other in carrying out original activities. In Zama, the municipal office organized a signature campaign against the stepping in of the First Army headquarters and collected more than 60,000 signatures out of a population of 120,000. The city of Sagamihara followed suit and got 210,000 out of 620,000 citizens to sign.

Iwakuni: the Community Expresses its Will by Referendum In Iwakuni city, it was more than a signature campaign.

It was a statutory referendum by all citizens that was called to express the people's will vis- à -vis the government's decision. The U.S. air base in Iwakuni began to be expanded in 1996 and already a reclamation of vast sea areas has been completed where carrier-based airplane landing exercises are due to begin.

Informed of the plan, the city council at first expressed opposition to it, but under strong pressure from the LDP national headquarters, conservatives soon changed their attitude in favor of accepting it. Faced by their about-face, Iwakuni Mayor Ihara Katsusuke decided to go to a referendum over whether the proposed land exercise plan should be accepted or not. Ihara's term of office was going to expire in March 2006 as the result of the scheduled consolidation of Iwakuni city with six neighboring cities, requiring the election of a new mayor for the enlarged Iwakuni city. The pro-base forces were scheming to use the post-consolidation election as the opportunity to kick out the anti-base mayor. Mayor Ihara forestalled this move by proclaiming that a referendum would be held on March 12, immediately before the expiry of his term. This called forth vehement opposition from pro-base forces.

They launched an intensive boycott campaign against the referendum. According to the city regulation, a referendum fails to take effect unless more than the majority of the eligible voters cast votes. If the number of voters did not reach the majority of the eligible population, the votes would not even be tallied. To defeat the boycott campaign, "Go to the polls" became the main slogan of the peace groups and the municipal office. Support for the referendum campaign came not only from nearby Hiroshima and Kobe but from all over the country. On March 5, 1,500 people from Iwakuni, Hiroshima, Yamaguchi, and neighboring cities gathered in a spacious riverbed in Iwakuni and lined up in human letters: "3/12 Go (to vote)!" appealing the importance of participating in the referendum. The sky views of the human letters were televised all of the country.

The result was a resounding victory for the anti-base camp. Despite the anti-referendum drive by pro-base groups, close to 60% of the eligible voters cast votes, making the referendum valid. Moreover, 87% of them voted against the government scheme. This means that 51% of all the eligible voters (84,000) opposed the U.S. plane landing exercises in Iwakuni. On top of that, in the subsequent mayoral election in the expanded Iwakuni city held on April 28, Ihara came out victorious and became mayor again. This election became a national focus as the crisis-minded Tokyo government and the Liberal Democratic Party had sent their top leaders into Iwakuni to support their pro-base candidate Ajimura Taro. Among the big shots coming down to Iwakuni were Chief Cabinet Secretary Abe Shinzo, Foreign Minister Aso Taro, and LDP Policy Board Chief Nakagawa Hidenao. Their defeat was shattering as Ihara won 54,000 votes, more than double Ajimura's 23,000.

Yuasa Ichiro, a leading peace activist based in the nearby naval port city of Kure who played a key role in this struggle, remarked that this victory represented an "historic moment in Iwakuni's modern history." The citizens of Iwakuni, he said, by demonstrating their unequivocal rejection of the central government's policy, declared that the future of Iwakuni would be made by Iwakuni citizens themselves.

Yuasa is right that what is happening in Iwakuni, Zama-Sagamihara, and Okinawa embodies the assertion of people's sovereignty at the grassroots level and defies the central government's claimed monopoly of decision-making on defense matters and external relationships. While the Tokyo government and the LDP leave no room for local level decisions by referenda or other means on the big national issues, Yuasa argues that local citizens have the right to participate in the decision making on issues like military bases because they are bound to affect local people's daily lives.

Kaneko also makes the point that local governments nowadays do not hesitate to skip the Tokyo government and negotiate base issues directly with Washington. The Zama municipal government in fact negotiates directly with the United States government while anti-base Mayor Iba Yoichi of Ginowan city (where the Futenma base is located) flew to Washington more than once to present his city's demands directly to the U.S. government. In fact, more and more local governments are now speaking up and taking action, refusing to leave decision making to the central government on matters of security treaty and defense. "This is entirely new in the history of local autonomy in Japan," Kaneko observed.

In this climate, one recent development is worth special mention. That is the launching of a nationwide network of anti-base community groups in February 2006. At the call of Ashitomi Hiroshi from the Nago Council against the Helicopter Base Construction in Okinawa and Kaneko Tokio from the Association of No Welcome to the First Army Headquarters in Zama, 23 local community-based anti-base groups got together on February 3 in Naha, Okinawa. Coming from Iwakuni, Hiroshima, Yokota, Zama, Sagamihara, Yokosuka, Kadena, Futenma, and Nago cities, they set up a National Liaison Council to Struggle Against U.S. Base Reorganization and Reinforcement with Ashitomi and Kaneko as coordinators. This is a loose network for cooperation in action, information sharing, and for dissemination of information about Japanese activities to anti-base activities in other countries. This is the first time that anti-base groups of different places and backgrounds have come together on an equal footing in a single network.

Linking Hands beyond Borders

It should also be noted that peace and anti-base activists based in communities struggling against bases have created, sustained and strengthened links beyond national borders in the past few years. Activists are constantly coming and going, participating in each other's struggle and actions, between Okinawa and South Korea as well as between mainland Japan and South Korea. In 2005 and 2006, activists from Guam were invited to attend the June 22 Okinawa international action events. This is an important solidarity link at a time when the U.S. and Japanese governments are trying to drive a wedge between Okinawan and Guam people using the relocation of marines.

On this basis, preparation has begun to link the anti-base activities in Japan with those of neighboring Asian Pacific countries and territories, South Korea, the Philippines, Guam, and Hawaii in particular, and an Asia-Pacific Consultation is scheduled in November in Tokyo. This will be part of a global anti-base network that originated in an anti-base conference at the 2004 World Social Forum in Mumbai. A global anti-base network will be formally inaugurated in March 2007 in Ecuador.

The so-called defense transformation and alliance realignment of the United States is for Japan a vicious process that involves the remaking of the Japanese statehood, civil society, culture, and ideologies. While rising local resistance is a hopeful sign, we have yet to create a viable political front to cope with the whole weight of this process to break it up. At the moment, the issue is still seen and reported on by the media from the angle of problems faced and suffered by the specific local communities involved. On the basis of the spreading local resistance, we need to make it a sharp national political focus of broadly based people's action addressing the central issue of this country today — where Japan is going.

THE RISE OF CHINA

In 1999 the People's Republic of China celebrated the 50th anniversary of its founding, marking the end of a period corresponding almost exactly to the second half of the 20th century, in which China was restored to its role as a major player in international politics. Given that for the first 50 years of the 20th century China served simply as an arena in which the imperialist powers fought for spheres of influence, this transformation is of significance not only for China but also for international politics in East Asia. However, it was not until the 1960s that China stepped onto the international political stage as a more independent power. In the 1950s China had officially - though not always actually - adhered to a policy of "leaning towards the Soviet Union," and promoted a "China-Soviet Union monolith" during the Cold War as part of the Eastern bloc. The end of the 1950s saw this stance change to one of Sino-Soviet rivalry, and China's first successful nuclear test in 1964 introduced into the bipolar Cold War structure a new orientation towards "multi-polarity."

China's independence grew more prominent in the 1970s, as rapprochement with the US in 1971 brought considerable changes to the international political framework of East Asia. From that time until the early part of the 1980s, China adopted a policy of "a single line" to align with the US and Japan to oppose the Soviet Union's drive for domination.

The increasing independence of China's foreign policy from the 1960s through the 1970s did not, however, reflect a similar expansion of China's own strength as a nation. China was during this time still suffering the aftereffects of the Great Leap Forward of the 1950s, the subsequent Great Famine, and the widespread chaos stemming from the self-destructive Cultural Revolution that began in the mid-1960s. China under Mao Zedong sought rapprochement with the US for no other reason than a very keen awareness of the threat posed by the Soviet Union in light of the domestic disorder in China. Thus, the Chinese threat perception of the Soviet Union and the US Asian Strategy seeking an "honorable withdrawal" from Vietnam, coincided well, leading to the Sino-US rapprochement in 1971.

Deng Xiaoping, who after the death of Mao Zedong seized the reins of power, sought through a policy of "reform and opening to the outside world" to revolutionize the "self-reliance" economic approach that had been pursued theretofore. Beginning with the introduction of a "production by contract" system, he set out on a bold course to introduce into China elements of a market economy.

This marked the country's first earnest attempts in the 20th century to establish the foundations for expanding its national strength. China began seeing the Soviet Union as somewhat less of a threat in the 1980s. Although the Soviet invasion of Afghanistan did cause considerable alarm, reinforcing the view of the Soviets as a danger to Chinese security, it was apparent thereafter that the USSR had become bogged down in Afghanistan. Causing greater unease for the Chinese was the new Reagan administration, and above all its Taiwan policy, amid the building of a strong "new Cold War" structure to counter the Soviet Union. China began around 1982 unilaterally to revise its policy of rapprochement with the US, aspiring to what it termed "an independent and autonomous foreign policy," and sought to put a certain distance between itself and the US. Another factor behind these changes was that the China-Vietnam War, which had stemmed from an overwhelmingly powerful sense of the Soviet threat, had not gone as China had wished and, in fact, had for all practical purposes been a "defeat." China thus became more convinced that enhancing its own national power had to take precedence over pursuing an active foreign policy.

As China began making adjustments to its foreign policy, the new US-Soviet Cold War posed little direct threat, with China not particularly favoring either side. Over-dependence on the US might be seen as an attempt to intimidate the Soviet Union, and it might also leave China unable to speak out against US policy towards Taiwan. In any case, the success of the "reform and opening to the outside world" policy was Deng Xiaoping's highest priority, as he strove to increase the country's own strength. Apparently, China firmly believed that the "peaceful international environment" needed to achieve this aim could be established without drawing particularly close to the US. From that point on, China assumed a rather passive and reactive attitude towards foreign affairs.

The Tiananmen Square Incident of June 4, 1989, seriously impaired China in its pursuit of a peaceful international environment, as China found itself isolated internationally for about a year thereafter. Another factor setting China apart was its insistence that rule by the Communist Party would be maintained, by force if necessary, following the dramatic end to the Cold War in the latter half of 1989.

There were those in the international community who hoped to sweep China into the subsequent wave of democratization, but the Japanese government and the Bush administration in the US feared that this would result in internal chaos, and both instead worked towards normalizing relations with China. As the country began normalizing its international relations, Deng Xiaoping at the beginning of 1992 again issued a dictate on reform and liberalization (during his inspection tour through the southern provinces of China), and the Chinese economy returned once more to rapid growth.

The growth of the Chinese economy in the 1990s allowed China for the first time in the 20th century to wield power as an important member of the international community on the sole basis of its own national power, free from alliances and partnerships with other countries. The Chinese economy began to grow at an annual rate of more than ten percent from 1992, and in that same year, the IMF and the World Bank released estimates of per capita GDP for individual countries calculated using purchasing power parity, the results of which astonished the world. On an exchange rate basis, China's per capita GDP at the time was less than US$500 but, using purchasing power parity, this figure climbs to about US$2000. Thus, the actual per capita GDP of China was more than four times the level calculated through exchange rates; multiplying this new per capita GDP by the population of China, the result is an economy on par with Japan and other major countries. If the present rapid growth continues, the Chinese economy someday might even surpass that of the US in scale.

Besides economic growth, there are other indicators showing China's growing national might, some of which could generate concern in other countries. Publicly released figures reveal a surprising 15% annual increase in defense expenditures. There have also been press reports of China eagerly buying up a vast supply of the weapons that Russia has been selling off since the end of the Cold War. 1992 saw the promulgation of the Law of the People's Republic of China on Its Territorial Seas and Adjacent Zones, and its activities in the Spratly Islands have sparked anxiety among the countries in Southeast Asia. Also noteworthy are the frequent proclamations of PLA naval personnel that their duty is the protection of the "maritime rights and interests" of China.

Given all of these trends, a perception of China as a threat has emerged in the post-Cold War era. Certainly there were those in the 1960s, even in Japan, who considered China a threat.

The danger posed by China during this part of the Cold War, however, was an ideological one, which would at most constitute a threat through "indirect invasion." By contrast, the view of China as a threat in the 1990s arises entirely from the power and policies of China itself. Though not allied now with any other country, China's presence has become a concern to other countries, one important consequence of the reform and liberalization policy initiated by Deng Xiaoping.

What is one to make of the emergence of China in this fashion? Since the mid-1990s this question has become a key focus of attention among policymakers in countries such as the US and Japan with ties to East Asia. In the US the debate has centered on whether to opt for engagement with China or for containment of China, with much argument over whether to classify China as a "strategic partner" or a "competitor." The balance of military power between China and other countries, recent patterns of behavior exhibited by China, and other important elements.

CHINA'S SOFT POWER STRATEGIES TOWARD SOUTHEAST ASIA

China has been more practical in making strategic arrangements with partners and more flexible in attracting international supporters. New policy initiatives such as "smile diplomacy" (weixiao waijiao), "public diplomacy" (gonggong waijiao), and "good neighbor diplomacy" (mulin waijiao) have been instrumental in Beijing's pursuit of a benign hegemony. These initiatives have one thing in common: a sophisticated use of soft power resources.

Soft power is an art of persuasion—and Chinese wielding of soft power has expanded its Western definition as well as extended its scope. Since the 1990s, China has strengthened its relations with ASEAN states in fields of foreign aid, trade, finance, infrastructure, business, labor, environment, and development as well as tourism. China's soft power diplomacy is intricate and comprehensive. It operates at four levels: first, establish firm political and fiscal connections with Southeast Asian governments through assistance aid; second, explore a comprehensive cooperative framework through FTA-plus development plans; third, enhance cultural attractiveness and promote pro-China understanding among ASEAN states by means of quasi-governmental projects; and fourth, less often noted, expand the influence of the private sector and its relations with Chinese overseas and local business networks in Southeast Asia. Among these, foreign aid, comprehensive economic networking and cultural transmission as state-initiated prongs form the core of its soft power resources.

A Reliable Partner or Laissez-Faire Politics

That China has transformed from a development aid recipient to a bilateral donor is a recent accomplishment for this nation of 1.3 billion. According to Chinese official statistics, its annual aid amounts to $970 million, but the real figure is probably higher. In Southeast Asia, Chinese foreign aid has surpassed that of the United States. For example, in 2002, China's aid to Indonesia was double that of U.S. aid. In 2006, China provided four times more aid to the Philippines s than the United States while the amount to Laos was three times that of the U.S.. Most of the aid contributes to local infrastructure and capacity-building programs. Beijing provided over $10 million to the government of Burma to assist regional reconstruction in cyclone Nargis-devastated areas in 2008. Through foreign aid, China has set itself up as a reliable supporter for its Southeast Asian neighbors. On the other hand, this government aid has facilitated the expansions of Chinese state-own-enterprises (SOEs) in Southeast Asia, such as the exploration of Indonesian natural gas reserves, investment in infrastructure in the Philippines, and the establishment of transportation links through Cambodia, Thailand to Singapore. These projects, based on Beijing's guideline of "going out," seem to align with local economic and developmental needs, but the underlying logic serves Chinese geo-political and geo-economic goals.

Opportunities for Co-prosperity and Co-development or Economic Mercantilism

Comprehensive economic networking is another Chinese soft power resource since the substance of China-ASEAN relations is mainly based on trade. ASEAN states regard China not only as an engine for economic grouping but a potential market with business opportunities. Therefore, China leverages its comparative advantage by employing economic diplomacy with soft power resources to formulate a multilateral framework based on free-trade agreements.

Beijing attempts to chart a win-win partnership based on the China-ASEAN Free Trade Area (CAFTA) for the purpose of easing regional anxieties about the intensified competition for export markets (i.e. high-value manufacturing goods) , and foreign direct investments (FDI). In 2007, the GDP of the China-ASEAN FTA exceeded $2 trillion while its total trade was amounted to more than $200 billion. According to China's official statistics, from January to September 2008, trade between China and ASEAN was $180 billion, an increase of 23 percent over last year. These large numbers are used by Beijing to demonstrate China's integral role in regional integration.

China's economic diplomacy toward ASEAN is sophisticated. It encompasses business investment, tourism and new integral development initiatives. Regarding the business realm, to expand Chinese business network corresponds to Beijing's economic and strategic interests in Southeast Asia. In October 2008, China held the 5th China-ASEAN Expo and China-ASEAN Business & Investment Summit, inviting 1,154 ASEAN-based companies to participate in the exhibition, signing 1,372 investment agreements, and attracting a turnover of $1.6 billion. Meanwhile, people-to-people interactions among young leaders and business elites from ASEAN and China are paralleled with 16 forums and meetings. Strategically, this annual China-ASEAN Expo promotes various business links with an eye to helping Chinese SOEs and small and medium enterprises (SMEs) invest in and cooperate with Southeast Asian business communities. This expo and other similar initiatives backed up by the PRC government are important for Beijing's soft power diplomacy. That is, by linking with local business in Southeast Asia, these efforts have drawn attention from ASEAN states, promoting China as a window of commercial opportunities and expanding Beijing's sphere of economic influence in ASEAN markets.

Promoting tourism is another way to bolster Chinese soft power. In the 1980s, only tens of thousands of Chinese (per year) traveled to Southeast Asia. Fueled by rapid economic growth, there have been more than 15 million arrivals per year in the ASEAN region (especially in Thailand, Singapore and Malaysia) in the 2000s. The figure is increasing by 30 percent each year. In 2007, 3.4 million Chinese tourists visited ASEAN, surpassing the number of Japanese tourists. Though some Chinese tourists create bad images , for ASEAN, the travelers provide important income sources. Moreover, a flourishing tourist industry will provide a sound basis for ongoing projects such as the Open Sky Initiative, ASEAN Common Area, and ASEAN Cruise Tourism. China's activism in tourism cooperation creates a situation of co-development while facilitating socio-economic interaction directly with Southeast Asian counterparts.

Currently, several China-ASEAN cooperative programs are underway. For example, the ASEAN-China Center for Trade, Investment and Tourism Promotion—whose MoU is currently being negotiated—will be established in the near future. This Center is expected to work to upgrade the quality and collaboration of tourism. Otherwise, initiatives of cultural and eco-tourism are emerging domains of further cooperation. In the Mekong River basin, for instance, China publicizes its cooperation with ASEAN states in the ADB-GMS-Xishuangbanna Biodiversity Conservation Corridors project. This project will connect 9 ecological zones scattered across the Indochinese Peninsula for the purpose of ensuring sustainable economic, cultural and environmental development. Beijing, having abundant economic and political resources, keeps reminding Indochinese states of its importance in shaping the eco-tour complex.

As bilateral relations progress and recession in the advanced economies deepens, ASEAN states will need greater Chinese engagement in their economic development. Take Singapore for instance. Singapore has worked on an "eco-city" project with China since 2007. This project aims to build a modern town in Tianjin based on the idea of ecological sustainability. This initiative represents an integral plan of economic, environmental and investment collaboration for both sides. For Singapore, this joint project will both gain considerable profit and consolidate it political partnership with China. For Beijing, the Singaporean experience in economic advance is of particular relevance to its investment in sub-regional economic zones. Increasing amount of similar proposals not only accounts for a closer relationship between China and ASEAN region, but also illustrates China's practice of "economic first" approach, which integrates geo-economic strategy and domestic needs.

In 2008, the global financial crisis touched off, in part, by the U.S. subprime mortgage meltdown resulted in financial and market turmoil in Asia. Leaders from ASEAN states such as Cambodia, Laos, and the Philippines have called on China to invest more in ASEAN. Such appeals from ASEAN states signify that a rising China is regarded as a source of economic support. Whether Beijing can see this regional bloc through global financial tsunami is still in question, but the demands from ASEAN make clear that one cannot overlook the growing influence of China's soft power in Southeast Asia.

A New Cultural Center or Cultural Imperialism

For China, in particular, the core of soft power is the promotion of Chinese culture and language. Since 2004, China has built more than 295 "Confucius Institutes" in 78 countries. A total of 500 are projected before 2010. In Southeast Asia, there are 21 Confucius Institutes providing language courses, including 13 in Thailand and others in Indonesia, Malaysia, Burma (Myanmar), the Philippines, and Singapore. These Institutes are sites for cultural transmission, intercultural exchange, and Chinese learning, conveying China's soft power resources to its ASEAN neighbors.

To be specific, overseas Confucius Institutes have at least two purposes. One is educational. The Institutes function as Alliance Française, Goethe-Institute, British Council, Insituto Cervante, which mainly deal with language and culture learning. Although Beijing heralds that the Institute is a non-profit and non-governmental organization, its principle and its budget are guided and sponsored by "the Office of Chinese Language Council International" (Hanban) affiliated with the PRC's Ministry of Education. Such an orientation naturally associates the institutes with the underlying strategic goals of the Chinese state.

Great powers both employ cultural commodities to exploit economic markets and to pursue ideological hegemony. Undoubtedly, the statement reminds us of U.S. foreign policy since the 1950s. The United States Information Agency (USIA). The USIA exerted influence on information sharing and made efforts to broaden dialogues between the States and the rest of the world. Moreover, it sponsored exchange programs such as the Fulbright Scholarship to inculcate overseas grantees with American culture and values.

Likewise the Confucius Institute also employs at least three kinds of soft power resources. First, the very notion of Confucius Institute is to nurture a worldwide cordial atmosphere conducive to Chinese learning. Language learning is associated with Chinese art, cinema, cuisine, fashion, and lifestyle. The pop culture itself may forge a pro-China ambiance (i.e. the fervor extending from Chinese language learning to supporting the 2008 Beijing Olympic Games), and reinforce the influence of Chinese soft power. Second, the Institute also provides a "Chinese Bridge Fund," sponsoring college student exchange program and supporting the research and development of overseas Chinese education. These funding programs and activities will intensify Beijing's international cultural attractiveness and magnify the influence of its soft power at the grassroots level. Third, since 2004, China has dispatched more than 2000 volunteers and teachers to 35 countries to work on Chinese education abroad in such ASEAN states as Indonesia, Lao, Philippines, Singapore, Thailand and Vietnam. These "civil diplomats" become vital human resources to wield cultural and social influence in the region.

Beijing has reiterated the politically neutral stance of the Confucius Institutes. However, political and ideological strings are evident in organizational governance, and relevant activities and publications.

For example, the grantees of the "Chinese Bridge Fund" determined by the Hanban may reflect Beijing's strategic considerations based on national interests. In addition, the disposition of 21 Confucius Institutes and hundreds of volunteers in Southeast Asia is also decided in accordance with cultural intimacy and political amity. China has made great efforts toward its neighbors in Southeast Asia to increase its cultural centrality in the region. It is plausible that the "China Fervor" intensified by Confucius Institutes and relevant projects will lay a foundation for the perception of a "benign China" and foster an even closer relationship between China and ASEAN states.

5

Asian Security: Impact of the North East Asia Strategic Quadrilateral

Asian security and stability is nowhere more impacted than by the power-play and balance of power in North East Asian strategic quadrilateral comprising Russia, Japan, China and the United States and this is a strategic reality that has prevailed ever since 1945 when the United States and Russia emerged as superpowers.

The North East Asia Strategic Quadrilateral comprises Russia, Japan and China as the resident powers in North East Asia and the United States as the non-resident power but perceiving North East Asia as strategically crucial for American Homeland security and for its balance of power politics to ensure its continued global predominance.

The power play and the ensuing balance of power in North East Asia is not only confined to this strategic quadrant of Asia but spills over all the way to South East Asia and South Asia or more succinctly put impacts the entire Indo Pacific Asia. It also impacts the entire Asian Heartland.

North East Asia in the last decade stood strategically neglected by both the United States and Russia as the two most dominant powers. United States stood strategically distracted by its military imbroglios in Afghanistan and Iraq. Russia's strategic resurgence had not extended to North East Asia mainly because of its strategic compulsions visa-a-vis the so-called Russia-China strategic nexus which failed to add or complement Russia's strategic weight and postures.

This strategic vacuum in North East Asia facilitated an exponential military rise of China without any checkmating by the United States and Russia as the two dominant powers which could have done so.

The onus of facilitating the emergence of the 'China Threat' which now envelops Indo Pacific Asia lies squarely on the shoulders of the United States as after 1991 disintegration of the Former Soviet Union it had emerged as the sole Superpower and global policeman. The United States had not only contributed handsomely to the economic rise of China fuelling its military rise but also endangered Asian security as a whole by molly-coddling China ignoring the imperatives of facilitating the rise of Japan and India as the other legitimate Asian powers.

North East Asia has been forcefully thrust in the global strategic consciousness as in the run-up to 2014 China has switched over from its much publicised and much trumpeted 'peaceful rise of China' to a robust and unabashed use of China's 'hard power' accumulated in the last decade without any checkmating. Gone are the US think tanks treatises emphasising and glorifying the use of China's 'soft power'.

China after signalling the world in 2009 with its public display of its stupendous military might felt strong enough to indulge in its use of 'hard power' first in the South China Sea against Vietnam and the Philippines and now in the East China Sea against Japan. Both South China Sea and East China Sea conflict escalations by China have now emerged as global 'flash-points'. Concurrently, China also started displaying its use of 'hard power' on the India-Tibet border encouraged by India's timid strategic responses.

The ripostes to China's military rise in North East Asia and its wider strategic impact, and so also its threatening contours, have emerged in the shape of the United States Strategic Pivot to Asia in2009 and Russia's Strategic Pivot to Asia Pacific in 2012. Both implicitly are targeted at checkmating China's unrestrained military adventurism in Asia Pacific.

The strategic landscape in North East Asia today presents a complex and challenging picture as Russia, Japan and the United States are all engaged in reassessing their strategic postures and re-positioning themselves to cope with an overly overbearing China obsessed with a single-point fixation of emerging as a superpower and fashioning a new bi-polar global strategic structure of United States and China which regrettably United States also endorsed spasmodically.

North East Asia in 2014 is visibly in a state of strategic churning resulting from the attempts of Russia, Japan and United States for recreation of a new balance of power to cope with China's switch-over to employment of 'hard power 'strategies.

Russia though still avowing its strategic relationship with China has put China on notice by its declaration in 2012 of the Russian Strategic Pivot to Asia Pacific. The implications stand examined by me in a number of my Papers in 2013. Strategic literature covering North East Asia have started highlighting the Chinese threat to Russian sovereignty where China is said to have subtly but mutely encouraged Russia's Far East provincial administration to secede from Russia. Also highlighted in this direction is the Chinese demographic invasion of Russia's Far East Regions by illegal migration with the end-aim of complete Sinification of Russia's Far East Region.

Seemingly in response to the above developments Russia has embarked on a military build-up in its Far East Regions, expansion and modernisation of the Russian Navy Fleet based in Vladivostok and holding large-scale integrated military exercises in proximity of its borders with China.

In terms of regional power-play with corresponding effects on global power-play, Russia made a significant political and strategic reach-out to Japan as the contending power of China in not only in North East Asia but also in Asia as a whole. This was manifested in the unprecedented Russia-Japan 2+2 Meet in Tokyo last year between the Russian Foreign and Defence Ministers with their Japanese counterparts to discuss strategic and military cooperation.

Japan in recent times has been subjected to intense military brinkmanship, coercion and provocation actions by China using the East China Sea islands territorial disputes as an excuse. The overall underlying reason of China is to effect a strategic diminution of Japan and lower its image as a serious peer competitor of China in North East Asia and in Asia. Japan as it is over the years has been seriously concerned about China's exponential military rise and its effect on Japanese security. Of particular military concern to Japan is the emergence of a powerful Chinese Navy threatening Japan's maritime lifelines. Japan's response to its perceived China Threat has been three- fold. Militarily Japan is currently engaged in a substantial military build-up especially of its Navy and Air Force. Redeployment of Japan's Armed Forces to a Southern alignment has been put into operation. Japan's national security structures have been reinforced and new mechanisms for more integrated functioning have been ordered.

In terms of political and strategic reachout in North East Asia, the significant move by Japan to Russia stands recounted above. The signalling to China of this reachout to Russia by Japan would not be lost on China.

External to the region, what is also visible is Japan's political and strategic reachout to the maritime nations of Asia's littoral located astride the sea-lanes emanating to and from Japan. Particular reference needs to be made to the continuing reinforcement of the Japan-India Strategic and Global Partnership.

Significant for North East Asia strategic power-play is that while Japan continues to swear that its security alliance with the United States is the cornerstone of Japan's security, what is becoming more visible is Japan's thrust of creation of an independent self-reliant Japanese defence capability. This presumably arises from Japan's concerns on the credibility of American support in the event of a Japanese show-down with China.

United States is forecasted as being able to continue with its military global predominance well into the better part of this century. However what has significantly happened are two major developments which affect the credibility of the United States to stand up to the militarily debilitating effects on Asian security of China's bid to achieve superpower status. The first is that of the United States strategic appeasement of China which in Asian capitals appears as American kow-towing to China. The second development is that China is progressively reducing the differentials in its strategic and military might with the military predominance of the United States thereby robbing America of its deterrent power against China even if the United States had the political will to face-off China.

United States Strategic Pivot to Asia is a hostage to the US Congressional moods and its credibility therefore in Asian capitals is that much reduced.

In the strategic quadrilateral of North East Asia, the foregoing analysis would have by now suggested that China is the 'villain of the piece' and that Russia, Japan and the United States are currently involved in reassessing and repositioning of their strategic formulations and policies to cope with the China Threat arising from its switch to use of 'hard power' strategies to achieve strategic superstardom.

Finally, in terms of strategic losses and gains to the powers that comprise the North East Strategic Quadrilateral's ensuing power-play it appears that China and the United States would be the major losers. China is headed towards emerging as the prime loser because its switch to 'hard power' strategies against its Asian neighbours is resulting in an Asian nation's polarisation against China. China today stands strategically alone notwithstanding the United States 'China Hedging Strategy'.

The United States is the second major strategic loser in that it's continued 'China Hedging Strategy' which simply amounts to 'China Appeasement' typecasts it in Asian capitals as a strategically diminished superpower and incapable of providing the required countervailing power against China going 'strategically berserk' in Asia.

In whatever pattern the North East Strategic Quadrilateral power-play emerges in the years to come, what is certain is that the resultant strategic pattern will significantly impact Asian security as a whole. Two impacts are already in evidence, namely, the Asian strategic polarisation against China following the South China Sea conflict escalation by China and the reinforcing of the Japan-India Strategic and Global Partnership.

THE CHANGING TRENDS OF SECURITY IN SOUTH ASIA

Post cold war era has witnessed changing trends in security. The traditional concept of security is now being replaced by non traditional security which stresses upon broader view entailing vast concerns of social, political, economic and environmental issues leading to the comprehensive security which is becoming a more popular version of security. This shift in security paradigm is being felt in South Asia also, which comprises of world's 1.5 population, which remains a deprived and a poor region because of the huge defence spendings. But now there is realization that the region needs to divert its resources from military towards economic and social uplift of the people, thus the stress from high politics to low politics. Both Pakistan and India need to go for more cooperative relations as to bring peace in the region which in turn will bring comprehensive security leading to the betterment of the people of South Asia.

In recent times with fast pace of globalization and complicated issues being faced by states, the understanding of security has become crucial for betterment of humanity. New and complex concerns have replaced traditional issues. The same goes for security which is undergoing changes, new concept of security is becoming more acceptable to that of traditional military security, which only stresses on military and defence aspects. But now states so as to secure security need to pay more attention to the present day problems being faced. These contemporary concerns include terrorism, poverty, population growth, health, environment, cultural, religious and ethnic antagonism. In coming years the above mentioned issues will be posing more problems, thus making states more insecure. If we take the most general meaning of security, it implies being secure from threats. Then how much are the states nowadays secure from the number of threats being faced other than military ones?

The concept of security is ambiguous and elastic in meanings. Generally security is taken as to be free from threats. It is a complicated and a contested concept. It is iridescent and manifold if seen in different perspectives or from different angles. Broadly speaking the concept of security can be divided into two categories: traditional concept of security that emphasizes the importance of state security, and non- traditional or broadened concept of security that seeks social security. Before we go into the graphic detail about what constitutes traditional concept of security and non-traditional concept of security and their implication in the South Asian region, let us briefly look into the theoretical evolution of these two concepts.

The traditional military oriented security was seen in world politics in 1940s till the end of cold war, by the then prevalent Realist scholars, who emphasized on attainment of military power. The Realists were the traditionalists who dominated the international relations in 1940s. They believed in 'power politics' with states as the main actors, giving stress on attainment of more and more military power.

Throughout the cold war the traditional concept of security remained dominant paradigm as both policy makers and experts strongly adhered to the conviction that international relations are essentially conflictual and that war is the only solution, a bitter reality that cannot be overlooked or denied. State security remained primary concern and objective of the followers of traditional concept of security. For them state is the pre-eminent actor in world politics and all other actors such as individuals, international organizations, NGOs etc. are either secondary or unimportant. From the Realist perspective, states face security dilemma and national security is achieved through the military means. The core values of traditional concept of security are national security and state survival; foreign policy of any state is formulated around these two basic priorities or values.

A growing number of contemporary writers have sought for an 'expanded conception' of security, including a wide range of considerations. After the end of cold war, the concept of security became a hot subject of debate, dissection and discourse not only among the scholars but also among the strategists, policy makers and economists.

The traditional concept that had emphasized the "centrality of state as pivot of political life" or state-centric security throughout the cold war was questioned and post cold war realities rendered it somewhat implausible and untenable.

The fast pace of globalization and immense interaction amongst states demonstrated that security stakes of states are interlinked and interdependent, thus requiring role and contribution of all, leading to collective action for satisfaction of human security. However post cold war era and 9/11 incident brought abut shifts in understanding of security. A number of non orthodox approaches have emerged viewing security differently.

Now the concept of security is not confined only to military threats. Non-military threats have gained much more importance and attention, thus leading to emergence of the concept of 'soft' security rather than the 'hard' security which prevailed during the cold war era. Non-military issues such as economy, trade, environment and terrorism etc. have become part of 'low' politics or 'soft' security which is the current broader view, leaving behind the only military issues captioned as 'high' politics or 'hard' security, coming under the narrow view in security studies. In early 1990's a new approach emerged as the 'Copenhagen School' led by Barry Buzan, which believed in a profound widening of security to non-military issues and also made an attempt to include sub- state groups into security analysis. This school has established itself in a decade.

Further beyond the above mentioned school is the 'deepening' approach led by Pluralists and Social Constructionists; these embrace the idea of human security arguing that object of security should be individual people and not the state or sub state groups. In 1990s United Nations Development Program (UNDP) further developed this concept of human security.

'The concept of security must change from an exclusive stress on national security to much greater stress on people's security, from security through armament to security through human development from territorial to food, employment and environmental security. 'The broad goal of security is to enable people to live without fears for their survival, well-being and freedom. Security thus, is not only the absence of war and conflict, but also the control of infections, diseases, the prevention of poverty, the elimination of illiteracy and the protection of sudden reversals that threaten the quality of their daily lives'. Nowadays governments are giving more stress on issues such as drugs, health and global warming, which fall under the 'comprehensive security'. In the late 1950s Prime Minister of Japan Ohira for the first time used the term comprehensive security. The concept was based on the idea that security was comprehensive in nature and should not be restricted only to military issues. It however did not exclude military capabilities. This approach became quite popular.

Later on in 1990s the concept of cooperative security emerged, it carried a few of elements of all others and included cooperative efforts for achieving security. These efforts would be towards issues of common concern. This has become a attractive security concept as it works around the welfare of all parties going for cooperative measures.

There is growing awareness among the people especially of the developed world that international boundaries are a weak barrier to the problems that afflict the poorest parts of the world. No doubt concept of security is undergoing changes. Military oriented security is being replaced by comprehensive and cooperative security, which gives a broader view of security.

ADVANCING SUSTAINABLE SECURITY IN SOUTH ASIA

The spotlight on U.S. Afghanistan and Pakistan policy is shining even more brightly today as the region copes with a series of attacks, including a car bomb in the northwest Pakistan city of Peshawar that killed at least 90 people and targeted attacks against United Nations workers in the Afghan capital of Kabul President Barack Obama is moving closer to making one of the most important decisions of his presidency, and today's events and the uptick in violence in Afghanistan and Pakistan in recent months underscore the need to advance stability in the region. The trick will be to react appropriately and proportionately to these recent events—almost certainly more attacks will occur—while continuing to advance a proactive and constructive strategy aimed at helping stabilize the region and integrate it with the rest of the world.

One key element of developing the right response to today's challenges is to lay out a series of positive end goals for the region. A fundamental problem with U.S. policy in the region since the 1979 Soviet invasion of Afghanistan is that it has been reactive to events and stuck in operational and tactical issues, with no overarching strategic objectives or realistic end state in mind.

The challenge that the Obama administration faces is not simply turning the page on the Bush administration's years of neglect, inattention, and misguided policies in Afghanistan and Pakistan—it is moving beyond a reactive mode of security policy in South Asia. Even in this new era of change and hope, President Obama continues to frame objectives in Afghanistan and Pakistan in the negative—"to disrupt, dismantle, and defeat al Qaeda in Pakistan and Afghanistan, and to prevent their return to either country in the future." President Obama has a chance to set a broader vision and set positive goals—an opportunity he missed in March when he announced the results of his administration's initial policy review.

One fundamental of the Obama administration's national security approach seems clear—that its centre of gravity and attention in the broader Middle East and South Asia is shifting eastward. The simplest metric demonstrating this shift are the costs—the federal government will spend more in the coming fiscal year on Afghanistan and Pakistan than Iraq, a broad measure of the recalibration of focus. It is not that the Obama administration will neglect the Arab-Israeli front or Iraq, which continue to pose difficult challenges. But dealing with Iran and addressing the security challenges in Afghanistan and Pakistan will likely consume more energy, resources, and high-level focus in 2010 and beyond.

Pakistan is perhaps the most complicated of these challenges. It is a nuclear-armed country of about 170 million people with one of largest militaries in the world—a fighting force of 1.5 million including reserves—and has been used as a staging ground for global terror attacks for years. The country's sheer size—it's more populous than Iraq, Afghanistan, and Iran combined—along with the major security challenges that exist there—means that the Obama administration will likely focus even more resources there.

Secretary of State Hillary Clinton is in Pakistan today on a trip aimed at advancing bilateral cooperation on a range of issues—diplomatic, economic, and development assistance, in addition to the military and security cooperation. The Obama administration has sought to move beyond the "transactional" nature of the bilateral relationship and has worked to build enduring ties, and much work needs to be done here. As I argued after my last trip to Pakistan earlier this year, it is not enough to simply triple nonmilitary assistance to Pakistan, although that is a step in the right direction.

The United States needs to revive a partnership with Pakistan's leaders and its people, as well as address the full range of human security challenges that plague the country. Pakistan will likely be the ultimate test case for whether the Obama administration can make its rhetoric on "smart power" actually work. Advancing sustainable security through development and diplomacy is easier said than done given the decades-long overinvestment in military means to advance U.S. national security. The brutal car bombing in Peshawar today should not distract from the long-term work that needs to be done to bring America's relationship with Pakistan into the 21st century.

The Obama administration is also facing some difficult policy choices to the west in Afghanistan. More than two months after the flawed presidential elections and less than two weeks before the second round elections, the Obama administration is still considering all of its options.

The massive fraud in the first round of the presidential elections was just the tip of the iceberg in a set of problems related to the question of whether the United States has partners in Afghanistan's leaders—whether those leaders are working to fight the drug trade that fuels the Taliban insurgency and dealing with massive corruption problems. President Obama is likely to make his decision on Afghanistan in the coming weeks, and it seems likely that he may send more resources, including more troops.

But much of the debate over the past few months has focused on operational tactics, as opposed to strategic goals, and the Obama administration has remained locked in the decades-long reactive mode in South Asia. The one major exception are the threads of a fundamentally new policy approach in development in Pakistan—typified by the Kerry-Lugar bill that triples nonmilitary assistance. But the devil is in the details of implementation there, and more diplomatic, intelligence, and security cooperation between the two countries are needed. The second review of Afghanistan policy is presenting an opportunity to develop a fundamentally different proactive strategy.

Two key elements are missing at this stage in South Asia policy—a set of clearly defined positive goals for the region and more discussion on India's important role on regional security dynamics. First, whatever choices President Obama makes at the conclusion of his second policy review on Afghanistan, he should take care to outline a positive vision and a set of goals that explains a viable end state in the region.

The American people are open to spending more resources if it achieves tangible results, despite recent warranted skepticism about the war in Afghanistan.

President Obama should make the case that America and its allies are working to build a sustainable security framework for South Asia—one that moves beyond the decades of war and violence that have claimed millions of lives and been a source of global instability.

The Obama adminsitration should set two clear end results for South Asia: 1) a stable and peaceful region of the world that is more integrated socially, economically, politically, and culturally; and 2) a region that has a functioning, just, and sustainable system of governance that provides security and the basic needs of its people.

These are lofty goals, and it will take years to achieve. America cannot do it on its own. But it can be a leader in advancing a sustainable security agenda for South Asia. The second missing element in the policy discussion is India's role in achieving these goals.

India, a regional power in South Asia and a rising global power, is a key partner for the United States, and we need to maintain a close and positive working relationship with India. Given how India is perceived in the region—particularly by Pakistan—it is vital to have a clearer discussion on the role that India can play in advancing a sustainable security framework in the broader region. This means addressing difficult issues such as the unresolved conflict between India and Pakistan in Kashmir, but also looking for ways to better leverage India's role in contributing to economic prosperity in the region.

The Obama administration is poised to make important operational decisions on Afghanistan—but as it does so, it should take care to keep its eyes on the ultimate prize, which is a broader South Asia region that has a functioning sustainable security framework that no longer requires so much attention and resources from the United States by the end of the next decade.

SECURITY POLICY: TRANSITION, AND BEYOND

The Obama Administration policy goal is to prevent Afghanistan from again becoming a safe haven for terrorist organizations.

The Administration has defined that goal as enabling the Afghan government and security forces to defend the country and govern effectively and transparently. Under an agreement announced after a meeting between President Obama and President Karzai in Washington, DC, on January 11, 2013, the U.S. security mission was to change from combat leadership to a "support" role by the end of June 2013. That transition was announced on June 18, 2013. Even with Afghan forces now in the lead, many of the pillars of U.S. and NATO security strategy will remain intact at least until the end of 2014 and possibly, to some extent, beyond that. The United States remains partnered with 49 other countries and the Afghan government and security forces. On February 10, 2013, Marine General Joseph Dunford succeeded Lieutenant General John Allen as top U.S. and NATO commander in Afghanistan.

Who Is "The Enemy"? Taliban, Haqqani, Al Qaeda, and Others

Security in Afghanistan is challenged by several armed groups, loosely allied with each other. There is not agreement about the relative strength of insurgents in the areas where they operate.

Groups: The Taliban/"Quetta Shura Taliban"(QST)

The core insurgent faction in Afghanistan remains the Taliban movement, much of which remains at least nominally loyal to Mullah Muhammad Umar, leader of the Taliban regime during 19962001. Although press reports say even many of his top aides do not see him regularly, he and those subordinates reportedly still operate from Pakistan, probably the city of Quetta but possibly also Karachi. This accounts for the term usually applied to Umar and his aides:

"Quetta Shura Taliban" (QST). In recent years, Umar has lost some of this top aides and commanders to U.S.-led military action or Pakistan arrests, including Mullah Dadullah, Mullah Obeidullah Akhund, and Mullah Usmani.

Some of Umar's inner circle has remained intact, and the release by Pakistan of several top Taliban figures close to Umar has helped him restore the leadership circle. Mullah Abdul Ghani Bradar, was arrested by Pakistan in February 2010 for purportedly trying to engage in negotiations with the Afghan government without Pakistani concurrence; he was released to house arrest/close surveillance in September 2013.

Other pragmatists around Umar include Akhtar Mohammad Mansoor, a logistics expert and head of the Taliban's senior *shura* council; Shahabuddin Delawar; Noorudin Turabi; and several other figures released by Pakistan since late 2012.

Umar and the pragmatists reportedly blame their past association with Al Qaeda for their loss of power. Signals of Mullah Umar's potential for compromise have been several statements, including one on the 10th anniversary of the September 11 attacks, acknowledging there have been some settlement talks; and another on October 24, 2012, that the Taliban does not seek to regain a monopoly of power.

The pragmatists are facing debate from younger and reputedly hardline, anti-compromise leaders such as Mullah Najibullah (a.k.a. Umar Khatab) and Mullah Abdul Qayyum Zakir. Zakir, a U.S. detainee in Guantanamo Bay, Cuba until 2007, is the top military commander of the Taliban and purportedly believes outright Taliban victory is possible after 2014. The Taliban has several official spokespersons, including Qari Yusuf Ahmadi and Zabiullah Mujahid. It operates a clandestine radio station, "Voice of Shariat" and publishes videos.

Al Qaeda/Bin Laden

U.S. officials have long considered Al Qaeda to have been largely expelled from Afghanistan itself, characterizing Al Qaeda militants in Afghanistan as facilitators of militant incursions into Afghanistan rather than active fighters.

U.S. officials put the number of Al Qaeda fighters in Afghanistan at between 50-100, who operate mostly in provinces of eastern Afghanistan such as Kunar. Some of these fighters belong to Al Qaeda affiliates such as the Islamic Movement of Uzbekistan (IMU), which is active in Faryab and Konduz provinces.

Until the death of Bin Laden at the hands of a U.S. Special Operations Force raid on May 1, 2011, there had been frustration within the U.S. government with the search for Al Qaeda's top leaders. In December 2001, in the course of the post-September 11 major combat effort, U.S. Special Operations Forces and CIA operatives reportedly narrowed Osama Bin Laden's location to the Tora Bora mountains in Nangarhar Province (30 miles west of the Khyber Pass), but Afghan militia fighters surrounding the area did not prevent his escape into Pakistan. Some U.S. officials later publicly questioned the U.S. decision to rely mainly on Afghan forces in this engagement.

U.S. efforts to find Al Qaeda leaders reportedly focus on his close ally Ayman al-Zawahiri, who is also presumed to be on the Pakistani side of the border and who was named new leader of Al Qaeda in June 2011.

CNN reported October 18, 2010, that assessments from the U.S.-led coalition said Zawahiri was likely in a settled area, and not in a remote area. A U.S. strike reportedly missed Zawahiri by a few hours in the village of Damadola, Pakistan, in January 2006.

Many observers say that Zawahiri is increasingly focused on taking political advantage of the Arab uprisings, particularly in Egypt where a Muslim Brotherhood leader, Mohammad Morsi, became president but then was ousted by the Egyptian military in July 2013. Other senior Al Qaeda leaders are said to be in Iran, including Sayf al Adl, although another figure, Sulayman Abu Ghaith, son-in-law of bin Laden, was expelled by Iran in March 2013. The United States has called on Iran to arrest and submit any Al Qaeda operatives to international authorities for trial.

U.S. efforts—primarily through armed unmanned aerial vehicles—have killed numerous other senior Al Qaeda operatives in recent years. In August 2008, an airstrike was confirmed to have killed Al Qaeda chemical weapons expert Abu Khabab al-Masri, and two senior operatives allegedly involved in the 1998 embassy bombings in Africa reportedly were killed by an unmanned aerial vehicle strike in January 2009. Following the killing of Bin Laden, three top operational leaders, Ilyas Kashmiri, Attiyah Abd al-Rahman, and Abu Yahya al-Libi were killed in Pakistan by reported U.S. drone strikes in June and August 2011 and June 2012, respectively.

Hikmatyar Faction (HIG)

Another significant insurgent leader is former *mujahedin* party leader Gulbuddin Hikmatyar, who leads Hizb-e-Islami-Gulbuddin (HIG). The faction received extensive U.S. support against the Soviet Union, but turned against its *mujahedin* colleagues after the Communist government fell in 1992. The Taliban displaced HIG as the main opposition to the 1992-1996 Rabbani government. HIG's areas of activity include Kunar, Nuristan, Kapisa, and

Nangarhar provinces, north and east of Kabul, but it is not a major factor on the Afghanistan battlefield.

The group is ideologically and politically allied with Al Qaeda and Taliban insurgents, but its fighters have sometimes clash with the Taliban over control of territory. A suicide bombing on September 18, 2012, which killed 12 persons, including eight South African nationals working for a USAID-chartered air service, was allegedly carried out by a female HIG member. HIG claimed responsibility for a suicide bombing in Kabul on May 16, 2013, that killed six Americans, including two soldiers and four Dyncorps contractors. On February 19, 2003, the U.S. government formally designated Hikmatyar as a "specially designated global terrorist," under Executive Order 13224, subjecting it to a freeze of any U.S.-based assets. The group is *not* designated as a "Foreign Terrorist Organization" (FTO).

Although it continues to conduct attacks, HIG is widely considered amenable to a reconciliation deal with Kabul. In January 2010, Hikmatyar outlined conditions for reconciliation, including elections under a neutral caretaker government following a U.S. withdrawal. On March 22, 2010, both the Afghan government and HIG representatives confirmed talks in Kabul, including meetings with Karzai, and Karzai subsequently acknowledged additional meetings with group representatives. Some close to Hikmatyar attended the consultative peace *loya jirga* on June 2-4, 2010, which discussed the reconciliation issue. HIG figures met government representatives at a June 2012 academic conference in Paris and a follow up meeting in Chantilly, France, on December 20-21, 2012.

Haqqani Faction

Another militant faction, cited by U.S. officials as perhaps the most potent threat to Afghan security, is the "Haqqani Network," founded by Jalaludin Haqqani, a *mujahedin* commander and U.S. ally during the U.S.-backed war against the Soviet Union. He subsequently joined the Taliban regime (1996-2001), serving as its Minister of Tribal Affairs. Since 2001, the network has staunchly opposed the Karzai government, and his faction is believed closer to Al Qaeda than to the Taliban—in part because one of the elder Haqqani's wives is Arab. Over the past few years, he has delegated operation control to his sons Siraj (Sirajjudin), Badruddin, and Nasiruddin, although Badruddin was reportedly killed in a U.S. or Pakistani strike in late August 2012. Suggesting it may sometimes act as a tool of Pakistani interests, the Haqqani network, which reputedly has 3,000 fighters and supporters, has primarily targeted Indian interests. It claimed responsibility for two attacks on India's embassy in Kabul (July 2008 and October 2009), and is considered likely responsible for the August 4, 2013 attack on India's consulate in Jalalabad.

No Indian diplomats were injured in the Jalalabad attack, but nine Afghans were killed. U.S. officials attribute the June 28, 2011, attack on the Intercontinental Hotel in Kabul; a September 10, 2011, truck bombing in Wardak Province (which injured 77 U.S. soldiers); and attacks on the U.S. Embassy and ISAF headquarters in Kabul on September 13, 2011 to the Haqqani group as well.

That the faction is tolerated or protected in the North Waziristan area of Pakistan and also its purported ties to Pakistan's Inter-Services Intelligence Directorate (ISI) has caused U.S. criticism of Pakistan. The ISI is believed to see the Haqqanis as a potential ally in any Afghan political structure that might be produced by a political settlement in Afghanistan. The most widely cited criticism was by then Joint Chiefs of Staff Chairman Mullen, following September 2011 attacks on U.S. Embassy Kabul, who testified (Senate Armed Services Committee) on September 22, 2011, that the Haqqani network acts "as a veritable arm" of the ISI.

Other senior officials issued more nuanced versions of that assertion. Many consider the faction less ideological than the Taliban—interested primarily in earning funds through licit and illicit businesses in Pakistan and the Persian Gulf and in controlling parts of Khost Province. Such interests could make the faction amenable to a political settlement. On November 13, 2012, a top Haqqani commander said that the Haqqani Network would participate in political settlement talks with the United States if Taliban leader Mullah Umar decided to undertake such talks, and a Haqqani representative reportedly was stationed at the Taliban office in Doha, Qatar that was opened on June 18, 2013 but later closed. It has also been reported that U.S. officials met with Haqqani representatives in 2011 in UAE.

The faction's calculations might be affected by how the United States characterizes the group. In July 2010, then-top U.S. commander in Afghanistan General David Petraeus advocated that the Haqqani network be named as an FTO under the Immigration and Naturalization Act. Some in the State Department reportedly opposed an FTO designation because that could complicate efforts to conduct reconciliation talks with the faction or create pressure for Pakistan to be named a state sponsor of terrorism.

A number of Haqqani leaders had already been sanctioned as Specially Designated Global Terrorists (SDGT) under Executive Order 13224. In the 112th Congress, S. 1959 (Haqqani Network Terrorist Designation Act of 2012), enacted on August 10, 2012 (P.L. 112-168). It required, within 30 days of enactment, an Administration report on whether the group meets the criteria for FTO designation and an explanation of a negative decision. On September 9, 2012, the Administration reported to Congress that the Haqqani Network meets the criteria for FTO designation.

Pakistani Groups

A major Pakistani group, the Pakistani Taliban (Tehrik-e-Taliban Pakistan, TTP), primarily challenges the government of Pakistan, but it supports the Afghan Taliban and some of its fighters reportedly are operating from safehavens in Taliban-controlled areas on the Afghan side of the border. Based in part on a failed bombing in New York City in May 2010 allegedly by the TTP, the State Department designated the TTP as an FTO on September 2, 2010. Its current leader, Hakimullah Mehsud, was named as terrorism supporting entities that day. He succeeded Baitullah Mehsud, who was killed in a U.S. drone strike in August 2009.

Another Pakistani group said to be increasingly active inside Afghanistan is Laskhar-e-Tayyiba (LET, or Army of the Righteous). LET is an Islamist militant group that has previously been focused on operations against Indian control of Kashmir.

Some assess the group as increasingly active in South Asia and elsewhere, and could rival Al Qaeda or Al Qaeda affiliates as potential threat to U.S. interests. Another Pakistan-based group that is said to be somewhat active in Afghanistan is Lashkar-i-Janghvi—it was accused of several attacks on Afghanistan's Hazara Shiite community during 2011-2012.

Insurgent Tactics

As far as tactics, prior to 2011, U.S. commanders worried most about insurgent use of improvised explosive devices (IEDs), including roadside bombs. In January 2010, President Karzai issued a decree banning importation of fertilizer chemicals (ammonium nitrate) commonly used for the roadside bombs, but there reportedly is informal circumvention of the ban for certain civilian uses, and the material reportedly still comes into Afghanistan from at least two major production plants in Pakistan.

U.S. commanders have said they have verified some use of surface-to-air missiles. It does not appear that sophisticated missiles were involved in the shootdown of a U.S. Chinook helicopter that killed 30 U.S. soldiers on August 6, 2011. Some insurgents have used bombs hidden in turbans, which had, until October 2011, generally not been searched out of respect for Afghan religious traditions. Such a bomb killed former President Rabbani on September 20, 2011, as noted above. A suicide bomber who wounded intelligence chief Asadullah Khalid in December 2012 might have had explosives surgically sewn into his body. A major concern, particularly during 2012, has been "insider attacks" (attacks on ISAF forces by Afghan security personnel, also known as "green on blue" attacks). These attacks, some of which apparently were carried out by Taliban infiltrators into the Afghan forces, declined by late 2012 but have continued occasionally in 2013.

MILITARY SCIENCE AND NEW SECURITY THREATS

If we take a critical look at the situation with ensuring the state's military security, we will see, among many other problems, the ineffectively tapped intellectual potential of the domestic military science. As a result, we have yet to hear coherent, clear-cut answers to these questions: What kind of war against Russia is possible in principle, considering the evolution of and the current status of the military sphere and the character of international relations? In this context, how should the country's defense be organized? And, what are the reasons for the prevailing situation?

On the one hand, public opinion tends to ignore the knowledge about the nature, essence, and substance of modern warfare. Many Russian politicians, who have rapidly risen to prominence (oftentimes riding on the crest of criticism against the military), failed to competently assess the military-political and military-strategic situation and organize the country's force development in compliance with the requirements of science, not propaganda slogans. They saw any argument by military experts in defense of Russia's security as a manifestation of the corporate survival instinct. The character of the ongoing polemics around military reform is indicative in this respect. Remember Kozma Prutkov's comment to the effect that an ignoramus feels absolutely at home in any sphere unknown to him.

Politicians who have little knowledge of the military or who have a personal agenda, are heavily influenced by the U.S. simplistic ("stand-off"), high-tech vision of warfare, forgetting the essential, marked difference between U.S. and Russian military policy, predetermined by the specifics of the geopolitical situation, history, development, and values of these states. Blind projection, transplantation of the U.S. worldview and methodology in the defense sphere to Russian soil naturally leads to their rejection, and will never ensure the American standard of quality in defense here.

Russia is a special country and it needs its own, specific defense and security (by all parameters). They say that "aliens" during the era of Peter the Great and Catherine II greatly benefited Russia. Indeed that was the case because their influence was offset by a powerful counterbalance within the country, comprising various restrictions on their will and the clearly defined limits on manifestation of their creative activity in Russian land. Foreign experience did not replace but supplemented Russia's capabilities. Today, however, we are witnessing attempts to replace the national defense system with another, based on a different worldview, other principles and methods of organization. Furthermore, what is disregarded is the great difference in the resource capabilities of Russia and the United States at present, as is the danger of ending up completely dependent on powerful "assistants" (once a foreign worldview, methodology, and principles of practical operation have been adopted, foreign specialists take charge of the defense sphere).

On the other hand, our military scientists have lost a unified scientific-methodological basis for analysis of warfare—a view thereof as a complex, integrated, systemic phenomenon, connected, through a multitude of threads, with various spheres of life. So, in their majority, they generate sound, good-quality fragments of knowledge that are easy to manipulate at will.

This fragmentation and one-sidedness is especially manifest in analysis and summarization of combat experience, in particular, in the Persian Gulf area, Afghanistan, the Balkans, on the Tajik-Afghan border, and in Chechnya.

Granted, scientific analysis is necessary in any particular event, but it should not be made a fetish of and extrapolated to entirely different situations. Say, it is wrong to build the entire personnel combat training system exclusively on the experience in mountain terrain warfare. After all, tomorrow it could be flatland or forest terrain.

What then? The fact is that for all the importance of the combat experience in the counterterrorist operation in Chechnya, it is inexpedient to use it as the basic component of the state's military organizational development. This also applies to the choice of weapons and military hardware and the correlation of precision and traditional and nuclear and conventional weapons. Otherwise we will have to keep acquiring new knowledge about warfare in the process of warfare itself. The cost of this kind of education is well known from history.

Experience, history and present-day reality show beyond any doubt that there has never been, nor will there ever be, a "pure" war, conducted according an "armchair" scenario. The very outbreak of any war brings in a multitude of new circumstances that can substantially change its course. Remember World War I. No one had ever especially planned it. It was simply that the political situation went out of control, and the war began to follow its own logic, producing so many unexpected twists and turns that baffled the collective brain power of the smartest of general staffs. Today, in order to attain their objectives, Russia's opponents will seek an assortment of methods to exert pressure, special operations, and weapons (above all precision guided weapons). "Decisive intentions" against Russia could arise from the instability of its domestic situation, criminalization of society, and concern about the security of nuclear facilities or of the environment. The aforementioned circumstances are, essentially, but an excuse, not a real cause of war, because the latter lies in the sphere of vital interests of states, resulting in acute contradictions between them. These include the struggle for natural resources, material values, means of communication, land and subsoil, and water and air space; elimination of competition (obstacles) in the way to world and regional leadership (including the establishment of amenable political regimes in other countries); the aspiration by multinationals in developed countries to promote their products, and so forth.

Deterrents against any forms of ag gression against Russia are: the progressive character of its development, pro-active diplomacy, the stability and effectiveness of state administration, constant protection of state interests both at home and on the international arena, and military power (the quantitative and qualitative characteristics of military organization).

Proceeding from the logic of the evolution of the present-day military-political situation and the specifics of the country's geopolitical status, it is essential to single out, among the possible kinds of wars, first of all, wars against Russia, the aims of military aggression by one or several states being the country's population, its material and spiritual values, natural and scientific-production resources, and change of the sociopolitical system; second of all, wars into which Russia could get involved for various reasons.

In that event its military power, international authority, and leverage over other countries could become a means (instrument) of the military policy of other states or coalitions thereof. Russia's entry into World War I is indicative in this respect. There was no pressing need for Russia to participate in it; there was no evidence of large-scale military aggression, but there were excessive military-political ambitions and heavy dependence on the allies. Here is what the military historian A.A. Kersnovskiy wrote: "For all its mediocrity, the Russian strategy in the Great War was not so bad as it might seem judging by its results. But it was tied hand and foot by the most deplorable of policies.

Russia unquestioningly followed even the most absurd demands of its allies, readily sacrificing its vital interests to their petty, mercantile designs (under the guise of the 'allied cause'). We never knew how to deal with foreigners, and in the Great War, in particular, were unable to take a fitting place, failing to use our highly advantageous political situation. We should have been selling our assistance to them just as they were selling their to us." (1) History repeated itself in 1945.

The Red Army, having reached the Wisla, was unprepared for a new strike. Yet, in response to a request from its allies, it precipitated, to the degree possible, the preparation of an offensive operation to rout the Nazis deployed between the Wisla and the Order. Soviet troops save d the allies from routing in the Ardennes, but at the cost of several hundred thousand lives. Meanwhile, when celebrating the 50th anniversary of their landing in Normandy, the "greateful" allies did not even invite those who had saved them in the winter of 1945. Why is it that no historical lessons are being learned? Why it is that the dialectics of international politics and the military sphere are not being studied while important state decisions concerning the country's defense interests are made without the necessary substantiation? These also are questions for the military science.

There is yet another peculiar method of warfare—the arms race. The moral, intellectual and financial costs of the arms race are huge and can be compared to the economic damage caused by a real war. The entirely different character of the aforementioned types of war dictates different priorities in ensuring the state's military security. Thus, the main brunt in the arms race is borne by the national economy, the defense complex, and the high-tech branches of industry. Participation in a war as an ally requires strenuous efforts by politicians and diplomats while in the event of outright armed aggression, the main burden will be borne by the state's military organization,. primarily its Armed Forces.

Forms of armed aggression will be predicated on the war's political objectives and the capabilities and methods of the employment of weapons and military hardware. The form of war against Russia will to a very large extent be contingent on the experience and achievements in the military sphere of states and coalitions intending to use force to destroy us or to impose their will on us. They will above all use strategy and tactics enabling them to use precision guided weapons and weapons based on new physical principles, delivering massed strikes in a stand-off mode. These strikes will be accompanied by strong EW and psychological impacts and acts of sabotage. The experience in antiterrorist operations in Chechnya points to the reality of non-classic (unconventional) wars. In these wars, the Armed Forces have to act according to the laws of unconventional warfare. Furthermore, it needs to be borne in mind that the scale of such wars is contingent on support from the outside.

Hence their complexity. Armed forces have to deal not only with the actual perpetrators of various terrorist and criminal acts, but also with their economic, political, and military sponsors, who cover up and hide their activities from the public and are based far away from the area of operations. So it is wrong, say, to compare the effectiveness of combat operations by Soviet troops in Afghanistan with U.S. strikes on Taliban bases. In the first instance, a limited contingent had to deal not simply with mujahedin guerrillas but with a well organized opposition to the Soviet Union on the part of the United States, Pakistan, and other states. In their operations against international terrorism i n Afghanistan, however, the Americans were objectively assisted by the Northern Alliance, supported by other countries. This problem is of principal importance to Russia as long as there are forces that intend to resort to a strategy of dismembering this country to prevent it from emerging as a strong competitor, especially a superpower.

A new approach to ensuring military security is based on the premise that the main threat in the future will originate not from the regular militaries of various countries, but from all sorts of terrorist, criminal, and other organizations whose participants are united into the so-called network structures. The latter are known as SPINs, or Segmented, Polycentric, Ideologically Integrated Networks. In this set-up, the main thrust is placed on what is known as operations other than war. A new term has even been coined: "network warfare."

There are several key characteristics that distinguish "network warfare" from conventional warfare. The first is the use of geographically distributed force. The second is that forces involved in "network warfare" are highly intellectual. By using knowledge acquired as a result of comprehensive surveillance over the battle area and an in-depth penetration of command plans, these forces are able to synchronize their actions while operating more effectively in an independent mode. The third is the availability of diversified and reliable communication channels (links) between their elements in a combat area, enabling them to carry Out joint operations, quickly adapting to the situation on the ground.

By relying on the laws of dialectics, we have every reason to believe that owing to the specifics of its geopolitical position, the complexity of the internal situation and the fact that Russia has yet to complete the building of a modern defense system, a whole spectrum of forms of warfare and operations other than war, including special operations, could be used against it. Everything will hinge on the wisdom of the country's military-political leadership, its reliance on the constructive sections of society, the dynamic development of the national economy, and the state of its Armed Forces. The army and the navy have always been the most effective political instrument of the state. There are three main tasks in the structure of state policy: acquisition of power, the exercise of state power in a particular sphere (for the military, in ensuring defense of the state), and maintenance of power, The principle of depoliticization prohibits the Armed Forces from engaging in the fulfillment of the first and the third task. But this does not applied to the second. Furthermore, any evasion (including by the military science) of problems confronting the state in the defense sphere that are essentially political, has to do not with depoliticization but inaction, which should be judged on an entirely different set of standards. Virtually all matters pertaining to force development are of great state and, therefore, political significance. So an oversimplified approach to the principle of depoliticization can provide fertile soil for the emergence of irresponsible people in the military, unable to prepare o bjective, well substantiated material for decision-making on the state level.

Military operations are complex in many respects. Here, it is impossible to do without expert opinion. This is especially important when it is war that is at issue. There is a view that war is too responsible a matter to be entrusted to the military. Yet it is even more irresponsible to prepare for and conduct a war without the military, whose ultimate mission is in fact to strengthen the country's security.

So, what needs to be done to fulfill this paramount state task?

First, it is critical to understand that just like all countries, Russia has its own interests whose realization is designed to ensure the existence and development as an independent and sovereign state. The population, the territory, the mineral resources and production assets, transport communications and facilities and installations beyond its boundaries-all of this must be protected (there is no shortage of those wanting to appropriate "no-one's" or poorly protected facilities). It is essential to declare national interests in a fitting and utterly comprehensible manner. They should be reflected in the Russian Constitution and other laws and regulations.

Second, establish at the top state level exactly what Russia should have and what resources and instruments it actually has to uphold its interests. To this end, a program and technology to advance state interests should be worked out.

Third, define the priorities of military organizational development and identify the resources to meet this need. Here, well substantiated proposals and calculations should be presented by the military since state security is at stake. It is perfectly clear that if a target is 1,000 kilometers away, it is senseless to fill a bomber with fuel to last only for 500 kilometers, invoking considerations of economy.

Either the fuel should be provided in full or the mission should be canceled. Until recently, things in the military sphere have been done exactly in reverse. Development of the military-industrial complex and the Armed Forces was planned not in terms of what they should be in accordance with the logic of the evolution of the military-political situation but what we could afford them to be, proceeding from considerations of economic expediency, which tended to decline with crises.

Furthermore, there were attempts to mechanically downsize the military and reduce the number of enterprises in the defense i ndustry as a means to address economic and social problems although it has long been known that when security and defense become hostage to other interests, a country sooner or later turns into a military camp, paying a very high price for negligence—in the lives of its citizens. Unfortunately, with regard to this country, history has been repeating itself with striking regularity. Chechnya is a good case in point.

Fourth, it is critical to drastically review the attitude of state structures as well as individuals toward defense, toward those who defend the country's interests with weapons in hand. Unfortunately, it has yet to be fully appreciated that the armed forces of any state are not only a major institution, not only a highly complex system with state-of-the-an weapons and equipment at their disposal, but also a specially organized, large mass of people designed for action under extreme conditions.

Not only many individuals but even politicians have yet to understand military service as a specific, special state service. What is even more important is the military's attitude to society which is apparently ignored by the majority of politicians, presumably believing that people in uniforms should have endless patience, be like robots, denied civil right and isolated from society and ongoing processes. The fact is that after all is said and done, a military serviceman, just like any other person, needs a clear-cut answer to the question why he should risk his life. The military itself always stays out of politics. It is being pushed into political battles by short-sighted politicians—through humiliation, disregard for the military, and abuse of its patience and organization.

If Russia is to advance and prosper, preserving its independence in a less-than-favorable external environment, it ought to realize that military science is not simply necessary—it is objectively the state's highest priority. It is not time-serving politicians but above all scientists who should provide clear-cut answers to topical questions in the practical sphere and make appropriate recommendations to the country's political leadership.

DEFEATING FUTURE ENEMIES

The contributors to this book examine a range of potential adversaries across a broad spectrum of conflict. They range from the challenges of peace enforcement in failed states where First World forces confront feudal clans, to combat operations against terrorist forces and their statebased supporters, to full-scale open warfare against state-based armies. For the most part, the authors consider the advantages and disadvantages that arise from Western dominance in the fields of military technology and military information. In most contemporary conflicts, potential adversaries are unlikely to possess these advantages and are therefore more likely to act unpredictably in order to gain a comparative advantage. This observation is as true for a terrorist organisation as it is for a warlord who controls a country. Unfortunately for us, in the current environment of protean insecurity, it is quite possible that a rogue actor might have access to weapons of mass destruction and might consider that their use is quite legitimate. The existence of this threat has preoccupied the Bush Administration since 11 September 2001, and it is the strategic concern that has the greatest influence on our immediate future.

Although the operational methods employed by information-age forces will vary considerably according to the nature of the conflict in which they find themselves engaged, the most likely enemies that we will meet share one thing in common. No force—whether from the industrial or the pre-industrial era—will think of challenging information-age forces in their area of strength. During the 20th century, even the most bitter battlefield confrontation was fought according to certain rules and within a broadly shared perception of reciprocity. Even the horror of the trenches during World War I was justified according to principles of attritional warfare—however misguided. In World War II the use of terrorbombing techniques was explained by reference to the effect that it had on the ability of the opposing side to support their war machine. Even the use of nuclear weapons was justified by a cost–benefit analysis of the value of immediately terminating the war. Those (Western) calculations of advantage are not necessarily shared by fundamentalist ideologues who know that they have God on their side and do not feel constrained about the ways in which they might further His ends (in their theology there is no question that 'He' might be a 'Her').

Religious fanatics are not alone in rejecting conventional notions of proportionality and restraint, much less state-based notions of what constitutes victory. The work that is likely to have the greatest long-term effect on war in the 21st century is Unrestricted Warfare. Senior Colonels Qiao Liang and Wang Xiangsui of the People's Liberation Army (PLA) published this vision of the future of conflict in 1999. The authors argue that, given the overwhelming military power wielded by the United States, those that wish to challenge America or its Western allies will have to adopt other means than conventional military attack. They consider terrorism, cyber warfare, economic attack and weapons of mass destruction.

They conclude that: Non-professional warriors and non-state organisations are posing a greater and greater threat to sovereign nations, making these warriors and organisations more and more serious adversaries for every professional army. Compared to these adversaries, professional armies are like gigantic dinosaurs which lack strength commensurate to their size in this new age. Their adversaries, then, are rodents with great powers of survival, which can use their sharp teeth to torment the better part of the world.

Perhaps most frightening is that the two colonels suggest that information-age warfare may be beyond the capabilities of traditional armies and traditionally trained 'managers of violence'. It is no use preparing to fight a conventional state-on-state war that will be a contest of strength fought out on an identifiable battlefield and governed by mutually accepted conventions if the enemy attacks in other ways. The recent spate of masscasualty terrorist attacks has served to demonstrate that plural democracies are vulnerable to attack anywhere. We confront 'Mad Max'-style warriors who have the option to use our own advanced technology against us, but who are often more effective fighting the war of the rodent, gnawing away at our social structure and avoiding open conflict with our security and defence forces. In the West, this is a theme that has been expounded by authors such as Ralph Peters and Martin van Creveld, and it is a concern that lies at the heart of this book.

The development of the essays that form the content of this book took place in the eighteen months following the events of 11 September 2001. During that time we saw the United States use military forces in innovative and novel ways in order to deal with a very different enemy. In Afghanistan, the internationally recruited forces of al-Qa'ida and their Taliban allies sought to use the country's traditional obstructions of terrain, weather and remoteness to stave off invasion. They were brought to battle by the forces of the Northern Alliance—armed, equipped and constituted very much like themselves. However, what proved decisive in this conflict was the presence of modern and highly unconventional special forces as well as coalition light forces that were able to deploy into the theatre and establish a presence with a facility not dreamt of by earlier armies. Despite the Cassandra-like lamentations of those pessimists who prophesied that the operation would come to grief in the mountains of Afghanistan, the international coalition, under the no-nonsense leadership of the US military, designed a smart campaign. It was a campaign that was appropriate given the nature of the enemy and the particular circumstances of the conflict. It was unlike any war we had seen before—perhaps because, in order to defeat this enemy, the United States selectively used its military strengths. The US military did not, however, resile from the fact that, in order to contend with this enemy, its forces had to become partly like those of the enemy. It was innovative, information-age warfare against an opponent whose lack of information resources caused it to fight blind.

The images that emerged from Afghanistan were markedly different from those that we imagine when we consider conventional state-on-state conflict. Instead of armoured formations battling it out in rolling open country or desert, the United States committed small teams that prepared the political conditions for victory well in advance of the deployment of ground forces. These groups included teams from the Central Intelligence Agency's Special Operations Group (SOG) whose mission was to win the support of the Northern Alliance and coordinate their efforts with those of the coalition forces coming into the theatre of operations. As combat operations developed, special forces troops fought alongside their Afghan allies travelling with them on horseback, but using hand-held laser designators to bring overwhelming aerial firepower to bear on their enemies.

This strategy maximised the technological superiority of the United States, but enabled it to exercise political influence on events on the ground. The same forces were able to employ lethal force with a degree of discrimination that is not possible when a weapons platform and its pilot are moving at high speed at an altitude of 30000 feet. Where appropriate, the use of light forces capable of bringing accurate but overwhelming firepower to bear will be the 21st-century equivalent of the guerrilla tactic of 'grabbing a superior foe by the belt'. In Afghanistan, instead of the technologically superior force being rendered helpless by an inability to use close fire support, the Taliban and al-Qa'ida were brought to battle and destroyed. The aim of contemporary operational commanders should be to possess the advantages of Lieutenant Colonel Leonhard's 'man-in-the-light', while leaving the opponent in the dark.

A similar principle will apply to future conflicts, though the methodology will differ according to circumstances. This theme is developed, who points out that the point of battle is not the combat itself, but the effects that it achieves. In any major conflict—whether it be against a fundamentalist non-state movement, a Third World warrior state, a Second World totalitarian dictatorship, or a combination of all three—First World forces will employ capabilities that are more joint, integrated, precise, lethal and decisive than previously considered possible.

What is more, as Colonel Cousens points out, planning such operations will involve a greater level of complexity than ever before. When engaging enemies that wage war using civilisation rather than terrain as the battleground, strategies need to be developed that use all elements of national and supra-national power to achieve victory. As Colonels Qiao and Wang concluded: Faced with warfare in the broad sense that will unfold on a borderless battlefield, it is no longer possible to rely on military forces alone to achieve national security in the larger strategic sense, nor is it possible to protect these stratified national interests. Obviously warfare is in the process of transcending the domains of soldiers, military units, and military affairs, and is increasingly becoming a matter for politicians, scientists, and even bankers. How to conduct warfare is obviously no longer a question for the consideration of military people alone.

In the era of asymmetric and unrestricted conflict, armies, the other services and their professional-officer classes only possess partial responsibility for the human, cultural and social security of the societies that they represent. Traditional, state-based military forces do, however, have a special responsibility in this changing, protean security environment. The military has traditionally been entrusted by states with a monopoly on the legitimate use of force. Consequently, the military possesses the greatest expertise in the development of strategies to use force in the defence of the state. In the information age, the military must share that knowledge and learn to rely on other aspects of national and transnational power.

Perhaps the greatest challenge to military men, politicians, policy-makers and theorists will be to accept that violent and destructive conflict has moved beyond the bonds of state-based entities and that all parties now share the responsibility for understanding and, if necessary, prosecuting war. The challenge that the transformation of conflict poses to military professionalism. His prescription is utterly correct. The military is no longer merely responsible for the mechanics of war against identifiable enemies. Defence forces are an integral part of the national security establishment; they must therefore assist in preparing and coordinating national and transnational responses to attack. Although the future of warfare remains uncharted, military professionals retain the special responsibility that their training and position in society bestows upon them. In this complex new world they have more, rather than fewer, roles to play.

Asymmetric War

At the heart of the new insecurity lies confusion about the implications of the varieties of asymmetric warfare being waged against Western societies. It is easy to become bogged down in the confusion of definitions and competing explanations of the phenomenon. As the discussion of terrorism in demonstrates, even among experts from a broadly similar background, there exists a wide range of opinions concerning the best way to respond to attacks that target our communities' vulnerabilities rather than contend with our military power. There does, however, appear to be little disagreement that asymmetric warfare—in the sense of an attack on areas of weakness by an intrinsically incompatible opponent— is here to stay.

The essence of asymmetric strategy is that an antagonist must step beyond accepted norms of armed conflict in order to achieve its desired outcome. For a variety of reasons, states cannot usually do this. There is nothing particularly unusual about asymmetric warfare. In fact the internecine slugging matches indulged in by great states during the 20th century are more the exception than the rule. Throughout history, most armed conflict has not been between states. Military power has most often been employed for the purposes of what we now call 'operations other than war'. During the 19th century, the great European imperial states most commonly employed their troops in what we now call constabulary tasks. Many of the non-state actors that they fought have since evolved into states themselves, but that does not negate the fact that the military forces of states were engaged in warlike activities against other types of human organisation. In our own age, peace operations and interventions in failed states require armed forces to conduct military operations that are often difficult to distinguish from combat operations. The challenge of the present and the future is to deal with the realisation that Pandora's box has been opened once again. The ability to wage war is no longer the monopoly of states, and armed forces must now contend with an infinite variety of potential opponents and allies. The assertion that all war between dissimilar states is asymmetric is a meaningless proposition that fails to deal with the true threat posed by those parties that choose to target our civilisation's soft spots.

Asymmetric modes of violence as well as attacks on the civil infrastructure of a state have already been adopted by non-state actors such as religious and political groups, criminals, warlords in failed states, and even single-issue groups such as radical environmentalists and economic luddites. These acts of propaganda by the deed have even won partial acceptance in some circles—a worrying postmodern trend that will make it more difficult to combat future terrorists. Some pundits have made great cause of blaming the United States for the attacks of 11 September 2001, and voices have been raised in Australia and elsewhere warning against participating in the international war on terrorism for fear of inviting another attack like the bombing in Bali.

In the meantime, Australians and other Westerners travelling and working abroad must accept that they are the targets of indiscriminate violence simply because of who they are. War is being waged, not just on conventional military establishments, but on all of us.

Inexorably and largely unnoticed, a novel and extremely unpleasant environment of global insecurity is being thrust on us. Western liberal pluralism is under attack and its own characteristics of the open society, freedom of speech and tolerance are being used against it. Those that would wish the threat away by ignoring the existence of fundamentalist terrorists, or the participation of their state sponsors, are simply feeding it. For that reason, if no other, we need to develop a more profound understanding of this new face of warfare.

In earlier this book, Group Captain MacFarling suggested that the Combined Bomber Offensive against Germany during World War II represented not only a war of attrition, but an asymmetric approach. His argument was based on the contention that all opposing forces are dissimilar. To accept this notion is to perpetuate the misapprehension that, in a globalised world, armed conflict is only an affair of states.

World War II might have been metaphorically a struggle between apples and pears, which the pears with considerably inferior industrial power were doomed to lose. However, the adversaries, being Western states, at least belonged to the same genus. They had more in common than they had differences.

It is not as if they were fighting a completely different type of organisation. What is more, Group Captain MacFarling pointed out that the allies were waging total war with the intention of bringing about unconditional surrender, not a political accommodation. In fact waging a war with the objective of bringing about the total surrender of the enemy represents the antithesis of asymmetric strategic objectives. As Colonel Qiao and Wang argue, the new objective of waging war is not just to use 'armed force to compel the enemy to submit to one's will'. Instead, they suggest it is 'using all means, including armed force or non-armed force, military and non-military, and lethal and non-lethal means to compel the enemy to accept one's interests'.5 The point is that, in a complex and multilayered global society, battlefield success and a consequent political settlement no longer represent the sole definition of victory. For many antagonists it may be enough to assert their world view and to deter interference in their program. It may even be to promote a militant ideology or religious belief with no thought of achieving a political objective.

Consequently, it is important to draw a distinction between the asymmetries of power that exist between all states and the application of asymmetric strategy in armed conflict. The use of violent strategies to achieve political or criminal ends is not confined to states. In the 21st century, the international community consists of a diverse collection of states, non-state actors, corporations and supranational social movements. Consequently, armies are going to have to contend with a potentially wider variety of opponents than ever before. Asymmetric warfare represents a completely different paradigm than state-on-state warfare.

Group Captain MacFarling's argument about asymmetric warfare relies on classical and medieval precedents to define the state and the part that it plays in conflict. Yet the system of states that we possess in the 21st century bears no resemblance to the states' system that existed even 100 years ago. Where once the sovereignty of the state was indefeasible, now states voluntarily forego or pool their authority in a great many areas.

More significantly, there are so many different types of states, ranging from illegitimate 'rogue' states to a solitary superpower, that any attempt to discuss asymmetry as a matter for states only is nonsense. Group Captain MacFarling uses the example of the Melian dialogue to promote the notion that asymmetric strategies are natural.

That conclusion is not supported by the end of the Melian affair. After some limited successes resisting the Athenian colossus in conventional fighting, the Melians were overrun; the Athenians killed all the men of military age, and sold the women and children into slavery. An asymmetric power relationship was a fact, but it was not a strategy that this particular small state without allies was able to apply. While dissimilar power relationships exist between all states, conventional and legitimate states are limited in the types of asymmetric strategies that they can employ. On the other hand, an organisation without the responsibility of sovereignty and without the liabilities of land, kin and international legitimacy can apply asymmetric strategies effectively against a state made vulnerable by its very success. Steven Metz and Douglas Johnson of the US Army's Strategic Studies Institute have proposed what is perhaps the most comprehensive definition of asymmetry yet devised. It is only one of many such definitions, but it has the distinct advantage of telling us what asymmetric strategy is not. It is not behaving in a similar way to an opponent, as occurred when the Allies matched German terror bombing with their own disproportionate response. Metz and Johnson argue that: [A]symmetry is acting, organizing, and thinking differently than opponents in order to maximise one's own advantages, exploit an opponent's weaknesses, attain the initiative, or gain greater freedom of action. It can be political–strategic, military strategic, operational, or a combination of these. It can entail different methods, technologies, values, organizations, time perspectives or some combination of these. It can be short-term or long-term. It can be deliberate or by default. It can be discrete or pursued in conjunction with symmetric approaches. It can have both psychological and physical dimensions.

6

Emerging Countries and New Globalization in Asia

Emerging countries are having an ever greater impact on politics and economics. China and India in particular—both of which have strong ties with Japan—form the kernel of the BRIC group of rapidly developing nations (Brazil, Russia, India, and China). In terms of scale, the BRICs include the world's largest nations, and account for about 40% of the global population and 30% of the world's land. The international community was formerly dominated by a cluster of European nations with populations on the order of 50 million people, but with the assimilation of countries having over a billion people, the international community is taking on a very different complexion.

This affects not only politics and economics but also science. For example, the International Society of Nephrology (ISN), of which I am a member of its Executive Committee, is illustrative of this new influence on the international scientific community within Asia-Pacific countries, including Japan. Since its inception 50 years ago, this international scientific organization has seen its membership expand to include scholars from 127 countries. Until 1990, Japan and Australia were the only Asia-Pacific countries to be represented on the governing council, with Japan holding an honorary seat as Asian representative, but at present, 10 of the 32 council members—more than from any other region—represent Asia-Pacific countries, namely Japan, Taiwan, China, South Korea, Australia (2), India (2), and Thailand, and 4 of the 10 elected Executive Committee members are also from Asia-Pacific countries. This example illustrates how many Asian nations now have a voice in the international community and a direct line to the rest of the world, giving the world a window into the activities of its many countries. As a result, Japan's position, vision, and actions are also under the spotlight.

Huge Pharmaceutical Markets and New Medical Needs

Until now, large pharmaceutical companies have mainly targeted the developed-world markets of the United States, Japan, and Europe. Success in these countries was largely due to high levels of pharmaceutical use against the background of comprehensive healthcare systems and advanced medical technologies. With their high levels of economic growth, the emerging countries have also recently seen a growing need for more advanced healthcare and medicines, and this need, coupled with improvements in medical technology and the expansion of healthcare systems, has led to a rapid expansion in the scale of the pharmaceuticals market.

In 2011, the pharmaceuticals market in emerging countries was estimated to be worth between $170 billion and $180 billion, completely eclipsing the Japanese market. According to information published by IMS Health, a healthcare information service, the pharmaceuticals market in 2009 was worth $90.3 billion in Japan, $31.7 billion in China, and $10.3 billion in India, but by 2011 the market had rapidly increased in the BRICs to $66.7 billion in China and $14.3 billion in India, compared to $111.2 billion in Japan. The estimates for 2016 are $120 billion in Japan, $160 billion in China, and $30 billion in India. The BRICs market has seen a growth rate of 10% to 20%, compared with just single-figure growth in the United States and Japan, currently the world's largest markets. China's growth rate is particularly impressive.

The rise of the emerging countries is also giving rise to new, unmet medical needs. Take dialysis treatment for example. Dialysis in emerging countries is certain to develop along a path different from dialysis in the developed world, where, for instance, hemodialysis is the main form of renal replacement therapy used to support patients with end-stage renal failure (this is true of about 90% of Japanese dialysis patients and about 70% worldwide). The emerging countries are also facing a sudden burgeoning of problems seen in the developed world such as aging societies and changes in disease patterns. Aging societies and lifestyle diseases such as diabetes mean that the emerging countries have a huge number of future end-stage renal failure patients, and that the medical costs of treating these patients is already an important policy issue in a number of these countries. However, unlike the developed countries, which have seen a gradual increase in patients, the existence of untreated patients in emerging countries has become an issue overnight. But the cost of hemodialysis-centered healthcare for renal failure is too high to be adequately met by the BRICs. It would not be possible to simply introduce into these countries the full suite of cutting-edge medical technologies developed by the advanced nations, and it could be argued that the most advanced levels are not what is needed in emerging countries. To meet these large-scale medical needs that have suddenly emerged, the priority must be to deliver healthcare to a much larger number of people at an economically feasible level. It seems that there may be points of commonality between this situation and the failure to penetrate emerging markets with hi-tech, high-quality consumer electronics so successfully sold to the developed world.

Some emerging countries are, in fact, already exploring a different framework for renal replacement therapy. For example, in June of 2011, China's Health Ministry announced that it would be promoting peritoneal dialysis, which costs less than hemodialysis. It also announced the creation of 30 centers in China to promote broad adoption of this method. These policies were supported by the Chinese Society of Nephrology. The ISN itself has launched a program focusing on education and awareness of peritoneal dialysis to help kidney disease patients in Africa and other emerging countries. Though peritoneal dialysis is received by only 5% of all end-stage renal failure patients in Japan, it is likely to become the de facto standard in emerging countries, and this will necessitate the development of, for example, therapeutic drugs to deal with issues such as complications associated with long-term peritoneal dialysis. As these examples illustrate, this new phase of globalization involving emerging countries will continue to give rise to new medical needs, and if we are to seize the opportunities found in the pharmaceuticals markets in these countries, it is essential to understand their new medical needs and respond to them as quickly as possible.

INDIA AND THE GLOBAL POWER SHIFT

The international security environment is witnessing a power shift from the developed Western states to Asia led by the rise of China and India. This power shift will have a significant impact on global geopolitics. Although a unipolar global order has been in place for a decade and a half, a non-polar world (as against a multipolar world) is in the making. Political, economic and demographic trends have made it inevitable.

As Richard Haass has noted, "In contrast to multipolarity — which involves several distinct poles or concentrations of power — a nonpolar international system is characterized by numerous centers with meaningful power. " He adds that while "the United States is and will long remain the largest single aggregation of power... power and influence are less and less linked in an era of nonpolarity. " According to Haass, "today's nonpolar world is not simply a result of the rise of other states and organizations or of the failures and follies of U. S. policy. It is also an inevitable consequence of globalization. "

Analysts assess that despite its pre-eminence in military, scientific and economic fields, the US remains a country in relative decline. Even if that decline is unlikely to make a difference in the near future, the certainty of new powers rising to be global players augurs for a new global power balance. Explosive rates of population and economic growth in Asian states are indicators of a new world order in which power will be more dispersed. The critical question is, if this multipolar world will have a benign or malign form. There are two likely possibilities on this.

The world could fragment into competing blocs that attempt to resolve their differences through power politics as nation states did in the 19th and 20th centuries. Robert Kagan has talked of an 'axis of democracy', including the US, EU, India and Japan, counterbalancing a 'club of autocrats', including Russia, China and Iran. 2 The other possibility is of existing and rising powers choosing to manage their relations through mutual interdependence, as has been attempted successfully in Europe over the second half of the last century.

Global shifts happen rarely and are even less often peaceful. The transfer of power from west to east will dramatically change the context of dealing with international challenges.

In the early 20th century the imperial order and the aspiring states of Germany and Japan failed to adjust to each other. That led to wars which devastated the better part of the world. The coming shift in power will have a greater impact globally and will require assimilation of diverse political and cultural systems. Today's rising powers seek redress of past grievances, are proudly nationalistic and want to claim their rightful place in the comity of nations. Asian rise in economic terms will translate into greater political and military power, thus increasing the potential damage from conflicts. Former British Prime Minister Tony Blair has noted that "In the next two decades China and India will undergo industrialisation four times the size of the United States and at five times the speed... For the first time in many centuries, power is moving East. " Blair added that

"In this new world, we must clear a path to partnership, not stand off against each other competing for power. The world...cannot afford a return to the 20th century struggles for hegemony. "

It is also clear that military power, however strong, is in itself insufficient to obtain the political objectives of a war. The capacity of weaker opponents to impose high costs through asymmetric or 4th Generation War fighting is enough to make even the strongest military power think carefully before embarking on a military option.

The costs of managing Iraq after an easy military victory offer a clear indication of a fundamental shift in military affairs. As Fareed Zakaria has written, "On every dimension other than military power — industrial, financial, social, cultural — the distribution of power is shifting, moving away from U. S. dominance. That does not mean we are entering an anti-American world. But we are moving into a post-American world, one defined and directed from many places and by many people.

Recent studies on managing the consequences of the waning US hegemony have in turn led to the need to choose between two policy approaches. One reflects a desire to use US military capacity in 'full spectrum dominance' and its global reach to contain rising powers.

The other looks at the evolving global power shift as an opportunity to build a new basis for global order, which would be predicated on cooperation and equity. According to Kishore Mahbubani, "The application of the three western principles of democracy, rule of law and social justice will go a long way towards creating a more stable world order.

But the West will not be able to apply them on its own... Hitherto the most successful partnerships have been West-West, for example the Trans-Atlantic Alliance. Equally strong East-West partnerships must be created. But in working with partners from other cultures and civilizations the West will have to curtail its ideological impulses and learn to be more pragmatic."

Bill Emmott has noted that "both the US and the EU should, as a matter of urgency, scrap or reform all the top organizations of global governance in which China, India and Japan are not properly and fully represented." This would include the G8 and the UNSC. He also recommends that "the US should support the EAS (East Asia Summit) as Asia's principal political and economic forum and state that it sees Asian integration and intra-regional cooperation as desirable.

"Recent US policies in the wake of 9/11, clearly demonstrated the former approach. Its consequences in Iraq and the anti-American mood in the Islamic world have raised doubts on the viability of such a policy. What strategy initiatives will emerge from the principal determinant of the global order, i.e. the US, remains to be seen.

US Seeks to Maintain Primacy

The US has sought to maintain its position as the pre-eminent power by following a policy of defence transformation, which leverages its technological superiority. As the US National Security Strategy states, "Innovation within the armed forces will rest on experimentation with new approaches to warfare, strengthening joint operations, exploiting US intelligence advantages, and taking full advantage of science and technology. "7 Transformation is designed to help address not only the traditional threats but also the emerging asymmetric threats from both state and non-state actors.

According to the US Quadrennial Defence Review, "although the U. S. military maintains considerable advantages in traditional forms of warfare, this realm is not the only, or even the most likely, one in which adversaries will challenge the United States during the period immediately ahead. Enemies are more likely to pose asymmetric threats, including irregular, catastrophic and disruptive challenges. " The National Security Strategy notes that the US is "pursuing a future force that will provide tailored deterrence of both state and non-state threats...while assuring allies and dissuading potential competitors. "

Thus the US simultaneously has to prepare against threats from state as well as non-state actors, which have acquired greater significance post 9/11. With respect to non-state actors, the primary threat comes from Al Qaeda and associated groups against whom the US is in the midst of fighting the so-called Global War against Terror, which it admits is going to be a 'Long War'.

The Global War against Terror includes overseas fronts like Iraq and Afghanistan and also homeland defence against future terrorist attacks on US soil.

The US recognizes the asymmetric nature of the threat from China, which is unable to match US military capabilities and is hence seeking to negate US superiority by targeting its technological dependence.

The Chinese anti-satellite test in January 2007 is an example of the new kind of asymmetric threat posed by China. Since the US depends heavily on space-based assets, this has led to fears of a new arms race in space. According to the US National Space Policy of 2006, "The United States considers space capabilities — including the ground and space segments and supporting links — vital to its national interests. Consistent with this policy, the United States will: preserve its rights, capabilities, and freedom of action in space; dissuade or deter others from either impeding those rights or developing capabilities intended to do so; take those actions necessary to protect its space capabilities;

respond to interference; and deny, if necessary, adversaries the use of space capabilities hostile to U. S. national interests."

With respect to state actors, the Quadrennial Defence Review suggests that the primary threat comes from China. As it notes, "Of the major and emerging powers, China has the greatest potential to compete militarily with the United States and field disruptive military technologies that could over time off set traditional U. S. military advantages absent U. S. counter strategies."

The US is strengthening its alliances in the Asia-Pacific with Japan, South Korea and Australia as well as building bridges with emerging powers like India. This quest for building up its alliances and partnerships is primarily designed to hedge against the possibility that the rise of China may place it on a collision course with the US. Although an outright war is unlikely, the possibility that tensions in the Taiwan Straits could escalate into military action, drawing in the US cannot be ruled out.

China's Emergence as a Peer Competitor

Pentagon's 2005 report to Congress on China's military power acknowledges that its goal of modernizing national defence is proceeding well: "China does not now face a direct threat from another nation. Yet, it continues to invest heavily in its military, particularly in programs designed to improve power projection.

The pace and scope of China's military build-up are, already, such as to put regional military balances at risk. Current trends in China's military modernization could provide China with a force capable of prosecuting a range of military operations in Asia – well beyond Taiwan – potentially posing a credible threat to modern militaries operating in the region. "

China has gone to great lengths to assure its neighbours that its path to development will be peaceful. A White Paper published in 2005 called China's Peaceful Development Road notes that, "China's road of peaceful development is a brand-new one for mankind in pursuit of civilization and progress, the inevitable way for China to achieve modernization, and a serious choice and solemn promise made by the Chinese government and the Chinese people, " adding that "China's development will never pose a threat to anyone. "

The Quadrennial Defence Review states that "shaping the choices of major and emerging powers requires a balanced approach, one that seeks cooperation but also creates prudent hedges against the possibility that cooperative approaches by themselves may fail to preclude future conflict. "

According to the US National Security Strategy of 2006, "as China becomes a global player, it must act as a responsible stakeholder that fulfills its obligations and works with the United States and others to advance the international system that has enabled its success: enforcing the international rules that have helped China lift itself out of a century of economic deprivation, embracing the economic and political standards that go along with that system of rules, and contributing to international stability and security by working with the United States and other major powers." The NSS adds that "our strategy seeks to encourage China to make the right strategic choices for its people, while we hedge against other possibilities."

China's military modernization is a function of its phenomenal economic growth, which has averaged 9. 5% for more than two decades. The dependence of China on foreign trade and investment for its economic modernization means that any disruption of the regional security environment in Asia will have adverse consequences for its objective of development which is still a long way away.

China's rising dependency on energy imports is leading it into an aggressive pursuit of overseas energy assets, which could lead to confrontation with the US over its links with regimes that are opposed to the US.

US policies towards Japan and India can be seen in the light of its stated desire to hedge against the possibility of the emergence of China as a revisionist power. However the US will have to be careful not to make the latter possibility self-fulfilling through its actions. For its part China would like to prevent a balancing coalition against it that could constrain its ability to prevent Taiwan breaking away to independence. China is aware that in its quest to achieve a moderately well-off society during the next two decades, it will remain vulnerable to external pressures.

Other Powers in the Region

Russia, the successor state of the erstwhile Soviet Union, is yet to play an international role in line with its size and military power, but its huge resources of energy underline its claim as a major player. Russia's relationship with the West remains tense in the light of Western efforts to bring democracy to countries in Russia's sphere of influence and US attempts to build missile defence sites in Eastern Europe. While Russia is wary of becoming a junior partner to China, its current friction with the West has led it towards a tactical embrace of China. The two countries held unprecedented joint military exercises in 2005 and have also joined hands to keep the US out of Central Asia, which they view as their backyard.

Ever since the end of World War II, Japan's status as a close ally of the US under the US-Japan Mutual Security Treaty has remained unchanged. The end of the Cold War did not have an immediate fallout on the division of labour within the US-Japan alliance, with the US continuing to bear the bulk of the responsibility for Japan's security. However Japan's inability to provide any military support towards the first Gulf War in 1991 came in for criticism and it responded by passing legislation that enabled the SDF to take part in UN peacekeeping operations. As the 1990s progressed, developments in the East Asian strategic neighbourhood gradually caused Japan to reassess its defence posture. The Taiwan Straits incident of the mid-1990s was an eye opener to Japan of China's military capabilities and intentions, while North Korea's withdrawal from the NPT and its missile tests had a direct bearing on Japan's security.

With frequent calls also coming from the US for Japan to take on an equal share of responsibility and to contribute towards collective security, Japan revised its defence doctrine and the guidelines of its defence cooperation with the US to provide logistical support for US military operations within the region. After 9/11, the nationalist government of Prime Minister Koizumi passed special legislation that allowed for Japanese forces to be sent to the Indian Ocean to provide logistical support for the US operation in Afghanistan. In 2003 Japan even approved a contingent of ground troops for the Iraq war although their mandate was to participate in humanitarian operations in a non-combat role, which restricted their effectiveness. These were the first signs that Japan was finally on the road to becoming a normal nation. In 2004, the New Defence Policy Outline institutionalized these changes in the realm of policy by making it part of Japan's defence doctrine to undertake a role outside East Asia in association with the international community and its alliance partner, the US.

Australia is a major regional power which has contributed to security in the region by maintaining peace and promoting state building in East Timor, Fiji and the Solomon Islands. Under Prime Minister Rudd, Australia is following a multilateral approach while preserving its traditional ties with the US. Although Australia invoked the ANZUS treaty for the first time after 9/11, it has indicated that this does not extend to a US-China conflict over Taiwan, apparently influenced by the benefits it could derive from China's economic growth. China is going ahead to improve ties with Australia as the agreement on the sale of Australian uranium to China showed. The US, Japan, Australia and India had initiated a quadrilateral dialogue in 2007 on the sidelines of the ARF summit in Manila. This had caused concern in China, which went to the extent of serving a demarche on all four countries seeking an explanation for the meeting.

THE TRADE IMPLICATIONS OF CHINA'S EMERGENCE

China's economic development has hardly been mono-dimensional. It is not simply a creation of Western capitalists seeking to outsource labour to the lowest bidder; nor is China any longer simply a manufacturing centre of cheap plastic and simple electronic products.

Chinese industry has moved rapidly up the production chain and is now producing a very large share of the world's office equipment, DVD players, digital cameras, personal computers as well as clothing and shoes and other simpler manufactured goods.

China's swift development has rerouted global supply chains forged over the last thirty years. It now runs large trade deficits with Eastern Asia while enjoying inexorably expanding trade surpluses with North America and Europe. It has become a trading nation par excellence and currently generates 70% of its national income through foreign trade. China's overall share of world trade has increased from 5% in 2000 to 10% today. (Rossi)

China is also exerting trade pressures on a range of developing and transition countries with which it is directly competing. Mexico and Turkey, for example, are losing market share in textiles to the Chinese without the kind of offsetting compensation that has proven so beneficial to much of Asia. Central and Eastern Europe now find themselves engaged in a global battle to win new investments. Hungary won important investments for basic assembly manufacturing in the mid-1990s; yet some of those plants have subsequently relocated to China. The Hungarians now recognize that in the face of serious Chinese competition, their best option is to move into ever more sophisticated production if they are to flourish in the emerging global division of labour (Visit to Budapest 2004, NATO PA Secretariat Report).

The net effect of China's rapid growth on the global economy has been highly positive, despite the inevitable dislocation suffered in certain sectors. Its booming economy is generating wealth worldwide. Those benefits accrue through countless channels. Yet, mercantilists and protectionists falsely argue that rising Chinese imports are invariably a bad thing and are simply sparking plant closures and job losses.

Trade economists counter that this is a misleading and partial economic interpretation of what transpires when a large country undergoes economic take-off and emerges as a major global commercial player. First of all, trading with that low cost producer invariably lowers prices for consumers as well as producers, who, as a result, are able to purchase lower cost capital goods. Price falls, in turn, check inflationary pressures in the importing economy, raise consumer welfare, and lower exporters' production costs. The resulting productivity gains help certain domestic industries win market share both domestically and internationally while rewarding workers employed in those sectors. It must also be noted that non-Chinese companies are currently generating over half of China's export earnings and 60% of import revenue. In 2000 alone, U.S corporate earnings generated in China reached $7.2 billion. (Hale and Hale) Western firms are also selling value added inputs to Chinese producers and are thus benefiting from China's place in the international division of labour. These are the winners in the game.

The losers are both the producers of import competing industries that cannot match the price/quality of imported Chinese goods and workers in those industries. Yet, those domestic import competing firms that manage to compete are likely to emerge even stronger. Most empirical work on the broad effects of expanding trade suggests that the gains of the winners in open trading systems significantly outweigh the losses of those suffering from new competition. In this process, moreover, trading countries are likely to grow more specialized in their production, leading to further productivity gains and wealth generation. Empirical evidence tends to confirm that precisely such processes are at work in those developed and developing countries with growing trade links to China.

The Economist recently estimated that if China continues to develop, and if parts of the developing world respond to its competitive challenge by adopting liberal commercial policies, the developed world could enjoy an additional 1% of growth a year, while the developing world would undergo a substantially larger rate of growth despite the dislocation which some economies would obviously undergo. (The Economist, October 2, 2004) The capacity of a single non-oil exporting developing country to have such a broad global economic impact represents an undeniable revolution in international financial and trading systems. As suggested above, it is an economic shift laden with political, diplomatic and strategic significance. Yet, in order to capture the potential gains, Western governments must ensure their economies are ever more agile and flexible. They should increase their respective capacities to shift both capital and labour into those sectors in which they are most competitive and out of those in which they are least productive.

The McKinsey Global Institute recently examined the fate of western workers who lost jobs because of firms moving production facilities to China or India. According to this study, 70% of such American workers find new work within six months, while in Germany only 40% do. This suggests that labour market rigidities can gravely complicate efforts to adapt to changing international market conditions. China is also having a strong effect on global demand. While many casual observers see its most substantial economic impact largely in terms of its enormous exports, China is also a large and growing capital and consumer goods market. It is estimated that if current growth and income distribution were sustained until 2020, China would offer the world 100 million consumers with an average income equivalent to the current income average of Western Europe. (The Economist, October 2, 2004.) Already it has almost single-handedly revived the previously flagging economies of East Asia through high demand for a range of manufacturing inputs, high technology components and consumer goods. Australia - like a range of other commodity exporters - is enjoying a veritable economic boom thanks to burgeoning Chinese demand.

China's imports are growing at a very rapid rate - 40% in 2003 alone. Since 2001, it has accounted for one third of the increase in global import volume. China is the world's third largest importer, and in 2004 accounted for 17% of Japan's exports, 16% of the European Union's, 8.5% of the United States', 38.5% of the rest of Asia's, and 20% for the rest of the World. (Rossi) It is now Japan's leading trade partner and the second largest trade partner of the European Union behind only the United States. EU-China Trade doubled between 1999 and 2003. (Eurostat, 14/6/2004, Kihara and Takeuchi) China is also providing an important market for developing countries; 45% of China's $400 billion in annual imports comes from developing countries, and these rose by $55 billion in 2003. It is, in fact, running a significant trade deficit with the developing world. (Kharas) Some optimistic forecasts suggest that if China continues down the reform path it could be the world's largest exporter and importer within ten years.

The US trade with China deficit has reached the enormous sum of $162 billion. (Teather) Yet, imports from China do not explain the explosive growth of the US current account deficit, now at 7% of GDP and rising, partly because China has, in fact, simply replaced other suppliers to the US market. In 1988, for example, only 2% of US shoe imports came from China, while 60% came from Taiwan and South Korea. Today China has 70% of the US shoe import market, having all but displaced South Korea and Taiwan from the US market, although the Koreans and Taiwanese effectively own many of the Chinese plants selling to the United States. Many of Taiwan's electronics companies have also relocated to the Chinese mainland and are playing a pivotal role in China's electronics exports to the United States. By the end of 2003, China's deficit with Taiwan stood at $31.5 billion; $13.1 billion with South Korea; $7.6 billion with ASEAN; $5 billion with Japan; and $1.3 billion with Australia.

(Hale and Hale) A similar trend can be traced in other goods markets including personal computers. While Asian countries are losing market share in the United States to China, they are being compensated by a massive increase in exports to China in higher end and more valuable products.

The Chinese economy is far more open than the Korean or Japanese economies were at similar points in their economic take-off, and the state seems to have rejected the more dirigiste model of development employed by the Japanese. China's general tariff rates have fallen precipitously from 40% in the early 1990s to 10.4% in 2004. (Beattie) It entered the WTO under highly stringent conditions that have helped to open its market even further. In 2004, exports and imports together accounted for nearly 75% of China's total GDP. This is an extraordinarily high share for such a large country, and more than double that of the United States. Part of the reason is that China's domestic non-tradable economy remains very underdeveloped.

China has also implemented exceedingly open investment rules, although foreign investors still complain about serious administrative burdens and creeping non-tariff barriers in areas like financial services and investment rules. Still, foreign investment in China accounts for some 35% of its GDP. (The Economist, October 2, 2004) It is now the world's fifth largest recipient of foreign direct investment (FDI) and is moving quickly up the list. FDI in the first ten months of 2004 reached $54 billion. These funds are fundamentally transforming China's manufacturing and transport infrastructure.

OTHER EMERGING POWERS: BRAZIL AND SOUTH AFRICA

Although China and India are the only countries likely to become global powers in the next decades, several other rising states are poised to exert markedly increased regional and multilateral influence. Russia, a member of the BRIC group of countries, is sometimes considered in that light. It is also, like China, both a nuclear power and one of the "permanent five" with veto power on the United Nations Security Council. Russia, however, is not yet a member of the World Trade Organization, which China joined in 2001. Moreover, Russia is a special case: it is less an emerging power than a re-emerging one – a successor state to a former superpower (the Soviet Union) attempting to regain a leading role in international affairs despite its reduced circumstances.

The two other non-Asian emerging powers that bear closest attention are both the leading diplomatic actors on the other continents of the developing world. Brazil, the most populous country in the Americas after the United States, has clearly become the dominant country in South America and a leading voice for developing-country interests internationally. In Africa, that leadership role seems to have been taken up by South Africa over a decade after emerging from the dark period of apartheid. While not the continent's most populous country (that distinction belongs to Nigeria), South Africa has its largest and most dynamic economy. South Africa has also achieved an enviable degree of democratic stability and it has become increasingly engaged in multilateral diplomacy both regionally and globally. Brazil and South Africa are the most likely candidates from their respective continents for membership in an enlarged UN Security Council. Both Brazil and South Africa have, along with India and China, become key members of the majority developing-country bloc within the WTO that has challenged traditional G7 leadership in the conduct of multilateral trade negotiations. Brazil and South Africa have joined the inner circle of countries (which does not include Canada) with real influence on whether the current WTO Doha development round can succeed.

Brazil and South Africa have also been in the forefront of promoting "South South cooperation." A significant development in that regard was the creation in 2003 of the Trilateral Commission of India-Brazil-South Africa (IBSA) Dialogue Forum with the explicit mission to develop a common agenda of multilateral action as leading democracies from three continents and to foster South-South partnerships.

The Forum meets annually and set out a plan of action for trilateral cooperation at its inaugural meeting in New Delhi in March 2004. How Brazil performs could set the pace for Latin America as a whole. The National Intelligence Council projection foresees that:

Brazil's success or failure in balancing pro-growth economic measures with an ambitious social agenda that reduces poverty and income inequality will have a profound impact on region-wide economic performance and governance during the next 15 years.

Luring foreign direct investment and advancing regional stability and equitable integration – including trade and economic infrastructure – probably will remain axioms of Brazilian foreign policy. Brazil is a natural partner both for the United States and Europe and for rising powers China and India and has the potential to enhance its leverage as a net exporter of oil.

At the same time, the Goldman Sachs study on the BRICs noted that, although Brazil had posted an average annual real GDP growth rate above 5% over the past 50 years, growth had faltered as a result of financial and currency woes in the 1990s. Compared to China and other large Asian economies, Brazil remains less open to trade, its levels of investment and savings are lower, and its public and external debt are much higher. Hence Brazil's advance into the front rank of world economies will be slower and less certain.

In the case of South Africa, there are additional public health and demographic risk factors in addition to the factors of poverty and crime.

Principally these are related to the HIV/AIDS epidemic, its impact on the labour force and the strains on public services. According to Goldman Sachs projections, South Africa could become a high-growth economy, though their long-range (50 years) forecast predicts a more moderate GDP growth rate per annum of about 3.5%.

South Africa will still have an economy much smaller than any of the BRICs in a few decades' time. However, as a result of declining population growth rates, it could have a higher per capita income level.

As well, on the diplomatic front, South Africa is reaching beyond its leading role in southern African regional forums and the African Union. Its role in the WTO has already been noted. But it has also been actively pursuing regional and bilateral free-trade and investment partnerships with the European Union, the European Free Trade Association, the United States, and the MERCOSUR bloc (Brazil, Argentina, Uruguay, and Paraguay), as well as growing links with China and India.

Implications for Canada

Canada will be unlikely to exert much influence in South America or in Africa without strong ties with Brazil and South Africa. Canada must also take into account these countries' increasing role in multilateral forums, notably the WTO and the UN.

Brazil has traditionally been Canada's largest trading partner outside of NAFTA in the Americas. There has also been a long-standing, if rather narrowly based, investment relationship. Progress has been made in recent years, with Canadian FDI in Brazil reaching about $7 billion in 2003, and Brazilian investments in Canada exceeding that amount. This is considerably greater than Canada's investment relationship with China and India combined. At the same time, Canadian exports to Brazil are well down from their peak level of 1997, and two way trade flows account for only about 0.4% of Canada's global total (just 0.2% of exports and 0.7% of imports in 2004).

Moreover, bilateral relations remain in question overall. A November 2004 visit to Brazil by the Canadian prime minister and trade minister, which gave a push to the negotiation of a limited free-trade arrangement with

MERCOSUR, was a positive sign coming after a series of frictions. These include a 2001 Canadian ban on Brazilian beef imports over BSE fears and the ongoing dispute over export subsidies for regional jets built by Bombardier and its Brazilian competitor Embraer. More broadly, Canada and Brazil have not been in sync over the now stalled negotiations over a Free Trade Area of the Americas (FTAA), and that appears to have also bogged down the bilateral negotiation with MERCOSUR. One analyst argues that, while Brazil is interested in a deal with Canada, it is intent on pursuing its own hemispheric strategy, not one driven by North American interests. Furthermore: "Canada does not control the agenda [of the FTAA] – the US and Brazil do. Canada will have an increasingly difficult time influencing the agenda, and creative thinking will be needed if there is to be a renewal of productive Canadian-Brazilian relations." In regard to South Africa, Canada has provided considerable bilateral assistance in support of the country's post-apartheid democratic transition (some $150 million in the decade after the new constitution of 1994).

South Africa is also Canada's largest trading partner in sub Saharan Africa. That total is still very small, however, accounting for only about 0.1% of Canada's global two-way trade (0.1% of exports and less than 0.2% of imports in 2004). Investment is also small and has been concentrated in the mining and resource sectors.

Diplomatically, Canada has sought to engage South Africa through the Commonwealth and through pan-African initiatives such as the New Partnership for Africa's Development (NEPAD) that was a centrepiece of the agenda for the G8 summit hosted by Canada in Kananaskis, Alberta, in June 2002. Bilateral relations have been mostly positive. However, Canada does not as yet appear to figure significantly in South Africa's ambitious approach to forging strategic free-trade and investment links outside of Africa.

THE STATE OF THE WORLD: A FRAMEWORK

The evolution of geopolitics is cyclical. Powers rise, fall and shift. Changes occur in every generation in an unending ballet. However, the period between 1989 and 1991 was unique in that a long cycle of human history spanning hundreds of years ended, and with it a shorter cycle also came to a close. The world is still reverberating from the events of that period. On Dec. 25, 1991, an epoch ended. On that day the Soviet Union collapsed, and for the first time in almost 500 years no European power was a global power, meaning no European state integrated economic, military and political power on a global scale.

What began in 1492 with Europe smashing its way into the world and creating a global imperial system had ended. For five centuries, one European power or another had dominated the world, whether Portugal, Spain, France, England or the Soviet Union. Even the lesser European powers at the time had some degree of global influence.

After 1991 the only global power left was the United States, which produced about 25 percent of the world's gross domestic product (GDP) each year and dominated the oceans.

Never before had the United States been the dominant global power. Prior to World War II, American power had been growing from its place at the margins of the international system, but it was emerging on a multipolar stage.

After World War II, it found itself in a bipolar world, facing off with the Soviet Union in a struggle in which American victory was hardly a foregone conclusion.

The United States has been the unchallenged global power for 20 years, but its ascendancy has left it off-balance for most of this time, and imbalance has been the fundamental characteristic of the global system in the past generation. Unprepared institutionally or psychologically for its position, the United States has swung from an excessive optimism in the 1990s that held that significant conflict was at an end to the wars against militant Islam after 9/11, wars that the United States could not avoid but also could not integrate into a multilayered global strategy.

When the only global power becomes obsessed with a single region, the entire world is unbalanced. Imbalance remains the defining characteristic of the global system today. While the collapse of the Soviet Union ended the European epoch, it also was the end of the era that began in 1945, and it was accompanied by a cluster of events that tend to accompany generational shifts.

The 1989-1991 period marked the end of the Japanese economic miracle, the first time the world had marveled at an Asian power's sustained growth rate as the same power's financial system crumbled.

The end of the Japanese miracle and the economic problem of integrating East and West Germany both changed the way the global economy worked. The 1991 Maastricht Treaty set the stage for Europe's attempt at integration and was the framework for Europe in the post-Cold War world.

Tiananmen Square set the course for China in the next 20 years and was the Chinese answer to a collapsing Soviet empire. It created a structure that allowed for economic development but assured the dominance of the Communist Party.

Saddam Hussein's invasion of Kuwait was designed to change the balance of power in the Persian Gulf after the Iraq-Iran war and tested the United States' willingness to go to war after the Cold War.

In 1989-1991 the world changed the way it worked, whether measured in centuries or generations. It was an extraordinary period whose significance is only now emerging.

It locked into place a long-term changing of the guard, where North America replaced Europe as the center of the international system. But generations come and go, and we are now in the middle of the first generational shift since the collapse of the European powers, a shift that began in 2008 but is only now working itself out in detail.

What happened in 2008 was one of the financial panics that the global capitalist system periodically suffers. As is frequently the case, these panics first generate political crises within nations, followed by changes in the relations among nations. Of these changes, three in particular are of importance, two of which are directly linked to the 2008 crisis. The first is the European financial crisis and its transformation into a political crisis.

The second is the Chinese export crisis and its consequences. The third, indirectly linked to 2008, is the shift in the balance of power in the Middle East in favor of Iran.

GLOBALIZATION OF INDIAN ECONOMY AND IT'S IMPACT ON ENVIRONMENT

Globalism, at its core seeks to describe and explain nothing more than a world, which is characterized by net works of connection that span multi continental distances. It attempts to understand all the interconnections of the modern world and to high light patterns that underline them.

In contrast, Globalization refers to the increase or decline in the degree of globalism. It focuses on the forces, the dynamism or speed of these changes.

In short consider globalism as the underlying basic network which Globalization refers to the dynamic shrinking of distance on a large scale (Joseph Nye, 2002) Globalization is a process by which capital goods and services and some times labour cross-national borders and acquire a transnational character. It is often accompanied by the flow of related taste ideas even values across boundaries thus helping to reshape local political institutions, social relationships and cultural pattern. (Md. Saidul Islam, 2007)

Globalization (a homogenization of global economic social and political order) is not synonymous with internationalization (a collaboration of nation states in their pursuit of mutual interests (Irogene ceme, 2005) As summarized in Mc. Michael (2004) both proponents and opponents of globalization can discern the following characteristics: Washington based consensus among global managers/policy makers favouring market based rather than state managed development strategies.

1. Centralised management of Global market rules by the G-8 states (USA, UK, France, Germany, Japan, Italy, Russia and Canada)
2. Implementation of these rules through multilateral agencies World Bank/IMF/WTO
3. Concentration of market power in the levels of TNCs and financial powers in the hands of transnational banks.
4. Subjection of all states to economic disciplines (Trade financial Labour) varying by position in the state system (North/South/East) global currency hierarchy debt load resource endowments and so forth.
5. Realisation of global debt via new gender, race and ethnic inequalities.
6. A counter movement at all levels, from marginalized communities to state managers to factions even within multilateral institutions contesting and second guessing unbridled market rule.

GLOBALIZATION OF INDIA AND ENVIRONMENT

Environmental Globalism refers to the long distance transport of materials in the atmosphere or oceans or of biological substances such as pathogens or genetic materials that affect human health and well being.

The impact of globalization on environment and sustainable development needs to be continuously addressed in Indian contest, which profoundly remains in the transaction. In spite of the potential of globalization the economic convergence it paved for an increase in inequality resulting in increased environmental impacts such as climate change, protection of O zone layer, bio diversity and desertification.

Trade and Environment

International Trade arrangement and Environment agreements contain very few provision for harmanising Trade and Environment. The increasing tendency of transnational corporation to establish global standards for environment performances enhances the Foreign Direct Investment to sustainable development

Pollution Havens vs. Haloes

According to the supporters of Globalization FDI introduces the latest environmental friendly technologies and commodities and trade regimes that impose stricter environmental regulations on less developed countries. These measures will improve environmental conditions in developing countries. Thus supporters declare that FDI wears a " pollution halo and economic globalization leads to more eco friendly industrial development (wheeler 2000).

But opponents argued that globalization has converted less developed countries into pollution havens for the dirty industries from being set up (Mani and Wheeler, 1997) In India the share of dirty industries in total FDI was 51 percent in 1991-2000. Of these 27.4 percent was in energy, 4.5 percent chemicals, 7.5 percent transport, 5.5 percent metallurgy and 3.5 percent in food processing, all classified as Red or most polluting industries, while hotels and tourism having 1.7 percent and textiles 1.2 percent came under orange industries (CPCB Annual Report 2003). Also the largest inflow to approvals of foreign investment was in the dirty industries chiefly chemicals with 37.7 percent.

Many goods produced by the public sector were de licensed to allow private and foreign firms to produce them. These include polluting industries such as mining power production, Chemicals etc., Though the law suggests that foreign firms should obtain licenses, the NEP does not prevent them from establishing hazardous industries in India.

For example, Hindustan Lever limited, a branch of unilever-a US-Dutch company started a mercury thermometer factory in the pure environs of Kodaikanal after its main factory was closed in USA. The thermometers were made for export. The resulting level of mercury poisoning was almost 250 times the permitted limits in this region and adversely affected the environment.

Other Side of Free Trade

India's 75000 km of long coastline had become the waste destination of the entire world. Lead Ash, Battery scarp, Zinc ash, waste oil and old ships laden with pollution control Boards and asbestos meant to be broken are increasingly being labeled " Destination India".

In case of Zinc and lead wastes alone, India import over 70,000 MT and 50,000 MT (1995) respectively through its 7 major and 100 minor ports (Ravi Agarwal, 1998). Toxic wastes imports are allowed under the Free trade Regime, Which violates the Basel protocol on Trade in Hazardous wastes. According to Green peace, Hundred of tones of plastics and metals such as lead, copper and other wastes are coming into India from countries like Australia, Canada, UK and USA apparently for recycling.

An Indian company Futura industries of Tamilnadu, has imported 10,000 metric tones of plastic wastes since 1992,out of which only 30-40 percent could be recycled. In 1992-93 imports of lead acid battery wastes from Australia increased nearly three folds from 126000 kg to 346000 kg (Kothari, 1998). 168 containers of waste oil were illegally imported via. Nharasheva contained terminal Nar Mumbai.

Hotrachem, a marine based chemical factory exported 118 tonnes of highly toxic mercury to India. In December 2005, The Britain Environment Agency (BEA) published a report that there were several companies exporting e-waste from UK to India. The distinction of Along being the world's largest ship breaking yard is another proof of India becoming the toxic dumping ground.

The grant MNCs – Coke and Pepsi, finding loopholes in the Indian Environmental laws on safe levels of pesticides in food, did not remove dangerous pesticides in residues from their bottled Drinks in Coca Cola Company has come under scrutiny once again for selling harmful products – this time, with high levels of ben benzene, a cancer causing chemicals.

In 2003, Center for Science and Environment, New Delhi found that Coca-Cola and Pepsi Company production in India contained extreme high levels of pesticides, DDT, Malathran, Lindane and Chlorpyijos.

Equally alarming is the pollution of scarce remaining ground water and land by the Coca-Cola Company. Coca-cola plant located in Mehdiganj, 20 kilometer from Varansi, draw electricity from 2 diesel power generators on which consumes 360 liters of diesel per hour. Two tube wells draw thousands of liters of under ground water lowering the water level from 15 to 40 feet (Kalyan, 2003).

Besides, Coca-Cola has indiscriminately discharged its waste into surrounding fields and the ground water has been rendered unfit for human consumption and the land has been poisoned. In a good will gesture, in Kerala, Coca-Cola was distributing the solid waste from its bottling plants to farmers in the area as fertilizer. BBC had the waste tested and found extremely high levels of heavy metals such as lead and cadmium in the waste, effectively making the solid waste toxic.

Indian companies are also squeezing natural resources at a faster pace for shrimp farming in most valuable brackish wetlands, and lakes. Industries have been cleared adjustment to marine National part and protected areas of wild life officially. The destructive potential of the liberalized economy could be identified in tropical islands, rain forests, coral reefs and marine wastes and genetic store houses.

As Vandha Shiva says, " Basmati, neem, pepper, bitter gourd turmeric-every aspect of the innovation embodied in our indigenous food and medicinal systems is now being pirated and patented. The knowledge of the poor is being converted into the property of Global corporations, creating a situations where the poor will have to pay for the medicines and seeds they have evolved and have used to meet their needs of nutrition and health care (Tonic solo,2003).

7

Changing Global Balance of Power in Asia 2020

GLOBAL POWER BALANCE 2020

The global power balance has been in a churning state ever since the turn of the millennium. The disintegration of the Soviet Union enabled the United States global strategic predominance to be unrivalled and unquestioned. Concerned by United States unilateralism., Russia and China as the two nations most strategically affected set in motion two significant initiatives to offset the US predominance. Russia under the dynamic leadership of President Putin set Russia on a course of strategic and military resurgence. This was facilitated by rising Russian oil revenues. China with significant economic resources at its disposal embarked on a strategic build-up of its strategic assets and military upgradation. The United States decade-old strategic global predominance was now to be under challenge by Russia and China. This strategic challenge by these two nations became further accentuated as a result of United States getting inextricably tied down militarily in Afghanistan and Iraq.

The current global economic turbulence has prompted many strategic analysts to re-examine the short-term global balance of power perspectives with 2020 taken as a more identifiable time frame. Some would like to believe that the current economic melt-down could affect the global power balance and the inter-se strategic equations between USA, Russia and China. They would like to suggest that the United States as the strongest economy in the world could weather the storms, but Russia and China, and especially Russia's resurgence and its strategic challenge to the United States could be diluted.

This Author would like to maintain that the economic meltdown today is globalised in its dimensions and would therefore affect USA, Russia and China without any exception. However, Russia and China's strategic programs directed at altering the global power balance would not be diluted. This besides other reasons, is valid, because Russia and China are not involved in any costly strategic distractions like the United States in Iraq and Afghanistan, requiring a significant outlay of financial resources.

Otherwise too, it is conceded by many economists that economies of the world surface more strongly after economic depressions. Strategically, the historical evidence cannot be ignored that the Second World War took place within a decade of the Great Depression in which the United States was the most vitally affected.

Therefore, in strategic analysis such economic depressions may act as "speed breakers" but definitely do not bring global strategic power rivalries to a "dead end".

With the above as an introductory background, this Paper attempts to analyse "Global Power Balance 2020: Perspectives" under the following heads:

- Global Power Balance 2020 Will be Bi-polar in Nature
- Multi-polarity is a Political and Strategic Myth
- United States Would Have Strategic Edge Over Russia in a Bi-polar World
- A New Cold War is Inevitable.

Global Power Balance 2020 Will be Bi-polar in Nature

Assertions of this Author in this direction stand examined in fair detail in earlier SAAG Papers and particularly those dealing with Russia's resurgence. This Author firmly believes that the global power balance in 2020 would be bi-polar in nature with the United States and Russia as the two poles.

Russia is being dismissively discussed in US and Western think-tanks and Russia's resurgence is de-emphasised and devaluated. This dismissive attitude is not born out of realistic strategic analysis but wishful thinking that Russia does not emerge as a strategic challenge to United States global predominance.

The moot question that needs to be considered is that who amongst Russia and China is more strategically potent to challenge United States global predominance?

Even on current analysis the following strategic realities suggest that Russia is the foremost candidate to challenge USA and not China (1) Russia's existing strategic nuclear weapons arsenal outnumbers the United States whereas China's nuclear arsenal at about 400 warheads is a remote comparison (2) Russia's existing power projection capabilities extend far beyond its immediate neighbourhood, in all dimensions – land, sea and air. China's power projection is limited to her periphery and limited to ground forces dimensions only (3) Russia is an "energy self-independent" state and this is an essential pre-requisite of national power. Japan and Germany lost the Second World War because they were not "energy self-reliant" (4) Russia has existing strategic partnerships with many countries across the globe. China has no "natural allies" to boost her strategic power (5) Russia's resurgence has been welcomed in many regions and more importantly in the Middle East. China is not viewed as a credible strategic challenger to the United States.

More importantly Russia has been a practitioner of global power politics in the bi-polar environment of the Cold War and successfully provided countervailing power to the United States for 45 years. Further, it needs to be noted that Russia was not defeated by the United States in the Cold War; it was Russia that defeated itself.

Russia's current strategic and political resurgence is precisely aimed in this direction once again, namely, to reclaim her former superpower status. It has won recognition in Europe, Middle East, Central Asia and South East Asia too. Reading between the lines one gets a sneaking feeling that the United States may prefer China as a manageable strategic rival rather than Russia. But the strategic realities indicate that the United States would in 2020 have to accept a bi-polar world with Russia as the second pole.

Multi-polarity is a Political and Strategic Myth

Multi-polarity as a desirable state in the global power balance was forcefully enunciated by China to begin with in the immediate period following the demise of the Soviet Union. To begin with, in the early 1990s, China advocated a multi-polar world incorporating China, India, Iran and Syria with Pakistan added. Later inducements were to include France and Germany. This enunciation never took off though being repeated periodically.

So the initial Chinese model of multi-polarity comprised Asian nations with no strong strategic linkages with USA as the unipolar power. China then as the only nuclear weapons state in this grouping may have been led to believe that it would emerge as the natural leader of its proposed multi-polar grouping.

Russia today also talks of multi-polarity but one suspects that it is more for political reasons in favor of China than any strategic conviction. Russia would strategically prefer a bi-polar world at the global level and without frowning on multi-polarity at the regional level.

China, Japan and India even with the full development of their strategic strengths cannot hope to equal the strategic potential of being super-powers in the classical sense of definition of the term.

They can sit on the global powers high table as associate global players, but not as "super powers". China, Japan and India therefore are incapable of emerging as multiple poles to bring about a multi-polar world. Only the United States and Russia qualify to be superpowers. Available indicators suggest that the United States and Russia would be the two super-powers in 2020 and no scope exists for any of the other global players intruding into that league.

THE CHANGING GLOBAL BALANCE OF POWER

Major power shifts between societies, countries, regions or empires are nothing new in world affairs. The only certainty about any given balance of power is that it will change. New powers arise as established ones, even the greatest, decline. While large shifts occur rarely, when that happens the impacts are usually momentous and far-reaching. Moreover, historically such shifts have seldom been peaceful. The collapse of the Soviet Union was an exception late in a century that had seen two devastating world wars. At the same time, the end of the Cold War gave way to new intra- as well as inter-state conflicts rather than a stable "new world order." International institutions and regimes are still struggling to come to terms with the ramifications of new states and of "failing or fragile" states.

Other factors, notably those associated with globalization, are combining to produce what Canada's recent *International Policy Statement* refers to as "a new global distribution of power." The dominance of the United States as the sole remaining superpower in the post-Cold War international system has led some to speak of a "unipolar moment." America's military prowess remains unrivalled, even if the burdens of that grow heavier. Yet in other respects, notably economic as well as scientific and technological, the United States is becoming less dominant in overall global terms. An expanded European Union of 25 (soon to be 27) member countries has emerged as a distinctive power centre within the West. Elsewhere, major "emerging powers" – China and India are the two most frequently mentioned – are seen increasingly to be challenging Western leadership, and eventually perhaps overtaking most if not all of the existing great powers.

The most evident immediate challenge, and a main focus of this chapter, is geo-economic, stemming from the growing power resources of emerging-market countries, the rapid advancement of which will have large implications for the current G7 industrialized countries. Many books and articles have been written in recent years about these apparent trends, many by Americans warning that the United States for all its present power is not ready for what is coming. For example, Jeffrey Garten, a former Under Secretary of Commerce in the Clinton administration, wrote almost a decade ago that: "Dealing with the big emerging markets will be key to our economic well-being and to our security in the decades ahead. It will require a new mind-set about our economic and social policies as well as fresh strategies for our involvement overseas. America is totally unprepared for this challenge."

Garten identified 10 "big emerging markets" (BEMs) selected according to the criteria of large populations and resource bases, expanding market reach, regional influence, international ambitions, high economic growth and liberalization. The group includes: China, India, and Brazil as the leading three, along with Mexico, Indonesia, South Korea, South Africa, Argentina, Turkey, and Poland. Garten argued that the BEMs would be at the crux of all the major global dynamics in the next decades, and that this would require a "massive shift" in how Western policymakers think about their strategic international interests. In particular, according to Garten: "It is likely that our [the United States'] relationship with China will emerge in the next decade as the most important focus of our entire foreign policy."

These predictions were made before the attacks of 11 September 2001 and the resulting renewed focus on global terrorism and events in the Middle East. The inclusion of Argentina and Poland in Garten's BEMs also predated the former's financial crisis and the latter's membership in the European Union. Subsequent outlooks of the major international powers have promoted into this front rank of countries several other candidates that are viewed as playing roles of global significance or in which developments are seen to matter in global terms. For example, one survey of foreign policies of 10 "great and emerging powers" includes Iran among the latter. Common to these contemporary perspectives is an expectation of rapid, even wrenching, change in a world of disorder.

At the same time as international policy agendas are growing ever more complex and interconnected, inter-state relations have also become more fluid and unstable. The foregoing analysis of 10 leading foreign-policy powers observes that: "World politics remains in a profound state of flux more than a decade after the Cold War. A coherent balance of power among nation-states has yet to emerge ...." Nevertheless, what has remained constant in all recent as well as earlier forecasts is the increasingly important role in global affairs of the Asian giants, China and India, superseding that of Japan. That is the one global phenomenon above all that seems not to be in doubt.

The significance of an Asia-driven shift in the global balance of power was underlined in a far-reaching exercise that was undertaken by the National Intelligence Council (NIC) of the U.S. Central Intelligence Agency in 2004. Looking ahead to the world in 2020, the report of the NIC's "2020 Project" summed up its findings as follows:

The likely emergence of China and India, as well as others, as new major global players – similar to the advent of a united Germany in the 19th century and a powerful United States in the early 20th century – will transform the geopolitical landscape, with impacts potentially as dramatic as those in the previous two centuries. In the same way that commentators refer to the 1900s as the "American Century," the 21st century may be seen as the time when Asia, led by China and India, comes into its own. A combination of sustained high economic growth, expanding military capabilities, and large populations will be at the root of the expected rapid rise in economic and political power for both countries.

- Most forecasts indicate that by 2020 China's gross national product (GNP) will exceed that of individual Western economic powers except for the United States. India's GNP will have overtaken or be on the threshold of overtaking European economies.
- Because of the sheer size of China's and India's populations – projected by the US Census Bureau to be 1.4 billion and almost 1.3 billion respectively by 2020 – their standard of living need not approach Western levels for these countries to become important economic powers.

Barring an abrupt reversal of the process of globalization or any major upheavals in these countries, the rise of these new powers is a virtual certainty. Yet how China and India exercise their growing power and whether they relate cooperatively or competitively to other powers in the international system are key uncertainties. The economies of other developing countries, such as Brazil, could surpass all but the largest European countries by 2020; Indonesia's economy could also approach the economies of individual European countries by 2020.

The sheer burgeoning economic size of China and India, both nuclear powers as well, provides the most impressive evidence of their global ascendance, with India's growth rate perhaps eventually exceeding that of

China. Looking forward 20 years, the Economist Intelligence Unit forecasts that, measured in terms of Gross Domestic Product (GDP) at purchasing-power parity exchange rates, India's economy will have surged far ahead of Japan's to be the world's third biggest in 2026 (at 9.9% of global GDP, compared to 4% for Japan). China's economy will have overtaken that of the United States by 2017 and will account for 21.8% of global GDP in 2026. (That compares to 2.5% and 2.4% respectively for the next largest "emerging powers," Russia and Brazil.) Meanwhile, the European Union 25's share of global output will decline to 16% from 21%.

Under such scenarios, China and to a lesser extent India will rise to the rank of global powers, rivalling the weight of America and Europe at least in economic terms. Their foreign policies will therefore be watched intensely in future international policy calculations.

GLOBAL POWER

China's insistence that Taiwan - a democratic country with all the attributes of independent statehood except recognition - belongs to China and has no right to an independent sovereignty strikes at the heart of China's legitimacy problem as a global power. For all its good-neighbourly diplomacy and calls upon the presiding superpower to exercise restraint in the exercise of its coercive power, China in domestic (Tibet, Xinjiang, democracy movements, human rights) and quasi-domtestic (PRC-Taiwan) affairs is seen as overbearing when handling the problem of dissent. Given that most states in the world accept Beijing's view on the matter, that is, the One China policy which states that there is one China and that Taiwan is a province of China, this does not appear to be a problem for the society of states. Irrespective of minority claims within its sovereign territory, China remains an accepted great power in the IR system.

In military terms it is also a superpower if one accepts that its nuclear arsenal is adequate to the task of global (deterrent) reach and that its conventional forces can defend China in the improbable event of attack. Unlike the US and other modern military establishments, China lacks the latest technology. However, it continues its program of modernization, which it is increasingly able to afford thanks to a strengthening economy. Thus while China is a *great power*, exercising a valued balancing and concerting role in the system, it has yet to be accepted as a *superpower* along US lines. In terms of *global power*, China demonstrates an ability to engage in global governance when state-managed (as in the UN and its agencies) and transnational business relations (benefiting from investments from transnational companies), but where issues of dissent and their wider ramifications are involved (particularly democracy and human rights issues), global civil society is not overly impressed with China. Social networks independent of the state, including human rights activists, as well as postmodernist views on diversity and tolerance, find the authoritarian government of China troubling and out of touch with the global ethos.

PERCEPTION OF BALANCE OF POWER

In general, there are two main theoretical schools of international relations: *realism* and *liberalism. Realism* identifies the entire system of state relations based on criteria such as strength, power, geopolitics, geostrategy and the correlation of forces largely among Great Powers. *Liberalism* emphasizes other factors, such as economic interdependence, "soft" sources of power, and the role of international institutions and multilateralism.

According to many scholars, while various approaches could be considered supplementary, realism is the more dominant theoretical tradition since the policies of Great Powers and their relations have so far strongly influenced international affairs. Moreover, the regional and multilateral institutions would not be able to function without the participation of Great Powers.

The theory on balance of power is associated with realism and remains the most fundamental framework for understanding international relations. The concept of balance of power has historically been used to explain the actions of states in an insecure environment. The system was first formed and operationalized among the applied though debate on it continues.

Balance of Power: Meaning

Balance of power is perceived *as the basic concept in the relations among states*. Modern theory on balance of power is connected to the Newtonian conception of an universe in equilibrium. The substance of this theory is: *Under normal circumstances, all states always seek to maximize their power and international positions through various methods and techniques, and because of the adjustments of the "invisible hand", no one gains hegemony and an equilibrium in the international relations systems is maintained*. This definition suggests a mechanism in which any attempt by any state to expand its power and attain dominance or hegemony that would allow it to impose its will on the other states will be resisted. No state, therefore, will be in a position to determine the fate of others.

Thus, a state of equilibrium in the international relations system is one in which no state becomes an absolute dominant power; more powerful states, in spite of pursuing various strategic interests, are satisfied with the existing territorial, adjustments may take place, no powerful state (or group of states) seeks to change the system fundamentally, as it would not yield additional benefits commensurate with the anticipated costs.

Consequently, the Great Powers have frequently supported the balance of power system throughout history, because they have both greater capacity to influence outcomes and the largest stake in the established order. In effect, balance of power mirrors the Great Powers' compromises on the distribution of benefits and spheres of influence in the world on the basis of their correlation of forces.

Rules of the Diversion

The aim of countervailing power is the protection of each state's security and the system in which these states exist as a whole. Therefore, the way to ensure each state's security is to prevent the emergence of any preponderant state that would lead to an upset of the existing status of equilibrium.

As Wolfer puts it, in balance of power terms, these rules can be stated in the following manner:

(a) Watch a potential adversary's power and match it.

(b) Ally oneself with a weaker state to restore the balance of power.

(c) Abandon such alliances when the balance has been restored and the common danger has passed.

(d) Regard national security interests as permanent; alliances must therefore change when a new threat rises.

(e) *Do not treat defeated states harshly through punitive peace treaties (today's adversary may be tomorrow's ally).*

Change of Balance

An international system is not maintained in a state of stable equilibrium when important shifts in the array of forces among states occur. There are two basic elements leading to the attempts to change the balance of power system:

- Differential growth in political, military and technological power that creates a change in the array of forces among states.
- Shifts in states' domestic political coalitions may necessitate redefinition of their "national interests" and foreign policies.

An equilibrium can be altered if there is a shift in political, military and technological capabilities of states and, as a result, *the expected benefits exceed the expected costs of bringing about a change in the system.* Victorious state or states would create the new peace settlements and status quo reflecting the redistribution of power in the system. The hegemonic wars in this view included the Thirty Years War from 1618-1648, the wars of King Louis XIV from 1667-1713, the Napoleonic Wars from 1792-1814, World War I from 1914-1918 and World War II from 1939-1945. However, resolution of crises is still possible through peaceful adjustment of the systemic disequilibrium, by compromises or moderation of the ambitions of emerging Great Powers. Essentially, it is the sharing of costs and benefits in keeping the status quo among the existing Great Powers.

The determinants of whether or not to create and maintain the international balance of power are the cost-benefit calculations that a state (or states) will make in the determination to change the existing equilibrium. The material environment (e.g., economic growth, demographic change, military technologies, communications and transportation conditions), the international system structures, and "internal" factors (e.g., leadership personalities, national identities, political-economic interests of groups and others in the society) provide incentives or disincentives for a state to attempt to change the international system.

Meaning of Implement a Balance of Power Policy

As J. Spanier explains, all states are very concerned about their strength or power for survival. To prevent an attack, a state must be *as powerful as potential aggressors; a disproportion of power may tempt another state. A balance of power is thus a prerequisite for each state's security.* When the balance is disturbed, the tendency is to take responsive action to return to a position of equilibrium. If states disregard the operational rule that power must be counterbalanced, they place their own security in jeopardy.

As Kissinger argues, *the balance of power serves to restrict the ability of states to dominate each other and to limit the scope of conflicts.* Kissinger views the balance of power not as an automatic mechanism, but instead as one of two possible outcomes of a situation in which states are obliged to deal with each other. One state can become so powerful that it dominates the others, or else the "pretensions" of the most aggressive member of the international community are kept in check by chosen by prudent leaders.

Harman, when studying the significance of theory on balance of power, asserts that *prudent states do not amass more enemies than they can effectively counter or handle at any one time. If states must deal with two or three adversaries, it would be wiser to concentrate on the strongest one by isolating and separating it from the others.* This principle is called the "conservation of enemies".

Chessmen on the New Strategic Chessboard

On the international strategic chessboard, the ranks of "chessmen" are classified by geopolitical, demographic, economic, military and traditional criteria in which geopolitics has significant importance. Generally, two ranks are identified: the first rank comprises *Great Powers,* whose scope of interests and capability of intervention reaches out beyond their borders. The second rank is comprised of *Middle and Small Powers,* which do not have (or have only a very few) of these roles to act, while the Middle and Small Powers are acted upon. The "chessmen" positioned on the strategic chessboard in the Asia-Pacific are ranked as follows:

- *First* is a group of Great Powers that includes the United States, China, Japan, Russia and India. These are the chief game players in the strategic chessboard. Their positions, however, are not necessarily equal to one another:
    - The United States is currently the single superpower having political, economic and military might, and global influence.
    - China is an emerging power with an increasingly important voice in the regional economy and greater political influence in the Asia-Pacific. -Japan is an economic power whose political and military stature are not commensurate with its economic abilities.
    - Russia's international prestige declined sharply after the collapse of the Soviet Union. In spite of this, however, Russia still has a strong military force, including nuclear weapons.
    - India is now exercising its clout mainly in the South Asian region and is also viewed as a rising power.
- *Second* is a group of Middle Powers. These countries do not have great influence on the developments in the region, but they play an important role in balancing power, as they occupy strategic geopolitical positions and are the Korea, and Vietnam.
- *Third* are Small Powers (Laos, Cambodia, Singapore) and some very small states like Brunei (with a population of 300,000 people), and the Marshall Islands (with a population of 40,000 people). Those countries can only make worthwhile stands when they are engaged in alliances or alignments with other actors.
- *In addition,* some scholars of liberalism have flirted with the idea that new transnational actors, such as international and regional organizations, NGOs and multinational corporations, are gradually playing a greater role in international affairs.

IMPLICATIONS FOR CANADA

What does all this mean for Canada? It is true that Canada's next-door relationship with the United States will always be an enormously important fact of international policy from a Canadian perspective. In fact, one possible response to competitive pressures coming from other regions, especially from rising Asia, could be to pursue closer integration of the North American economy in order to meet this competitive challenge from a position of regional strength. Alternatively, another possible Canadian response could be to seek to rely less on the North American market by developing new partnerships with the rising powers. In either case, as the world becomes more multi-polar – with major emerging powers forcing the pace of changes in the international system – there will be large implications for Canada, given our high exposure to international trade and investment flows. Canada will have to develop international strategies that take this into account or risk being left marginalized, not only in relation to the United States but multilaterally as well.

Canada can probably not avoid some diminution in its global weight. A recent prognosis by the Conference Board of Canada observes that: "In 15 years, Canada will account for less than 2 per cent of the world's gross domestic product (GDP), only 1 per cent of the world's military expenditure and just 0.5 per cent of the world's population. Our role in global dynamics will be marginal."

It is important to understand that this is a *relative* decline, and that it is *not* due to a more powerful United States. On the contrary, as Charles Doran points out, the United States will be "doing all it can to hang on to its own power share in an increasingly competitive world. ... A genuine reason for the Canadian relative decline in capability is that middle powers with huge capacity for growth, and experiencing rapid growth, are ascending from the bottom of the central system. As they ascend, they take power share away from the rich, middle powers like Canada that are not growing as fast. Three states in particular are in a position to challenge the standing of Canada. They are China, India, and Brazil, perhaps in the order of their size of impact."

Doran and others predict that Canada, despite its resource wealth and international reputation, will feel increased pressure from these emerging powers seeking to advance their interests within major international forums. Canada will therefore have to strategically focus its energies and use all of its skills if it is to maintain a significant presence in the international decision-making of the future.

GLOBAL POWER IN TODAY'S WORLD

The term *global power* is a more contemporary term for *great power,* as traditionally employed in the International Relations (IR) literature, and a better fit for 21st century conditions than *superpower. Superpower* was the creation of the politics of 20th century nuclear weapons technology, even though the coining of the term in 1944 did not take the nuclear dimension into account but rather the global reach of a nation. As the Cold War became more entrenched, that which distinguished a nuclear *superpower* from a 19th century *great power* was possession of the power of ultimate destruction and the strategic doctrine of nuclear deterrence that emerged from it. The processes of globalization that characterize the present century mean that 'great' power needs more than nuclear superpower capability. Indeed, it needs to broaden out to the more traditional *great power* attributes of maintaining sufficient diplomatic, economic, and military resources for preserving the international order in which *great powers* presume themselves to be the main actors. Beyond being merely 'great', or only 'super', they must now be 'global' and attain transnational competencies that permit interaction with non-state actors, regional forums and the instruments and institutions of global governance. In short, a*global power* needs to promote international order; possess formidable military capability and the communicated will to use it; and engage productively in transnational projects such as global justice, as well as deal effectively with transnational threats such as militant religious extremists.

Such is the meaning behind the term *global power* as used in the present discussion. Its meaning will be further elaborated on China's capacity to match these criteria of not only being (a) a *great power*in the traditional sense and (b) a militarily outstanding one, but also (c) a transnational performer.

Is China a great power *in helping to maintain the world order?* A *great power,* according to Hedley Bull's classic 1977 work, *The Anarchical Society,* belongs to a society of states that maintains a balance-of-power to prevent a global dictatorship emerging through imperial conquest. Besides the balancing-of-power in maintaining this socially constructed system, *great powers* also engage in the order preserving mechanisms of *international law, diplomacy, concerting* (or joint management of the system), and *war* when it acts to preserve (or defend) the system rather than destroy it.

As a member of the United Nations Security Council, the People's Republic of China (PRC) belongs to the elite club of recognized *great powers.* It is involved in more than 1000 international governmental organizations that deal with issues ranging from drug trafficking to the environment; and it is an ardent supporter of the United Nations and international law, warning against the exercise of military power when peaceful methods of diplomacy ought to be given greater scope for realization. This was especially notable with regard to China's reaction to American military interventions in the post-Cold War era, indicating China's understanding of the need for great powers to critique one another in the interests of a balanced state system. Even before its economic rise and military modernisation, China was a vocal critic of superpower conduct in world affairs. Indeed, China's role during the Cold War was one of balance in the strategic triangle (comprising the US, Soviet Union and PRC), whereby China pursued a policy of 'leaning to one side' (either the Soviet Union or the United States) from within a posture of strategic independence.

Even with the collapse of the Cold War structure, and the clear military and economic superiority that now rests with the remaining superpower, the United States still supports the prevailing state system and is sensitive to balance-of-power as well as concerting behaviour. Thus China may continue to exercise its role of superpower critic as the need arises. China is not alone in its balancing efforts, as the failure of the US to gain UN support for its war on Iraq in 2003 demonstrated. In this sense, the European Union (EU) and its member states, Russia and others act as both a concerting and balancing force. China, too, acted in concert with the US in its campaign against state-defying terrorism. But alongside other states, including France, Germany, Russia, and Turkey, it opposed the US war on Iraq. Even though the US went ahead regardless, it still returned to the UN to gain a mandate to continue in the aftermath of the war and to involve other nations. This indicates that the American hegemon is aware of the need to maintain its power through legitimacy, as well as reducing its foreign policy costs in material terms, in the rate of casualties, and hence in domestic public opinion terms. Another 'Vietnam' - both at home and abroad - would not be countenanced by the American public.

Unlike the characteristically unipolar structure of the state system over which Washington presides coupled with US unilateralist management tendencies, China has been a strong advocate of multipolarity and, of late, multilateralism. This would suit China in view of its subordinate power status in comparison to the US; a view which would suggest to some observers that if China surpasses the US and becomes the dominant state, it would behave in a similar fashion to the US. This is the 'strong states cast long shadows' proposition. Such a proposition supports the China threat thesis if (a) one is opposed to the emergence of an Oriental hegemonic power in the state system preferring an Occidental one, or (b) if one is opposed to unipolarity, preferring a closer semblance of balance-of-power in bipolarity or multipolarity. The first pertains to cultural affiliations and Samuel Huntington's 'clash of civilizations' thesis; the second has an aversion to hegemonic systems. In light of increasing opposition to US hegemonic leadership in the aftermath of the Iraq war, China may garner some support for its rise as a serious balancer to the US. However, the US would need to entrench itself in world-defying, self-aggrandising behaviour to warrant such an adversarial image. Indeed, the US would need to lose its hegemonic legitimacy and China to gain it.

THE PURSUIT OF GREAT POWER LEGITIMACY

It is unlikely the US will persist in such a self-destructive path of loss of legitimacy but it is possible that China will capitalize on it tactically in order to make strategic gains in its own legitimacy enhancement. To gain legitimacy of the order exercised by the US, there would need to be an acceptance of an Oriental superpower, the issue of dissent in its various forms (Tibet. Xinjiang, Taiwan, Democracy, human rights) would need to be addressed, China's championing of international law and diplomacy would need to be maintained and visibly supported, as would a consultative management style global affairs. And this is only in the political field. There is economic and military strength to consider too. However, it is in the political field that legitimacy comes to the fore; such legitimacy equates with 'honour' in ancient Greek or Occidental thought and 'virtue' in the classical Chinese or Oriental equivalent. Legitimacy, honour and virtue are indeed precious moral resources for a great power to cultivate and they apply to aspiring states across the East-West civilisational spectrum. Thus the acquisition of legitimacy may overcome 'clash of civilisations' objections, particularly if deployed along multilateralist rather than unilateralist lines. This, China appears to be doing. Ironically, it was China who acted as an imperial power in its hierarchical international tribute relations until the 19th century, and the United States that disdains imperial ambitions in its 'freedom and democracy' rhetoric.

China's consolidation of its role as a great power in a sovereign state system was evident in its socialist state persona when it emphasized the equality of states principle, criticized the superpowers for putting their own strategic competition ahead of global welfare, safety and justice and, since the Cold War's end, its assiduous cultivation of diplomatic relations with a host of nations and regions. Of interest are its more positive relations with traditional rivals Russia and India. With the former it is engaged bilaterally in a 'strategic partnership' that has developed into a Treaty on Good Neighbourly Friendship and Cooperation (2001), and the establishment of a mechanism of bilateral security consultations (2005) inclusive of joint military exercises - the first being planned for August 2005, as well as multilaterally through the Shanghai Cooperation Organisation. With the latter, now a nuclear power in its own right, China has not only worked to dispel threat perceptions but also supports India as a candidate for a permanent seat on the UN Security Council. According to Chinese State Councillor Tang Jiaxuan, during his visit to India in October 2004: 'India is a major country in Asia... China fully understands India's position and endorses its aspirations... We also hope to see India play a greater and constructive role in the UN Security Council.' Also of consequence is China's interest in promoting peace on the Korean peninsula through its hosting of the Six-Party Talks on prevent the nuclearisation of the Korean peninsula, and a planned common economic future with Southeast Asia. The end of this decade will see the emergence of a regional free trade agreement between China and the Association of Southeast Asian Nations (ASEAN). Tariffs are to be reduced to between 5% and zero and investment barriers removed. This trade region will create an integrated market of 1.7 billion people, forming what will become the world's most populous free trade zone. At the same time China has committed itself to a code of good conduct over the contested ownership of seabed resources in the South China Sea.

ECONOMIC AND MILITARY DIMENSION OF GREAT POWER

The issue of energy resources in the South China Sea, while seemingly contained within a code of conduct that is not legally binding but which appeals to China's honour and legitimacy, does not remove doubt in the minds political realists who see China's need for energy as an overriding concern, driving diplomacy as well as military expansion. 'China's appetite for energy resources,' notes Jeffrey Robertson, 'threatens to outweigh the trend toward great power responsibility epitomized by its dealings with Russia and India.' How strong are China's appetites in relation to its spirit and reason - or its traditional notion of power in terms of virtue?

The Economist of 2 October 2004 dedicated its *Survey of the World Economy* to China and the United States. It notes that China is the world's largest consumer of steel, copper, coal and cement, the world's second largest consumer of oil (after USA), and that in 2003, China consumed 40% of the world's coal and 30% of its steel. In 20 years (2024), it was projected that China's energy requirements would quadruple but its per capita use of energy would remain half that of the US.

The implication in China's growing appetite is whether it will seek what it wants with a carrot or a stick - with the soft or hard power option - or what combination of both? A classical source of Chinese strategic culture, Sun Tzu states that 'All warfare is deception'. How deceptive is China's military power? How soft is China's hard power? - as in (a) *vulnerable* and (b) a *disguise for soft power*? How hard is China's soft power? - as in (a) *compelling* and (b) a disguise and means for the *acquisition of hard power*? These combinations speak to a realist strategic culture which some commentators view as the natural outcome of China's rise to global power. As the November 2004 issue of the IISS Strategic Comments states, China has 'sought to promote a variety of new institutional arrangements that exclude the United States... [in Eastern Asia] where China can exercise a natural leadership role' and that its need for energy and raw materials has extended its resource diplomacy to Central Asia, the Middle East and Africa. Indeed, many of China's gains are in direct relation to American interests.

It is estimated that China's proven oil reserves will be depleted by 2018. China has been importing oil since 1993. Its dependence on oil imports has led it to energy investments in countries which are not only resource rich but also at polar extremes in terms of friend or foe in the American strategic spectrum. Thus, Australia - a firm US ally - won a AUS$25 billion contract in 2002 to supply liquid natural gas (LNG) to China. It was described by Australia's foreign minister, Alexander Downer, as 'the beginning of a long-term strategic partnership in energy'. As to oil imports, a fifth of China's imports (14 percent from Iran and 6 percent from Sudan) come from countries governed by what the US would regard problematic regimes. The imposition of sanctions on these and other 'rogue' countries would impinge on China's energy sourcing. Why would China choose to invest in such politically risky energy producers? The answer largely lies with the benefits to be gained by entering regions that are prohibited to American business interests. As China specialist Drew Thompson has remarked, '...China's presence in the energy and infrastructure sectors of Sudan, Iran and Syria is largely the result of longstanding sanctions that have largely marginalized multinationals and the "supermajor" oil companies...' It may be concluded that China pursues an opportunistic and pragmatic approach in relation to its energy needs, and as long as there are willing suppliers there is no reason for China to exercise military means for energy acquisition. For example, it is unlikely that China's expanding naval capability is directed to the forcible acquisition of the contested Spratly Islands in the South China Sea. It is more likely that it is a demonstration to Taiwan - an internal not international affair, as far as Beijing is concerned.

Nuclear Superpower Status

With regard to the China threat theory - the fear that China will grow into a military superpower, China's leadership deliberately adopted a policy of good-neighborliness (see above) under the concept of *heping jueqi*, meaning 'the peaceful emergence of China', also known as its 'peaceful rise'. This entails the non-hegemonic stance of China, the emphasis on development and the view that China's economic growth will benefit other nations, not hurt them. Indeed, 'peaceful rise' was replaced with 'peaceful development' to further emphasise the non-threatening nature of China's growth. If China's is a peacefully rising power, how does one explain its armory of over 30 intercontinental ballistic missiles (ICBMs), 110 intermediate-range ballistic missiles (IRBM) as well as its submarine-launch missile capability (which is still small)? While this nuclear force is by no means comparable to that of the US which has over a thousand nuclear missiles, or Russia with its 635 ICBMs, and its newly announced plan for nuclear modernization, China's nuclear force does bestow upon it the prestige and deterrent power sought by others in recent times - including India, Pakistan and even North Korea in its formative stages of becoming a nuclear power.

It may be argued that with its minimal deterrent force China is hardly a nuclear superpower to be taken seriously. On the other hand, China does have global reach - how many nuclear warheads are needed to constitute a threat and to be deemed a credible deterrent? Moreover, China's nuclear arsenal is not designed to compete (as occurred during the Cold War between the USSR and US in the accumulation of ever greater numbers and sophistication of nuclear warheads and delivery systems), but to deter threats to China. It does not have a strategic alliance system to defend or an umbrella under which allies shelter - as is the case with the US and its defence partners. Thus China can claim nuclear superpower status without arousing undue suspicion. The suspicion which it does arouse concerns Taiwan - and this is precisely what Beijing intends: to deter a Taiwanese bid for formal independence.

THE RISE OF THE "BRICS" AND THE "BRICSAM" APPROACH

In 2003, the U.S. firm Goldman Sachs published a seminal study that focused on four of the emerging-market economies in particular: Brazil, Russia, India and China (the so called "BRICs"). The analysis looked ahead to 2050 and compared probable growth scenarios for these four compared to the "G6" – the six largest industrialized countries with GDPs of over

US$1 trillion (in effect, the G7 minus Canada). Among the trends highlighted by this modelling projection were the following:

- The ranking of the world's largest economies will have shifted dramatically by 2050. Only the United States and Japan will still be among the six largest.
- By 2039, the combined BRIC economies will outweigh the combined G6 economies in U.S. dollar terms.
- By the same measure (GDP in U.S. dollars), China will overtake all but the United States by 2016, and the United States by 2041.
- In 2050, the world's largest economies will no longer be the richest measured by GDP in U.S. dollars per capita, although one of the BRICs, Russia, may have overtaken both Italy and Germany among the G6 on this scale.
- India's economy will overtake that of Japan by 2032 to move into third place, and India also has the potential to achieve the fastest growth over the next three to five decades.

A subsequent research project being undertaken by the Canadian-based Centre for International Governance Innovation identifies a considerably larger group of countries as the ones to watch. Labelled as "BRICSAM," these are the BRIC countries with the addition of South Africa, Mexico, and the countries of the Association of Southeast Asian Nations (ASEAN). Although the inclusion of smaller countries may be questioned, the general argument is that as a whole the BRICSAM group accounts for about half the world's population and, with average economic growth rates of 6% in the past five years, these countries are poised for moderate to high growth in the future. As two members of the BRICSAM project put it: "The reason for focusing on these countries is that global economic power appears to be shifting towards them and away from the [current] members of the Organization for Economic Cooperation and Development (OECD) and the G7."

If this overall trend is borne out, notwithstanding the many disparities and uneven rates of growth among the BRICSAM countries, this will indeed mark a major transformation of the world economy, especially given that as of 2003 they still accounted for only 12% of global GDP at market exchange rates. A BRICSAM orientation can be expected to result in a rapid expansion of trade flows in resource-based commodities to feed those countries' growing demand for energy and other raw materials. Led by the Asian economies, it could also lead to more emphasis on cultivating close contacts with these economic movers and shakers, and perhaps the negotiation of more regional and bilateral deals, at the same time as global economic institutions such as the World Trade Organization (WTO) would come under pressure to accommodate the interests of these new powers.

Implications for Canada

Whalley and Antkiewicz argue that the BRICSAM phenomenon poses a number of challenging adjustments for Canada, given this country's long dependence on U.S. markets (especially for manufactured exports), and that a BRICSAM strategy needs to be the focus of any potential diversification of Canada's commercial relations. At the same time, it might be argued that such a geographic diversification towards emerging markets could reinforce Canada's role as primarily a resource exporter. In that case, diversification would have to be accompanied by a broader strategy – involving education and skills development, scientific and technological innovation, and productivity gains – in order for Canada itself to emerge as a globally competitive trader in higher value-added goods and services.

Among the prospective factors that Whalley and Antkiewicz point to are the following:

- Taking advantage of fast-growing BRICSAM markets will especially spur resource export growth, and with that "the economic centre of gravity may well progressively tilt even more to the West and further away from Central Canada."
- Canada will face more competition from BRICSAM countries in its traditional export markets, as well as intensified competition for a share of their expanding import markets.
- "Contacts and networking will become more central to market access, and the precise legal text of trade agreements will probably matter less."
- "[I]mmigration policy may need to take into account the benefits of larger first-generation immigrant communities in Canada with direct network ties to BRICSAM countries."
- "Policy towards international agencies such as the WTO may also change as the BRICSAM countries either singly or jointly take a different approach to international economic issues."
- Traditional foreign policy concerns about these countries in terms of development, security, and governance may "become increasingly subordinated to the need to secure access for trade and investment ..." and "the key issue will become how to work jointly with them in pursuit of mutually advantageous global arrangements."

With regard to the last point, however, the suggestion of "subordination" could be misleading. The trend that other analysts have observed is not for diplomatic, development, and defence concerns to recede in importance, but rather for them to become more tightly integrated with trade and economic objectives.

For example, Louis Bélanger argues that "there is an unmistakable trend on the part of the emerging economic powers to treat trade policy as high politics. This trend reinforces the already strong movement of politicization of the global trade agenda." These new powers "join the game with the clear objective of using their trade policies to legitimize years of liberal reforms and to advance geopolitical objectives." According to Bélanger, if Canada is to be a significant player in the context of economic trade liberalization at this level, it will have to bring forward strong positions of its own in important debates on "not only economic issues, but also on ethical, social and environmental ones." That will require clear foreign and trade policy linkages in terms of "how the government sees the articulation between trade and development, democracy, security and good governance ...."

The House of Commons Subcommittee on International Trade, Trade Disputes and Investment put forward an integrated approach in a 2005 report based on its consideration of an emerging markets strategy for Canada. In making 44 recommendations to the government, the Subcommittee advocated that government policies and programs take into account social, environmental and human rights concerns and that Canadian business activities in promising emerging markets be pursued within a framework of corporate social responsibility.

These elements of a BRIC or BRICSAM strategy may be the most likely to arouse political controversy over their design and implementation. At the same time, it is clear that Canada still has a long way to go just in terms of building significant ties with most of these countries, at least in trade terms. While Canada's two-way trade with BRICSAM has been growing slightly in recent years, it still accounts for only about 18% of Canada's global total. Of that total, approximately 3.7% is made up of exports, compared to 14.5% which consists of imports from these countries. As a result, Canada is running trade deficits with all of the BRICSAM countries, in some cases equivalent to as much as 60% of total bilateral trade.

Moreover, as Whalley and Antkiewicz observe, "these flows are dominated by China in terms of the level and rate of growth." In fact, trade with China alone makes up nearly 60% of Canada's total trade with BRICSAM. (Mexico, which is also in this grouping, is a distant second as trade partner, and is a special case since it already has closer linkages to Canada as part of the North American Free Trade Agreement.)

Not surprisingly, Whalley and Antkiewicz argue that a BRICSAM strategy for Canada should consider bilateral negotiations with China and also India, which is the other economy with the most long-term potential.

The Subcommittee report referred to above recommended that the four BRIC countries be the "primary focus" of an emerging markets strategy. But here as well, China was highlighted as the major actor.

As the report stated: "In terms of the focus of a Canadian emerging markets strategy, it was clear from the outset of our hearings that China should be Canada's top priority. ... there was widespread agreement across businesses and associations that, while opportunities may exist around the world, China was in a class of its own."

THE EU: RESHAPING THE POWER PARADIGM?

The EU's identity is rather distinct from that of China. It is often perceived to be a normative actor, founding its policies on values, institutions and cooperation rather than power politics.

As such the EU constitutes an effort to reshape the power paradigm to reflect a new kind of power in global politics. As stated in its 2003 Security Strategy the EU aims at the "development of a stronger international society, well functioning international institutions and a rule based international order".

The rules underpinning this new international order are to be founded on Europe's liberal political norms, its views of an open global market and its preference for highly institutionalized multilateralism.

Similarly, the relations with the emerging powers are largely constructed from the belief that the latter should adapt their international political norms to the European standards. Normative convergence is thus the starting point for developing relations with emerging countries.

Europe's policy towards China has to date been one of conditional cooperation. The EU is prepared to help the PRC, to invest in the development of the country, but in turn, China must meet a number of standards and demands.

This is a rather unique way of dealing with a rising power. In contrast to the United States, Europe is not gearing up for a confrontation if needed. So-called "hard power" is hardly on the agenda. European nations are not taking up bases in Asia to curb Chinese influence in case this might be necessary. Power politics, based on military capabilities and threats with the use of force, seems to have disappeared from the diplomatic handbook all together.

On the contrary, Europe wishes to forge a tighter link and strengthen its influence through ever-increasing economic interdependence and shared values. In this process, Europe sees itself as the model China should aspire to. EU policy is based on the belief that "human rights tend to be better understood and better protected in societies open to the free flow of trade, investment, people, and ideas.

As China continues its policy of opening-up to the world, the EU will work to strengthen and encourage this trend."

British top diplomat Robert Cooper champions this approach in an often-quoted book, where, he talks about a post-modern security strategy with the emphasis firmly placed on values and international cooperation rather than hard power and control over territories. "Nationalism makes place for internationalism", he writes. "The final goal is the liberty for each individual."

The crucial question is to what extent this approach can be actually successful. Beijing has not put democracy and respect for human rights on top of its list of priorities.

In terms of foreign policy, it is unrealistic to think Beijing will comply with Europe's "post-modern" discourse. If one, in accordance with Robert Cooper, distinguishes between "modern states" and "post-modern states", then China is to be categorized as a "modern state", for which "internationalism" is but one modus operandi serving the national interest. The PRC is therefore by no means at a point where it can meet the European expectations.

Chinese officials, scholars and pundits all tend to indicate this when talking in private. It is crucial for the EU to be aware what power it has to sway policy in China. An important parameter in the EU's dealings with China will be the strategic weight Brussels will be capable of bringing to bear with Beijing. China perceives the EU foremost as an economic actor, far less as a political actor. One reason why Beijing for example wants the PCA negotiations to focus on trade and economic cooperation might be that it has doubts about the EU's capacity to deliver really in the political domain.

The EU should also be critical of its leverage as a normative actor. China may well recognize the advantages of cooperating with the EU and of learning from it in certain areas, but it is certainly not willing to accept the tutelage of the EU. China is not a prospective EU member, nor does it see itself as a weak nation, depending solely on the EU for support in its political and economic reform process. The most real incentive that the EU has to offer is access to its market.

The EU's success with China will to a large extent rest on recognition of common interests, in areas such as the environment and energy, but also in trade and investment. The degree to which China's interests match those of the EU will determine the success of relationship. As the constellation of world power is changing, the EU's strategy will have to change with it. Europeans must come to grips with the fact that "the West does not enjoy a predestined supremacy in international politics that is locked into the future for an indeterminate period of time.

The Euro-Atlantic world had a long run of global dominance, but it is coming to an end." The future is more likely to be shaped by Asia and China in particular.

China's mounting power and growing assertiveness poses a challenge to the EU's standing in the international order. The growing economic weight of Asia and China's reemergence is facing Europe with a process of de-centering. As David Kerr observes the "fact that most powers in Eurasia – and China foremost among them – are accumulating sovereignty or the means to stronger sovereignty, not sharing sovereignty as the European experience promotes, means that the European region remains quite exceptional in both its political dynamics and its strategic organization."

Even if China will continue to defend its interests in a peaceful way, partially by nourishing its bilateral relations, partially by working via multilateral institutions, its growing capabilities ask the EU to adapt with regard to its policymaking capacity.

In order to face common challenges with China and to fill the present strategic void, the EU needs to develop the capability to play a role of importance in the changing global environment. The EU has to pool the fragmented capabilities of its member states into real levers for exerting influence if it is to be taken seriously as a strategic international actor by Beijing.

TOWARDS A PRAGMATIC RELATIONSHIP

The Sino-European partnership has been going through turbulent times in the past few years. As it stands, the partnership is not strategic, but it has vast strategic potential. The challenge will be to work out a pragmatic consensus on how to gradually turn joint strategic interests into more result-driven cooperation. Given the distinctive identities of China and the EU and their different development paths, this process will inevitably have to be commensurate with the two partners' internal transformation.

After a period of difficulties over issues like Tibet, climate change and alleged economic protectionism, both sides are now figuring out how to best position themselves in the future. Beijing is executing an important review of its major relationships and one of the questions is where the EU will fit in. There is growing momentum for synergies with Washington, leading to speculation about a transpacific bargain. But in the multilayered multipolar world it will remain key for China to maintain good relations with the other powers too. For Europe, changes brought about by the Lisbon reform treaty may ultimately halt its descent into strategic redundancy and instigate the EU to assure protagonists like China that it has indeed the ambition to develop solid strategic partnerships.

The years ahead will thus be ones of relation therapy. Europe and China need to define for themselves what they consider to be the main interests driving their partnership.

For the EU in particular it is a matter of finding a remedy against the kind of diplomatic schizophrenia in which short-sighted policies of the member states counteracted the proselytizing European Commission. It would be a good start to evaluate the effectiveness of the current instruments for engaging China. More efforts should also be made in bringing member states around the table to deduce a common denominator from their often-diverging national interests. If Europe is to constructively engage China, it will have to engage itself collectively first.

Simultaneously, China and Europe have to agree on which interests they will build the pillars of their strategic partnership. One of the main setbacks in the EU-China partnership has always been its obsession with dialogues without a common view on how the new world order actually binds them together.

Obviously, the global financial crisis and the subsequent economic recession have confirmed the necessity to reshape our economies. Both countries face an important challenge to combat unemployment, to improve social welfare and to be more efficient in using scarce natural resources. Increased investment in innovation, a secure climate for creative development and a dynamic services sector will be vital for developing new and sustainable sources for growth.

This is an individual responsibility, but it can only be successful in a climate of trust and reciprocal openness.

Both sides are confronted with similar social challenges: an ageing population, a heterogeneous ethnic society, growing urban complexes and substantial internal economic differences.

They have a common interest in enhancing social equality and welfare. While facing different economic limitations, both sides are aiming to make their development inclusive and harmonious.

Rather than lecturing each other, this brings the opportunity to exchange lessons learned. The emphasis should not be on differences per se, but on commitment and progress.

China and Europe are both regional powers with broad global interests. As a consequence of increased international engagement and increasing economic interests abroad, Europe and China are geopolitically more proximate than ever before.

There is an important joint interest to promote stability and sustainable development in those regions that we share in our extended neighbourhoods. This is particularly the case of the Middle East, Africa, and South-Central Asia. We have to avoid that these regions develop into a belt of insecurity that endangers our development.

There is a strong need to work together to enhance security, to guarantee that our policies benefit lasting stability and development, to invest in the safety of our energy supplies, to limit the impact of environmental hazards, to support effective governance, tackle non-traditional security threats, and enhance maritime security. It is legitimate that growing interests bring the need to exert influence, but this should be cooperative and aim at sharing the costs of maintaining security.

We are moving steadily towards a new multipolar world order. In this order the major powers will have to balance between meeting increasing international expectations and persistent strong internal needs. The emerging multilayered and culturally diversified multipolarity will make global governance much more complex and is by no means a guarantee for multilateralism.

To be effective multilateral organizations need to reflect the emerging new international order, but effective multilateralism also implies that all parties are committed to overcome diverging expectations and try to reach a pragmatic consensus on how to make foreign policies complementary and mutually supportive. Europe and China could be in the vanguard here as well. As the unipolar moment fades, Europe and China have showed themselves anxious not to slide into another era of great power rivalry.

Such contest would severely weaken the two player's chances for sustainable internal development. In spite of all the friction and misunderstanding, both sides need each other if they are to develop an alternative for harsh international anarchy. Successful bilateral cooperation will be key in promoting global peaceful development. It will also give them the scope to strengthen their internal unity, which will be key in boosting positive power vis-à-vis others. If Beijing and Brussels are serious about changing the nature of great power politics, a pragmatic partnership between China and Europe build on mutual benefit, trust and understanding is mandatory.

CONCLUSION

Forecasts of global power shifts and long-term economic projections must be treated with caution, given the number of variables in play. They can, however, point to key trends that need to be taken seriously by prudent policymakers. Better preparation for probable international scenarios may also result in more effective responses to such anticipated events.

In the next several decades, it seems virtually certain that at least two Asian "emerging-market" countries, China and India, will move into the front rank of the world's economies and will increasingly exercise influence as global powers.

A change of such magnitude in the global power balance is likely to challenge the positions of even the most powerful Western countries. At the very least, the current G7 countries will have to adjust their policies to accommodate the interests of these rising powers.

Outside of Asia, several other countries – notably Brazil and South Africa – are also likely to exert growing leadership within their regions, within the developing world as a whole, and within important multilateral forums including the United Nations and the World Trade Organization. In addition, these countries are forging links among themselves and with Asian powers. They are building networks and alliances that promote common agendas of "South-South" cooperation.

As a smaller player in a world of contending giants, Canada is likely to experience a continuing decline in its relative power on the world stage. As a trade-dependent nation, Canada will also remain highly exposed to international economic trends.

And in an environment of intensified multi-polar competition, Canada may not be able to rely as much as it has on proximity to the United States, which will be preoccupied dealing with its own power shift challenges.

Canada's choice of competitive options within and beyond North America, whether that includes deeper economic integration, or more diversified relationships with other regions, perhaps a combination of both, will be greatly affected by the changes that China, India and other leading emerging-market countries bring to the international system.

If Canada is to avoid being marginalized, it will have to be innovative both at home and abroad, equipping Canadians for this new era of globalized competition with an increasingly "Asian face," and developing stronger Canadian ties to the emerging powers of the international system. It is certainly not too soon to be devising strategies to meet that challenge.

VISION 2020 : MODERNISING FOR AN ERA OF STRATEGIC UNCERTAINTY

In the prevailing era of strategic uncertainty, while terrorism is gradually becoming the primary threat, the external and internal threats and challenges faced by India are such that a large army is still required to be maintained. Also, a high degree of preparation and operational readiness are still necessary as conventional war, though improbable, cannot be categorically ruled out due to unresolved territorial and boundary disputes with China and Pakistan.

At the same time, heavy capital investments in modern defence equipment are undoubtedly a drain on a developing economy that is ill equipped to handle the burgeoning defence expenditure.

Several eminent analysts have recommended that qualitative upgradation should be accompanied by quantitative downsizing of personnel strength of the army to generate funds for modernisation. However, given its responsibilities for border management and the manpower-intensive sub-conventional operations that the army is involved in—this is easier said than done.

Future conventional conflict on the Indian sub-continent will in all probability result from the ongoing low-intensity limited war on the Line of Control (LoC) with Pakistan or the unresolved territorial and boundary dispute with China and will be predominantly a land conflict. The Indian Army lacks a potent firepower punch, especially in the mountain sector. Precision-guided munitions (PGMs) have still to enter service in numbers large enough to make a real difference. The reconnaissance, surveillance and target acquisition (RSTA) assets necessary for the optimum exploitation of even the existing firepower assets are grossly inadequate.

Automated command and control and decision support systems have been on the drawing boards for several decades but are yet to mature. According to former Vice Chief of Army Staff Lieutenant General (Retd.)

Noble Thamburaj, the modernization focus of the 11th Defence Plan is on "precision fire power, air defence, aviation, Future Infantry Soldier as a System, infrastructure development, network centricity and achieving battlefield transparency through improved surveillance, night vision and target acquisition.... Considering the receding span of technological cycle, (the) right balance has to be maintained between state-of-art, current and obsolescent technologies."

Main Battle Tanks: T-90S replaces Arjun

On Army Day 2010, Chief of the Army Staff General Deepak Kapoor admitted that a large number of India's battle tanks are 'night blind'. The indigenously designed Arjun main battle tank (MBT) has been in the pipeline for over two decades. Though the tank has many good features, it has consistently failed to meet the army's General Staff Qualitative Requirements for an MBT and orders have been placed for only 124 tanks to be manufactured.

The Defence Research and Development Organization (DRDO) had been repeatedly pressing for comparative trials of the Arjun with the T-72M1 and the T-90S. Success in these trials has led to orders being placed for another 124 Arjun MBTs.

Since the lack of progress on the Arjun MBT had significantly slowed down the pace of armour modernization, in 2000, India signed a deal with Russia to acquire 310 T-90S tanks and assemble 1,000 in India.

In 2008, the Ministry of Defence (MoD) decided to acquire another 347 T-90S tanks. The first India assembled T-90S (Bhishma) rolled off the production line on January 8, 2004. Ultimately, "The army's future armour profile could comprise approximately 1,700 T-90S, 1,800 upgraded T-72M1 and 250 to 500 Arjuns." Almost 1,800 T-72M1 (Ajeya) tanks are still awaiting modernisation. The lack of a suitable fire control system and night fighting capability are major handicaps. The upgradation of 500 to 600 of these has now commenced "at the rate of 200 tanks per year". The upgrade package includes a new fire control system comprising a TISAS (thermal imaging stand alone systems) night sight and TIFCS (tank integrated fire control system), new TADIRAN radios, a gyro-based navigation system and a Laser warning system. The ability to fire on the move is being improved with a better stabilization system. An add-on ERA (explosive reactive armour) package will enhance protection against APFSDS and HEAT rounds. Eventually, the T-90S 1,000 hp power pack, de-rated to 850 hp, will be retro-fitted.

The problem of defective indigenous ammunition is still to be resolved. The DRDO has commenced conceptual stage development of Future Main battle Tank and Future Infantry Combat vehicle for the 2020-25 time-frame.

T-90S Russian tanks have provided new teeth to India's strike formations in the plains and corrected the imbalance that had resulted from Pakistan's acquisition of T-80 UD from Ukraine and the Al Khalid tanks jointly designed with China. Hence, armour modernization is proceeding apace but cannot yet be classified as a success story.

Generating firepower asymmetries

In a future conventional war that will be fought under the nuclear shadow, manoeuvre will be extremely limited.

This restriction will lead to much greater emphasis being placed on firepower to achieve the laid down military aim. Hence, it is imperative that artillery modernization is undertaken with alacrity so as to generate firepower asymmetries on the future battlefield. After a long spell of keeping the powder dry, action on modernization of the Indian Artillery is livening up once again.

Beginning in January 2008, the MOD issued three global tenders for 155 mm guns and howitzers for the mountains, the plains and self-propelled guns for the deserts. Summer and winter trials were expected to be held over the next one year and it was anticipated that contracts would be awarded as early as in the first half of 2010. However, none of the manufacturers have as yet been invited for trials. It is a well-established fact that potent artillery firepower had turned the tide and eventually paved the way for victory during the Kargil conflict.

Despite the lessons learnt in Kargil, modernization of the artillery has continued to lag behind. The last major acquisition of towed gunhowitzers was that of about 400 pieces of 39-calibre 155 mm FH-77B howitzers with a range of 30 km from Bofors of Sweden in the mid-1980s.

This gun had proved its mettle in the Kargil conflict. After two decades of neglect during which the 100 mm and 122 mm field guns of Russian origin and the indigenously developed and manufactured 75/24 Indian Mountain

Gun joined the long list of equipment bordering on obsolescence but still in service with the army, tenders were floated and trials were held for a 52-calibre 155 mm gun to replace all field and medium guns.

Just when a contract for 120 tracked and 180 wheeled self-propelled (SP) 155 mm guns was about to be concluded after years of protracted trials, South African arms manufacturer Denel, a leading contender for the contract, was alleged to have been involved in a corruption scam in an earlier deal for antimaterial rifles (AMRs).

The other two howitzers in contention, from Soltam of Israel and BAE (Bofors) of Sweden reportedly did not meet the laid down criteria and Army HQ recommended fresh trials, setting the programme back at least three to four years. Another bone of contention was that the howitzers that had been offered were technology demonstration models and not guns that were in actual service with the home country armies.

BALLISTIC AND CRUISE MISSILES AND MISSILE DEFENCE SYSTEMS

In his special address, Vice Admiral Anup Singh traced the advent and development of missile technology since the 1950s up to the present and also reviewed the regional scenario with respect to missile capabilities.

He noted that in the history of warfare, the development of military technology had never been as rapid as it has been in the last five decades, with phenomenal surges in missile technology and intrusions into outer space.

He termed the growth in missile technology as revolutionary, not merely evolutionary. Vice Admiral Anup Singh pointed out that ballistic missiles are the ultimate manifestation of deterrence.

The introduction of ballistic missiles resulted in an arms race in both numerical and technological terms as the number of missiles, their reach and payload have come to represent the power of a nation.

Defence against ballistic missiles is difficult due to limited reaction time, speed and lack of predictability. At the same time economics have much to do with the proliferation of missiles. He expressed his concern over the geostrategic environment around India where Weapons of Mass Destruction (WMD), including nuclear and missile proliferation, are an acute and worrisome reality.

India requires credible defence against these threats, which must include ballistic missile defence assurance and offensive defence by way of retribution in line with the declared doctrine. There is also a need to enhance surveillance capability against ballistic and cruise missiles. India's Prithvi and Agni missiles have come to represent national pride and national power. In the cruise missile category BrahMos is a path breaking development.

The Vice Admiral said that the development of missile technology is in India's strategic interests. Vice Admiral A.K. Singh highlighted the concept of four layered BMD surveillance comprising satellites and long, medium and short range radars and noted that India requires a layered surveillance and defence system, including missile interception technology. He pointed out that a missile is most vulnerable in the boost phase and the terminal phase and not so much during the cruise and re-entry phases. Therefore, it is the first phase and the last phase which decide the Ballistic Missile Defence (BMD) system.

He also referred to ballistic trajectories which may be normal or depressed or lofted to make it difficult to intercept. He highlighted how it is a costly venture to develop ballistic missiles and cruise missiles and pointed out that the Indo-Russian BrahMos Aerospace had been unable to bring down the cost of its supersonic missile to that of the US Tomahawk (approximately US $800,000).

Cmde. Ranjit Rai expressed despair at the absence of a well-articulated defence strategy in India. He was also concerned about the lack of collaboration between the three services and ISRO. He highlighted the importance of developing a terminal homing seeker in a missile system.

He said that India is a satellite power and that the space recovery capsule is a great achievement for the military. He added that multi-satellite launch vehicles can also be used to launch missiles.

He concluded that the Indian military must be actively involved in issues relating to use of space and must develop an anti-satellite capability. Mr. Thyagaraj spoke about conventional ballistic missiles used in the context of firepower and its political implications.

He said that a nation's needs and capability to generate missile strikes are driven by its geostrategic location and command of intelligence, early warning and guidance.

It is important to consider the status of the entity to be attacked, whether it is a state or a non-state actor or a nuclear power as a missile attack may give rise to nuclear escalation. He concluded with the remarks that India's No First Use (NFU) nuclear doctrine may need to be reviewed in the current geo-political circumstances.

Discussion points were:

- ISRO has always maintained its civilian orientation in line with the national policy of peaceful uses of space. It has also helped ISRO in importing technologies and material from outside India. This has, however, created an undesirable gap between the military and ISRO. This gap needs to be bridged.
- It would be beneficial for both India and the US if they develop a future missile defence system jointly. This will enhance the strategic partnership between the two countries.
- The Government of India should lay down that all defence procurement will only be made from Indian companies. This will impel Western companies to assist India to develop its defence manufacturing infrastructure.

PRECISION GUIDED MUNITIONS AND PLATFORMS

There is considerable debate on whether technology drives weapon requirements or *vice versa*. Whatever the truth may be, excessive reliance on technology without checks and balances can be dangerous. The mistaken bombing of the Chinese embassy in Belgrade shows how fatal reliance on technology can be. It is, therefore, important to ensure adequate absorption of technology into the system.

Citing from Hindu mythology and Indian and world history, Dr. Pillai highlighted the Indian contribution to the art of war over the ages. He said that India has to move ahead in the technological field as future wars will be autonomous and net-centric using C4I2 and other advanced technologies.

Cyber warfare will aim to defend and destroy the NCW capabilities including space assets. Owing to various technology denial and control regimes such as the Missile Technology Control Regime (MTCR), in 1983 India started its own programme to develop missiles indigenously and the Integrated Guided Missile Development Programme (IGMDP) was launched.

Realising the need for indigenous cruise missile technology, India chose the supersonic route to develop BrahMos, which is the first of its kind in the world. BrahMos is a multi-platform cruise missile enabling it to strike from various types of land, sea and air-based platforms, including mobile and fixed ones.

It has better speed, kinetic energy and reaction time attributes than the Tomahawk missile. By 2012, BrahMos missile will be mounted on Su-30 aircraft of the IAF. BrahMos was also under further technological development towards propulsion and precison targeting. Referring to Indian ballistic missile capabilities, he stated that Agni-III is in the final stage of testing for induction into service. He also mentioned that India should focus on the emerging technologies such as scramjet, hyper-sonic, microwave, under water rockets, anti-torpedo defence system, micro-motors, nano-technology, hypersonic reusable missile and kinetic energy (KE) weapons. Citing the avowed aim of the DRDO to develop technologies that conform with the operational requirements of the three Services, Dr. Prahlada said that in order to ensure minimum collateral damage, small warheads with high precision are required, which can also be used in urban warfare and for countering terrorists.

These warheads would be capable of autonomous target recognition and homing to attack multiple targets simultaneously. They would be modular in nature and can be easily attached to any carrier (missile, rocket, UAV, bomb, etc.). Expressing his satisfaction with the progress in the field, he said that all the technologies like seekers, control components, warheads, ATR (Automatic Target Recognition), integration, simulation, mission planning and launching, are either already available or under development and will be achieved in the next few years.

Targeting is the *raison d'être* of any air force. In recent wars, the numbers of PGMs used has increased tremendously leading to decisive victory to the side with better PGM capability.

PGMs provide several advantages such as standoff capability, central resource planning, fast mission planning, battle damage assessment and boost the morale of own troops in combat. IAF weapon requirements include modular weapons with good standoff range, high precision assurance value, twin seeker head, changeable warhead, long shelf life, ease of storage, compatible platform, manned/unmanned and internal carriage.

The weapons should be developed keeping the reality of 'Western weapon and Eastern platform', in mind. There is a need to pay equal attention to enabling technologies such as satellites, AFNET and IACCS. The IAF is also coordinating ground-based needs with AWACS so that sensor to shooter loop can be reduced. Discussion points were:

- India is developing its own seekers to minimise dependence on other countries so as to reduce a critical vulnerability.
- India should concentrate on developing its own hardware to avoid over-reliance on Chinese and Taiwanese hardware, which are likely to be bug infested. Notably, the Chinese are hacking computers everywhere.

- There is also a place for dumb weapons in war and their production should not be neglected.
- Satellites are very useful in surveillance and battle damage assessment and India must launch its own military satellites.

No war has been won without firepower, but it may not be the only thing necessary to win a war. The definition of firepower is required to be broadened to include all destructive capabilities. Military planners must aim at cost effectiveness by maximizing combat potential. Application of combat power of the right amount, at the right place and at the right time will lead to a decisive outcome. Reiterating the axiom that "in war there is no silver medalist; either you win or you lose", Mr. Shekhar Dutt said that firepower contributes tremendously in enhancing defence preparedness. Effects-oriented planning, through real time networked approach and 24/7 surveillance to minimize the OODA loop, can make precision weapons more useful. PGMs address the need of modern day strike systems and improved integration and communication can be useful in avoiding friendly fire. In future, smaller but highly effective forces will be required. To address the present day battlefield requirements, the Indian Armed Forces need to substantially enhance their firepower capability.

The armed forces have to develop knowledge, precision, speed and lethality for the efficient use of PGMs which are true force multipliers. PGMs are traditionally thought of as conventional weapons. However, the destructive potential of the current terrorist organizations makes it necessary at times for PGMs to be used in the war against terror.

PGMs can be developed using indigenous technology and also by cooperating with other countries. It is highly desirable to change mindsets at all levels of leadership so as to ensure well defined strategies and doctrines. There is also a need to involve academics, scientists and journalists for the wider acceptance of enhanced military capabilities.

ARTILLERY GUNS FOR NEW WEAPONS

In view of the nuclear shadow under which the next conflict will be fought, offensive and defensive manoeuvres will be extremely limited. Consequently, it will be necessary to generate firepower asymmetries to destroy the adversary's war waging potential.

In such a scenario, the failure to modernize the Indian Artillery will have serious repercussions for national security. Hence, it is extremely heartening to note that in January 2008 the Ministry of Defence (MoD) began to make long-awaited amends by issuing Requests for Proposals (RFP) for various types of 155 mm howitzers. In the post-Kargil 1999 scenario in the Indian sub-continent, the artillery has proved to be a decisive arm. Indeed, even a battle-winning one. It was clear to all perceptive observers who followed the Kargil conflict closely that infantry soldiers had to repeatedly attack uphill to recapture the mountaintops at Kargil taken quietly by the Pakistan army. It was actually the artillery that had paved the way for victory.

The Indian Army deployed an overwhelming superiority of its concentrated firepower, and that enabled the infantry attacks to be launched for repossessing the lost territory. Operationally, the army also used the opportunity to test and fine-tune the indigenously-developed Pinaka Multi Barrel Rocket Launchers (MBRLs). The Indian Army has approved the 155 mm howitzer as the standard artillery calibre, but new, modern systems are yet to be acquired to replace the old units and augment the strength to requirement.

Precision-guided 155 mm artillery shells can destroy bunkers, bridges and small buildings with a single-shot kill probability (SSKP) as high as 80 per cent. Improved conventional munition (ICMs) shells carrying anti-personnel grenades and lethal 'air-burst' ammunition can be 'dispensed' over soft targets such as administrative bases, rations and fuel-storage dumps, headquarters and rest areas. When these are available in large quantities, the artillery can cause much greater destruction and indirectly reduce the number of casualties in the infantry. Approximately 400 FH-77B 155 mm guns that proved their combat superiority in the Kargil conflict, had been purchased in the mid-1980s from Bofors of Sweden to equip 20 medium-artillery regiments.

These guns had enhanced the effectiveness of the artillery by an order of magnitude. Notably, the 105 mm Indian field guns and the older 130 mm Russian medium guns in service since the early 1970s have reached an advanced stage of obsolescence; while World War II vintage 25 pounders, 75/24 Indian mountain guns, 122 mm field guns and 100 mm field guns have already been phased out of service. In the recent years, just when a contract for 120 tracked and 180 wheeled self-propelled (SP) 155 mm guns was about to be concluded after years of repeated trials, South African arms manufacturer Denel, the leading contender for the contract, was alleged to have been involved in a corruption scam in an earlier deal for Anti-Material Rifles (AMRs).

From Fire Support To Destruction

From its original status as a 'supporting' arm, artillery has now graduated to a full-fledged combat arm that dominates the battlefield with its inherently destructive firepower. In the classic 'fire and manoeuvre' tactics practised during operations on 20th century battlefields, artillery traditionally provided the firepower punch while armoured, mechanized and infantry units manoeuvred to gain tactical advantage. Artillery engagements were generally limited to the battle where own troops were in direct contact with the enemy.

'Covering fire' during attack and 'defensive fire' to beat back enemy attacks were provided in a supporting role. Artillery guns, mortars and rocket launchers were considered area weapons and the neutralization of large areas of ground with inherent dispersion of fire, rather than destruction, was the established primary task. Today, once a threat from across the borders has been discerned, the artillery, firing 155 mm precision strike ammunition can be employed to destroy the intruding forces quickly so that the aggression can be vacated and sanctity of the international boundary restored.

Targets that can be seen by the troops in contact with the enemy can be illuminated by a Laser beam by a ground-based artillery observer (spotter) carrying a Laser Target Designator. Those targets that are behind crest lines and on reverse slopes can be designated by an airborne artillery observer in an army aviation helicopter or an Unarmed Aerial Vehicle (UAV).

Improved conventional munitions (ICMs) shells carrying anti-personnel grenades and lethal 'air-burst' ammunition can be 'dispensed' over soft targets such as administrative bases, rations and fuel storage dumps, headquarters and rest areas. As these are not precision strike munitions, these have to be accurately directed using commando artillery observers or TV camera equipped UAVs to achieve the desired effect.

Precision munitions are expensive, but they turn out to be cheaper as only a few have to be used to destroy designated targets. Plus, they offer the advantage of Assured Kill, making operations that much easier and also saving lives that would otherwise be lost in an assault.

Long-range MBRLs such as Smerch can enable the enemy's sensitive command centres to be hit with impunity. Had Smerch MBRLs been available during the Kargil conflict, the Pakistani HQ and administrative base at Skardu and other targets deep inside Pakistan Occupied Kashmir (POK) would have been hit with devastating results.

Other force multipliers include Gun or Weapon Locating Radars (WLRs) for effective counter-bombardment, UAVs equipped with TV cameras and suitable for high altitude operations for target acquisition and engagement and damage assessment, powerful binoculars for target engagement by day and long-range night vision devices for the same purpose at night.

The Indian Army had in fact requested for the Gun Locating Radars in the mid-1980s, but their acquisition was approved by the government only after the Kargil conflict, in which a majority of the Indian casualties were due to the Pakistani artillery, which Indian forces could not detect and therefore could not neutralise effectively. Now, the Army has taken delivery of a dozen radars from the US arms major Raytheon under a government-to-government contract. More of these radars are to be made in India as required. The Indian Artillery is playing an increasingly important role in the successful execution of integrated land-air operations on the modern battlefield. The emerging philosophy of employment of artillery firepower visualizes the synergetic orchestration of all firepower resources across the length and breadth of the battlefield to cause destruction, systematic degradation of the enemy's fighting potential and suppression of specific combat echelons of the enemy from operating effectively for limited durations.

The latter function will include the suppression of the enemy's air defence (SEAD) assets to enable own attack helicopters to operate freely and to also enable ground attack aircraics, and India has taken up the gauntlet by building one at Cochin. Fincantieri, which is building the Count Cavour in Italy, has been roped in as the consultant to make the best use of its expertise and experience. This lesson has not been lost on UK which has not built carriers for years. Hence it is jointly planning to build two similar 60,000 ton aircraft carriers with France for interoperability. UK hopes to learn from the experience of the French Navy which encountered problems in the size of the nuclear powered Charles de Gaulle to operate the newer Rafale aircraft. Despite excellent calculations, the ship's landing deck had to be enlarged, *post facto.* The ship's bridge also was located too far forward and led to turbulence for aircraft landing and the vessel lost a propeller in the Caribbean islands. The ship limped back to France with a tug in escort.

All these issues are being rectified in the new UK French carriers. When there is no operational flat top platform for continuation training and deck landing qualifications, the consequence is a backlog of pilots rapidly losing their deck landing qualifications DLQ. Indian Navy pilots are being trained in USA and at IAF bases in India as the Indian Navy is set to receive its first MiG 29Ks in the coming months.

Notably, the first MiG 29K flew spectacularly at the MAKS aviation show outside Moscow recently. INS Viraat was to have been decommissioned by 2010 but now it appears it will have to bat on longer than anticipated, as both of India's aircraft carriers on order have been delayed. The Gorshkov—to be christened INS Vikramaditya on commissioning—being refitted at the Sevmash shipyard at Severnodinsk in Russia, is delayed for delivery from 2008 to 2010 and the head of the shipyard has been removed for the faux pas. Nevsokye Design Bureau has been asked to look in to this. A delegation led by UK-trained engineer Vice Admiral B.S. Randhawa, the Controller of Warship Production and Acquisition (CWPA), slated to be the next Chief of Material, had visited Russia mid May and inspected the Mk 1143.4 Admiral Gorshkov, and yet again in July. He confirmed that the ship is behind schedule. Strangely, the Russians also asked for price escalation, saying that they had made a mistake in calculating the required work, and despite also that the delay was due to their own problems.

Even then, Defence Secretary Shekar Dutt, who is now India's Deputy National Security Advisor (NSA), and Secretary Defence Finance V.K. Misra, visited Moscow in July to help resolve the issue. According to former Chief of Naval Staff (CNS) Admiral Arun Prakash, the Russians need to be penalized for the delay as they had already been afforded one escalation. The Navy Chief, Admiral Sureesh Mehta, is an experienced aviator who, like his predecessor, has flown off INS Viraat and Vikrant as a green horn Sea Hawk rookie pilot. He was looking forward to inducting the Vikramaditya during his tenure. He has indicated a new date for its induction, as after late 2008. It will be a challenge for the next Navy team in South Block to ensure that the vessel is transferred to India not far behind the schedule.

The 273 metre long, 30 year old 48,500 ton Gorshkov's keel was laid in 1976 at the Nikolayev Shipyard now in Ukraine, and when commissioned, it operated 14 Yakovlev Yak-141 vertical take-off and landing (VTOL) Fighters, eight Yak-38 Forger VTOL fighters, as well as 16 Kamov Ka-25 and Ka-252RLD Hormone and Ka- 252PS Helix anti-submarine warfare (ASW), reconnaissance and search and rescue (SAR) helicopters. The ship was earmarked for scrapping, and then offered to the Indian Navy free, provided India paid for its refurbishment and bought Russian aircraft to operate from it. Admiral J.G. Nadkarni was among those who supported its acquisition towards fulfilling the Indian Navy's need for aircraft carriers. After much delay and procrastination, India signed a US $1.5 billion Gorshkov modernization contract in 2004 under Defence Minister George Fernandes' direction. Its refurbishment was agreed at $ 700 million, and the rest was for the 16 MiG-29K fighters, helicopters, miscellaneous equipment and weapons from third parties.

Bibliography

Baviera, A. S. P.: *China's Relations with Southeast Asia: Political Security and Economic Interests*, Philippine APEC Study Center Network, 1999.

Bhat, T.P. : *India and China : Trade Complementarities and Competitiveness*, Bookwell, Delhi, 2008.

Carolina G. Hernandez: *How Japan Can Contribute to a Peaceful World*, London, Routledge, 2005.

Digumarti Bhaskara Rao: *Military Conversion : Impact on Science and Technology*, Discovery, Delhi, 2003.

Dittmer, L.: *The Strategic Triangle: An Elementary Game-Theoretical Analysis*, Cambridge, Cambridge University Press, 1981.

Friedman, G.: *The Future of War: Power, Technology and American World Dominance in the 21st Century*, N.Y., Random House, 1996.

Gowdy, J., *Coevolution Economics: The Economy, Society and the Environment*, Kluwer, Boston, 2012.

Hagström, Linus: *Japan's China Policy: A Relational Power Analysis*, London and New York: Routledge, 2005.

Huntington, S.P.: *The China Modernisation Military and the State*, N.Y., Vintage Books, 1964.

Ian Storey: *ASEAN and the South China Sea: Movement in Lieu of Progress*, Washington, D.C., Jamestown Foundation,2012.

Iriye, Akira: *China and Japan in the global setting*, Harvard University Press, 1992.

Itoh, Mayumi: *Pioneers of Sino-Japanese Relations: Liao and Takasaki*. Palgrave-MacMillan. 2012.

Jha, Prem Shankar: *India: A Political Economy of Stagnation*, Bombay, Oxford University Press, 1980.

Joon Ahn: *The Rise of China and the Future of East Asian Integration*, Asia-Pacific Review, London, Carfax Publishing Company, 2004.

Kalindi Randeri: *Narendra Modi : Make in India*, Rupa, Delhi, 2009.

Kapur, C.K. : *Chinese Military Modernisation*, Manas, Delhi, 2003.

Kenneth B. Pyle: *The Japanese Question: Power and Purpose in a New Era,* Washington, DC: American Enterprise Institute, 1996.

Leo Tansky, *US and USSR Aid to Developing Countries: A Comparative Study of India, Turkey, and the UAR,* New York, 1967.

Mahurkar, Uday: *Centrestage: Inside the Narendra Modi Model of Governanace.* Random House India. 2014.

Mary, W.: *Military Space Force: the Cultural Dimensions of Authority,* Cambridge, Belknap Press, 1985.

Max Beloff: *Foreign Policy and the Democratic Process,* Baltimore, Johns Hopkins University Press, 1955.

Michael Schaller: *Altered States: The United States and Japan Since the Occupation*, Oxford: Oxford University Press, 1997.

Moulder, F. V.: *Japan, China, and the Modern World Economy.* Cambridge: Cambridge University Press, 1977.

Mukhopadhyay, Nilanjan: *Narendra Modi: The Man, The Times.* Westkabd. 2013

Nininger, Robert D. *Minerals for Atomic Energy.* New York: D. Van Nostrand Company, Inc., 1954.

Ottomar, H.: *Distribution of Stock of Money,* Effingham, London, 1892.

Prasad, Lal Bahadur : *Indian Political System and Law*, New Delhi, Shree, 2005.

Raj, K.N.: *New Economic Policy*, Delhi, Oxford University Press, 1986.

Randeri, Kalindi: *Narendra Modi : The Architect of A Modern State*, Rupa, Delhi, 2009.

Robert M Cassidy: *Counterinsurgency and the Global War on Terror : Military Culture and Irregular War*, Pentagon Press, Delhi, 2008.

Rose, Caroline: *Sino-Japanese Relations: Facing the Past, Looking to the Future?* Routledge. 2005.

Saksena, N.S.: *India: Towards Anarchy, 1967-1992*, New Delhi, Abhinav, 1993.

Selig Harrison: *Japan's Nuclear Future: The Plutonium Debate and East Asian Security,* Washington, DC: Carnegie Endowment, 1996.

Shaun Narine, *Explaining ASEAN: Regionalism in Southeast Asia*, Boulder, CO: Lynne Rienner Publishers, 2002.

Storey, I.: *Southeast Asia and the Rise of China: the search for security*, New York, Routledge, 2011.

Tomlinson, B.R.: *The New Cambridge History of India : The Economy of Modern India, 1860-1970*, Cambridge, Cambridge University Press, 1993.

Ullman, D. G.: *Making Robust Decisions,* Trafford, 2006.

Vohra, Ranbir. *The Making of India: A Historical Survey.* Armonk, N.Y.: M. E. Sharp, 1997.

Index

R

S

T

W

❑❑❑